Teach Yourself VISUALLY™

Mac OS® X Lion™

Visual™

by Paul McFedries

WILEY

Wiley Publishing, Inc.

Teach Yourself VISUALLY™ Mac OS® X Lion™

Published by
Wiley Publishing, Inc.
10475 Crosspoint Boulevard
Indianapolis, IN 46256

www.wiley.com

Published simultaneously in Canada

Wiley also publishes its books in a variety of electronic formats and by print-on-demand. Some content that appears in standard print versions of this book may not be available in other formats. For more information about Wiley products, visit us at www.wiley.com.

Library of Congress Control Number: The Library of Congress Control number is available from the Library of Congress

ISBN: 978-1-118-02241-2

Manufactured in the United States of America

10 9 8 7 6 5 4 3 2 1

Trademark Acknowledgments

Contact Us

For general information on our other products and services please contact our Customer Care Department within the U.S. at 877-762-2974, outside the U.S. at 317-572-3993 or fax 317-572-4002.

For technical support please visit www.wiley.com/techsupport.

WILEY **Sales** | Contact Wiley at (877) 762-2974 or fax (317) 572-4002.

Credits

Executive Editor
Jody Lefevere

Project Editor
Lynn Northrup

Technical Editor
Dennis R. Cohen

Editorial Director
Robyn Siesky

Business Manager
Amy Knies

Senior Marketing Manager
Sandy Smith

Vice President and Executive Group Publisher
Richard Swadley

Vice President and Executive Publisher
Barry Pruett

Senior Project Coordinator
Kristie Rees

Graphics and Production Specialist
Andrea Hornberger

Quality Control Technician
Melanie Hoffman

Proofreading and Indexing
Melissa D. Buddendeck
BIM Indexing & Proofreading Services

Screen Artist
Ana Carillo

Special Help
Rebekah Worthman

About the Author

Paul McFedries is a technical writer who has been authoring computer books since 1991. He has more than 70 books to his credit, which together have sold more than four million copies worldwide. These books include the Wiley titles *Teach Yourself VISUALLY Macs, Second Edition; MacBook Air Portable Genius, Second Edition; iPhone 4 Portable Genius;* and *Macs Portable Genius, Second Edition.* Paul also runs Word Spy, a website dedicated to tracking new words and phrases (see www.wordspy.com). Please visit Paul's personal website at www.mcfedries.com, or follow him on twitter at www.twitter.com/paulmcf and www.twitter.com/wordspy.

Author's Acknowledgments

The book you hold in your hands is not only an excellent learning tool, but it is truly beautiful, as well. I am happy to have supplied the text that you will read, but the beautiful layout and colors come from Wiley's crack team of graphics specialists. The scope of the tasks, the accuracy of the spelling and grammar, and the veracity of the information are all the result of hard work performed by project editor Lynn Northrup and technical editor Dennis Cohen. Thanks to both of you for your excellent work. My thanks, as well, to acquisitions editor Jody Lefevere for asking me to write this book.

How to Use This Book

Who This Book Is For

This book is for the reader who has never used this particular technology or software application. It is also for readers who want to expand their knowledge.

The Conventions in This Book

① Steps

This book uses a step-by-step format to guide you easily through each task. Numbered steps are actions you must do; bulleted steps clarify a point, step, or optional feature; and indented steps give you the result.

② Notes

Notes give additional information — special conditions that may occur during an operation, a situation that you want to avoid, or a cross reference to a related area of the book.

③ Icons and Buttons

Icons and buttons show you exactly what you need to click to perform a step.

④ Tips

Tips offer additional information, including warnings and shortcuts.

⑤ Bold

Bold type shows command names, options, and text or numbers you must type.

⑥ Italics

Italic type introduces and defines a new term.

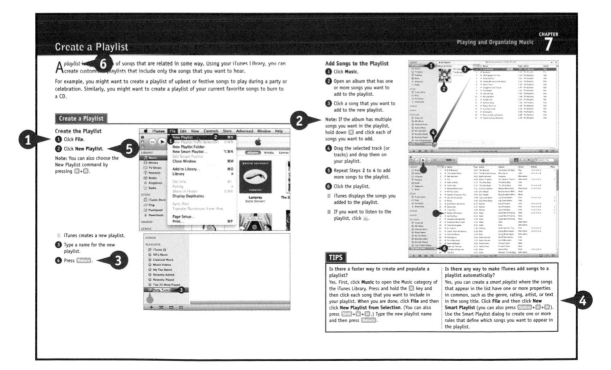

Table of Contents

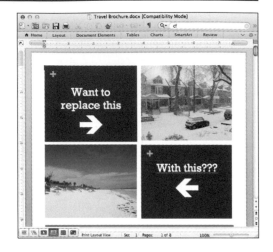

Chapter 3   Learning Basic Mac OS X Document Tasks

Chapter 4   Surfing the World Wide Web

Table of Contents

Chapter 7   Playing and Organizing Music

Chapter 8   Synchronizing an iPod, iPhone, or iPad

Table of Contents

Chapter 11 Customizing Mac OS X to Suit Your Style

Table of Contents

Chapter 14 Working with Your MobileMe Account

Chapter 15 Networking with Mac OS X

CHAPTER 1

Reviewing What You Can Do with Mac OS X

In this chapter you find out about the wide variety of tasks you can perform with Mac OS X, including creating documents; playing music; organizing photos, contacts, and appointments; surfing the web; and communicating with others.

Create Documents

Whether you use your Mac at home, at the office, or on the road, you can use Mac OS X to create a wide variety of documents. In general terms, a *document* is a file that contains information, which is usually text, but it may also consist of pictures, charts, lines, and other nontext items. With Mac OS X, you can create documents such as lists, letters, memos, budgets, forecasts, presentations, and web pages.

Text Documents

You can use text editing software on Mac OS X to create simple documents such as lists, notes, instructions, and other items that do not require fonts, colors, or other types of formatting. With Mac OS X, you can use the TextEdit application to create plain text documents, and the Stickies application to create electronic sticky notes.

> **TextEdit** File Edit Format Window Help
>
> To-Do List — Edited ▾
>
> Helvetica | Regular | 18 | B I U
>
> To-Do List
> ----------------------
> Pick up AA batteries
> Make dinner reservations at Joy Bistro (555-8642)
> Get flowers for Karen
> Call mom
> Drop off books for library
> Clean out office storage area

Word Processing Documents

You can use word processing software on Mac OS X to create letters, résumés, memos, reports, newsletters, brochures, business cards, menus, flyers, invitations, and certificates. Anything that you use to communicate on paper, you can create using Mac OS X. You can also use TextEdit to create formatted documents. Other examples include Microsoft Word for the Mac and Apple iWork Pages.

Spreadsheets

A spreadsheet is a software program that enables you to manipulate numbers and formulas to quickly create powerful mathematical, financial, and statistical models. Mac OS X comes with a test drive version of the Apple iWork Numbers application. Another example is Microsoft Excel for the Mac.

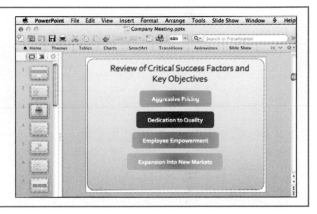

Presentations

A presentation program enables you to build professional-looking slides that you can use to convey your ideas to other people. Mac OS X comes with a test drive version of the Apple iWork Keynote application. Another example is Microsoft PowerPoint for the Mac.

Web Pages

You can use web page editing software on Mac OS X to create your own pages to publish to the web. You can create a personal home page, a blog, or pages to support your business. If your Mac comes with the iLife suite, you can use the iWeb application to create and publish entire websites.

Play and Record Music

M ac OS X is a veritable music machine that you can use to build, organize, play, and share your digital music collection. You can get music onto your Mac by copying it from audio CDs, or by purchasing music online. If you are musically inclined, you can even record or compose new tunes using an application called GarageBand (part of Apple's iLife suite). Once you have a collection of music on your Mac, you can use Mac OS X to create custom music CDs, or copy some or all of the music to a device such as an iPod or iPad.

iTunes

Mac OS X comes with the iTunes application, which stores your library of digital music files. With iTunes you can play albums and songs, organize tunes into related playlists, download and edit track information, and organize your music to suit your style. You can also use iTunes to listen to Internet-based radio stations.

iTunes Store

You can use the iTunes application to connect directly to the online iTunes store, where you can purchase individual songs, usually for 99 cents per song, or entire albums, usually for $9.99 per album. Mac OS X downloads the purchased music to your iTunes library, and you can listen to the music on your Mac or add the music to your iPod, iPhone, or iPad.

Import Music from a CD

You can add tracks from a music CD to the iTunes library. This enables you to listen to an album without having to put the CD into your CD or DVD drive each time. In iTunes, the process of copying tracks from a CD to your Mac is called *importing* or *ripping*.

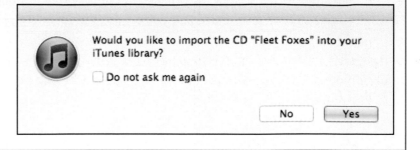

Record Music

Most Macs come with GarageBand, which enables you to record or compose your own tunes. You can attach an instrument such as a guitar or keyboard to your Mac and record your playing. You can also use GarageBand to add accompanying instruments such as drums, bass, piano, or another guitar.

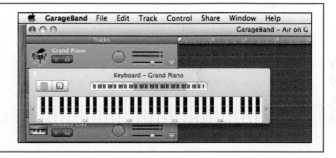

Burn Music to a CD

You can copy, or *burn*, music files from your Mac onto a CD. Burning CDs is a great way to create customized CDs that you can listen to on the computer or in a portable device. You can burn music files using the iTunes application.

Synchronize with an iPod, iPhone, or iPad

You can use the iTunes application to copy some or all of your music library to an iPod, iPhone, or iPad, which enables you to play your music wherever you are or on another audio device that connects to the device. When you attach the iPod, iPhone, or iPad to your Mac, iTunes automatically synchronizes the device according to the settings you specify.

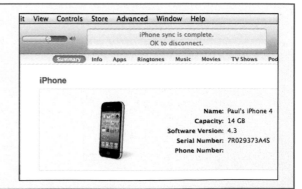

View and Organize Your Photos

Your Mac is perfect for showing your digital photos in their best light. Mac OS X comes with tools that enable you to view individual photos and to run slide shows of multiple photos. Mac OS X also enables you to organize your digital photos, import images from a digital camera or similar device (such as an iPhone or iPad 2), and edit your photos. Many Macs also come with a built-in camera that you can use to take simple snapshots.

View Photos

Mac OS X gives you many ways to view your digital photos. You can view photos within Finder using the Cover Flow view, or by selecting the photos and pressing Spacebar. You can also double-click a photo file to open it using the Preview application, or you can open a file using the iPhoto application, if it is installed on your Mac. Also, both Preview and iPhoto enable you to run photo slide shows.

Organize Photos

If your Mac comes with iPhoto, part of Apple's iLife suite, you can use it to organize your collection of digital photos. For example, you can create albums of related photos, and you can create folders in which to store photos. You can also rename and rate photos, apply keywords to photos, flag important photos, and sort photos in various ways.

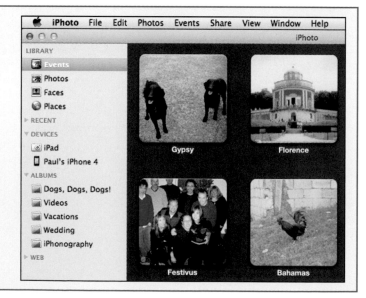

Import Photos to Mac OS X

If you have a digital camera attached to your Mac, you can use either the Image Capture application or the iPhoto application, part of Apple's iLife suite, to import some or all of the camera's images to Mac OS X.

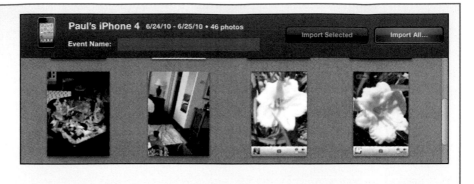

Take Snapshots

If your Mac includes an iSight camera or has a digital video camera connected, you can use the Photo Booth application to take snapshots of whatever subject is currently displayed in the camera. You can also apply various effects to the photos.

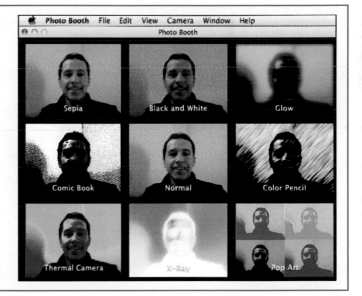

Edit Photos

If your Mac comes with the iPhoto application, you can use it to edit your digital photos. You can rotate, crop, or straighten a photo; you can modify a photo's exposure, contrast, and sharpness; you can fix problems such as red eye and blemishes; and you can apply special effects to a photo.

Play and Make a Movie or DVD

Your Mac's solid graphical underpinnings mean that it is a great tool for video playback. For example, Mac OS X comes with tools that enable you to watch movies on DVD. You can play digital video such as movies, TV shows, and podcast files that you download from the Internet, or digital video that you import from a camera. You can also use Mac OS X to create your own digital movies and your own DVDs.

Play a DVD

If your Mac has a DVD drive, you can use the DVD Player application to play a DVD movie. You can either use full-screen mode to watch the movie using the entire screen, or you can watch the movie in a window while you work on other things. DVD Player has features that enable you to control the movie playback and volume.

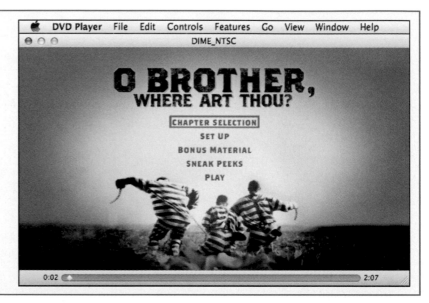

Play a Video File

Mac OS X comes with an application called QuickTime Player that enables you to open video files and control the playback and volume. QuickTime Player also includes many extra features, including the ability to record movies and audio, cut and paste scenes, and publish your videos on services such as YouTube and Facebook.

Play a Movie, TV Show, or Podcast

You most often use iTunes to play music, but you can also use it to play video files stored on your Mac, movies, and TV shows that you purchase from the iTunes store, as well as podcasts that you download from the iTunes store or subscribe to online.

Make a Movie

Most Macs come with an application called iMovie, part of Apple's iLife suite, that enables you to make your own digital movies. You can import clips from a video camera or video file, add clips to the movie, and rearrange and trim those clips as needed. You can also add transitions between scenes, music and sound effects, titles, and more.

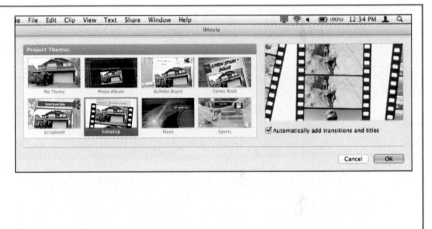

Make a DVD

You can use Mac OS X to create your own custom DVD discs. Using the iDVD application, part of Apple's iLife suite, you can create a DVD project that includes video footage, photos, and audio effects. You can enhance the project with a custom menu, titles, and sophisticated background and text themes. When you are done, you can burn the project to a DVD disc.

Take Advantage of the Web

You can use Mac OS X to connect to your Internet account. Once the connection has been established, you can use the built-in web browser to access almost any site that's available on the web. This means you can use your Mac to search for information, read the latest news, research and purchase goods and services, sell your own items, socialize with others, and more.

Surf the Web

Mac OS X comes with a browser application called Safari that you use to surf the web. With Safari you can navigate web pages, save favorite web pages as bookmarks, and view multiple pages in a single window using tabs.

Search for Information

If you need information on a specific topic, free websites called *search engines* enable you to quickly search the web for pages that have the information you require. You can search the web either by going directly to a search engine site or by using the search feature built into Safari.

Read News

The web is home to many sites that enable you to read the latest news. For example, many print sources have websites, some magazines exist only online, and there are more recent innovations such as blogs and RSS feeds. Some media sites require that you register to access the articles, but on most sites the registration is free.

Buy and Sell

e-Commerce — the online buying and selling of goods and services — is a big part of the web. You can use web-based stores to purchase books, theater tickets, and even cars, which gives you the convenience of shopping at home, easily comparing prices and features, and having goods delivered to your door. Many sites also enable you to sell or auction your products or household items.

Socialize

The web offers many opportunities to socialize, whether you are looking for a friend or a date, or you just want some good conversation. However, it is a good idea to observe some common-sense precautions. For example, arrange to meet new friends in public places, supervise all online socializing done by children, and do not give out personal information to strangers.

Take Advantage of MobileMe

You can use Mac OS X to set up a web-based MobileMe account that enables you to perform many activities online, including exchanging e-mail, maintaining contacts, tracking appointments, sharing photos and videos, and storing files online. You can also synchronize data between Mac OS X and your MobileMe account.

Communicate with Others

You can use Mac OS X to communicate with other people using online and wireless technologies. For example, once you have connected your Mac to the Internet, you can start sending and receiving e-mail, using either your Internet service provider (ISP) account or a web-based account. You can also use your Internet connection to exchange instant messages and perform audio and video chats. If you have a camera attached to your Mac, you can also place video calls to other people through your wired or wireless network.

Exchange E-mail

E-mail is the Internet system that enables you to electronically exchange messages with other Internet users anywhere in the world. To use e-mail, you must have an e-mail account, which is usually supplied by your ISP. The account gives you an e-mail address to which others can send messages. You then set up that account in Mac OS X's Mail application.

Exchange E-mail over the Web

You can also set up a web-based e-mail account. Although you can do this using services such as Hotmail.com and Yahoo.com, many Mac users create MobileMe accounts, which include web-based e-mail. A web-based account is convenient because it enables you to send and receive messages from any computer that has access to the Internet.

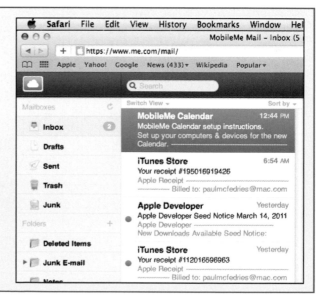

Exchange Instant Messages

Instant messaging allows you to contact other people who are online, thus enabling you to have a real-time exchange of messages. Communicating in real time means that if you send a message to another person who is online, that message appears on the person's computer right away. If that person sends you a response, it appears on your computer right away. On Mac OS X, you use the iChat application to exchange instant messages.

Audio and Video Chat

You can also use the iChat program to audio or video chat with another person. With an audio chat, you speak into a microphone and your voice is sent over the Internet to the other person, who hears you through his or her computer's speakers. You also hear that person's voice through your own speakers. With a video chat, a camera connected to your Mac sends your image over the Internet to the other person. You can also see and hear the other person on your Mac.

Place Video Calls

Mac OS X Lion comes with a program called FaceTime that enables you to make video calls to other people. With a video call, your image is captured by a video camera — such as the iSight camera built into many Macs — and a microphone captures your voice. Both the video and audio streams are sent to the other person, who could be using FaceTime on a Mac, an iPhone 4, or an iPad 2. The other person can also see and hear you.

Organize Your Contacts and Appointments

You can use Mac OS X to help you organize various aspects of your life. For example, Mac OS X comes with tools that enable you to enter, edit, organize, and work with your contacts, which means you can maintain a convenient digital version of your address book. Other Mac OS X tools enable you to schedule events such as appointments, meetings, and trips. You can even configure Mac OS X to synchronize your contacts and schedule among multiple devices.

Maintain Your Address Book

Mac OS X comes with an application called Address Book that enables you to store information about your contacts. For each contact, you can store data such as the person's name, address, telephone number, e-mail address, and birthday.

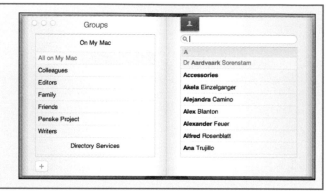

Work with Contacts

You can use your Address Book items to perform several different contact-related tasks. For example, you can use Mail to send a message either to individual contacts or to a contact group, which is an Address Book item that contains multiple contacts. Also, you can use iCal to set up a meeting with one or more contacts.

Schedule an Appointment

You can help organize your life by using Mac OS X to record your appointments on the date and time they occur. You do this using the iCal application, which uses an electronic calendar to store your appointments. You can even configure iCal to display a reminder before an appointment occurs.

Schedule an All-Day Event

If an appointment has no set time — for example, a birthday, anniversary, or multiple-day event such as a sales meeting or vacation — you can use iCal to set up the appointment as an all-day event.

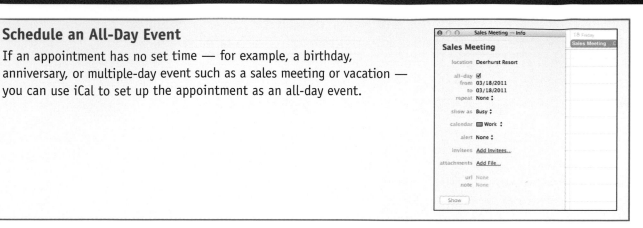

Schedule a Repeating Appointment

If an appointment occurs regularly — for example, once a week or once every three months — you do not need to schedule every appointment by hand. Instead, you can use iCal to configure the activity as a repeating appointment, where you specify the repeat interval. iCal then creates all the future appointments automatically.

Synchronize with MobileMe

If you have a MobileMe account, you can synchronize Mac OS X's contacts and appointments so that they also appear in the MobileMe Address Book and calendar. If you have an iPod touch, iPhone, or iPad, you can use MobileMe to sync those same contacts and appointments to your phone. If you have a second Mac, you can use MobileMe to keep your contacts and appointments in sync on both Macs.

CHAPTER 2

Learning Basic Mac OS X Program Tasks

A crucial Mac OS X concept is the application (also sometimes called a program), because it is via applications that you perform all other Mac OS X tasks. Therefore, it is important to have a basic understanding of how to start and manage applications in Mac OS X.

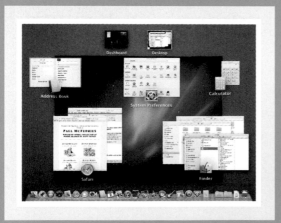

Explore the Mac OS X Screen

Before you can begin to understand how the Mac OS X operating system works, you should become familiar with the basic screen elements.

These elements include the Mac OS X menu bar, the desktop, desktop icons, and the Dock.

Understanding where these elements appear on the screen and what they are used for will help you work through the rest of the tasks in this book and will help you navigate Mac OS X and its applications on your own.

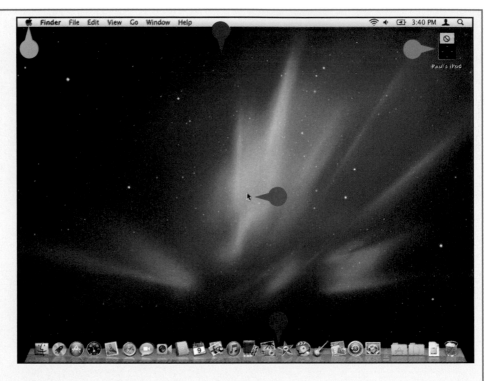

Menu Bar

The menu bar contains the pull-down menus for Mac OS X and most Mac software.

Desktop

This is the Mac OS X work area, where you work with your applications and documents.

Mouse Pointer

When you move your mouse, the pointer moves along with it.

Desktop Icon

An icon on the desktop represents an application, a folder, a document, or a device attached to your Mac, such as a disk drive, a CD or DVD, or an iPod.

Dock

The Dock contains several icons, each of which gives you quick access to some commonly used applications.

Tour the Dock

The Dock is the strip that runs along the bottom of the Mac screen. The Dock is populated with several small images, each of which is called an *icon*. Each icon represents a particular component of your Mac — an application, a folder, a document, and so on — and clicking the icon opens the component.

This makes the Dock one of the most important and useful Mac OS X features because it gives you one-click access to applications, folders, and documents.

The icons shown here are typical, but your Mac may display a different arrangement.

Finder

Work with the files on your computer.

Launchpad

View, organize, and start your applications.

App Store

Install new applications and upgrade existing applications.

Dashboard

Access several cool and handy mini applications called *widgets*.

Mail

Send and receive e-mail messages.

Safari

Browse the World Wide Web on the Internet.

iChat

Converse with other people in real time by sending each other text messages.

FaceTime

Place video calls to other FaceTime users.

Address Book

Store people's names, addresses, and other contact information.

iCal

Record upcoming appointments, birthdays, meetings, and other events.

Preview

View certain files on your Mac, particularly photos.

iTunes

Play music and other media and add media to your iPod, iPhone, or iPad.

Photo Booth

Take a picture using your Mac's camera.

iPhoto

Import and edit digital photos and other images.

iMovie

Import video footage and edit your own digital movies.

iDVD

Burn images or video to a DVD disc.

GarageBand

Create songs, podcasts, and other audio files.

iWeb

Create web pages and maintain websites.

Time Machine

Create and access backups of your files.

System Preferences

Customize and configure your Mac.

Applications

Display the contents of your Applications folder.

Documents

Display the contents of your Documents folder.

Downloads

Display the contents of your Downloads folder.

Trash

Delete files, folders, and applications.

Start an Application

To perform tasks of any kind in Mac OS X, you use one of the applications installed on your Mac. The application you use depends on the task you want to perform. For example, if you want to surf the World Wide Web, you would use a web browser application, such as the Safari program that comes with Mac OS X.

Before you can use an application, however, you must first tell Mac OS X which application you want to run. Mac OS X launches the application and displays it on the desktop. You can then use the application's tools to perform your tasks.

Start an Application

1 Click the **Finder** icon (🖥).

Note: If the application that you want to start has an icon in the Dock, you can click the icon to start the application and skip the rest of these steps.

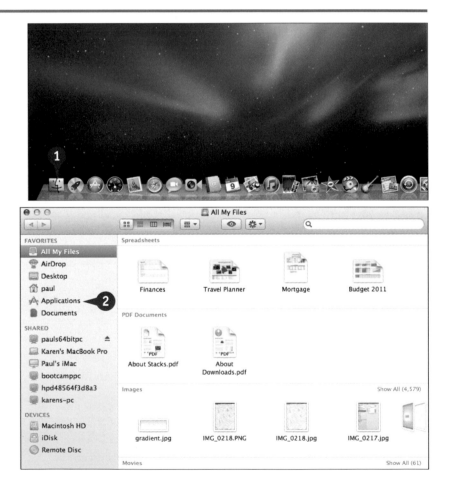

The Finder window appears.

2 Click **Applications**.

Note: You can also navigate to Applications in any Finder window by pressing Shift + ⌘ + A or by clicking **Go** and then clicking **Applications** from Finder's menu bar.

The Applications window appears.

3 Double-click the icon of the application that you want to start.

Note: If you see a folder icon (▢), it means that the application resides in its own folder, a storage area on the computer. Double-click ▢ to open the folder and then double-click the application icon.

- The application appears on the desktop.

- Mac OS X adds a button for the application to the Dock.

- The menu bar displays the menus associated with the application.

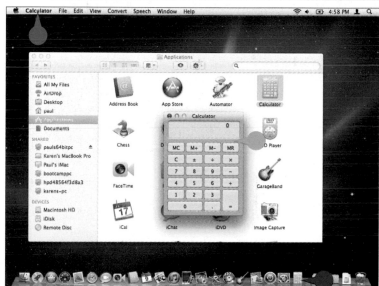

TIPS

How do I add an icon to the Dock for an application I use frequently?

First, start the application as described in Steps **1** to **3**. Right-click the application's Dock icon, click **Options**, and then click **Keep in Dock**.

How do I shut down a running application?

The easiest way is to right-click the application's Dock icon and then click **Quit**. Alternatively, you can switch to the application and press ⌘+Q.

Start an Application Using Launchpad

You can also start an application using the Launchpad feature that is new for Mac OS X Lion. This is often faster than using the Applications folder as described in the previous section, particularly for applications that do not have a Dock icon.

Launchpad is designed to mimic the Home screens of the iPhone, iPad, and iPhone touch. So if you own one or more of these devices, then you are already familiar with how Launchpad works.

Start an Application Using Launchpad

1 Click the **Launchpad** icon (⬤).

The Launchpad screen appears.

2 If the application you want to start resides in a different Launchpad screen, click the dot that corresponds to the screen.

Launchpad switches to the screen and displays the applications.

③ If the application you want to start resides within a folder, click the folder.

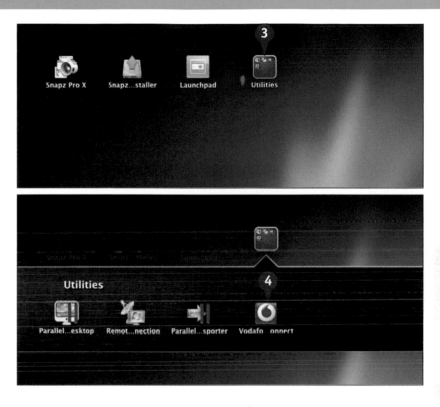

Launchpad opens the folder.

④ Click the icon of the application you want to start.

Mac OS X starts the application.

The dots that represent each Launchpad screen are quite small, making them hard to click with the mouse. Is there an easier way to navigate the Launchpad screens?

Yes. I mentioned earlier that Mac OS X Lion has designed Launchpad to look somewhat similar to the Home screens of the iPhone, iPad, and iPhone touch. Another similarity is how you navigate the screens.

On an iPhone, iPad, and iPhone touch, you navigate the Home screens by using a finger to swipe the screen right or left. With your Mac, you can also navigate the Launchpad screens by swiping. In this case, however, you must use two fingers, and you swipe right or left on either the trackpad or the surface of a Magic Mouse.

Note, too, that you can also use a trackpad gesture to open Launchpad: Place four fingers lightly on the trackpad and pinch them together.

Switch Between Applications

If you plan on running multiple applications at the same time, you need to know how to easily switch from one application to another.

In Mac OS X, after you start one application, you do not need to close that application before you open another one. Mac OS X supports a feature called *multitasking*, which means running two or more applications at once. This is handy if you need to use several applications throughout the day. For example, you might keep your word processing application, your web browser, and your e-mail application open all day.

Switch Between Applications

1 Click the Dock icon of the application that you want to switch to.

● Mac OS X brings the application's window(s) to the foreground.

● The menu bar displays the menus associated with the application.

Note: To switch between applications from the keyboard, press and hold ⌘ and repeatedly press Tab until the application that you want is highlighted in the list of running applications. Release ⌘ to switch to the application.

View Running Applications with Mission Control

The Mission Control feature, which is new in Mac OS X Lion, makes it easier for you to navigate and locate your running applications.

Mac OS X allows you to open multiple applications at once, and the only real limit to the number of open applications you can have is the amount of memory contained in your Mac. In practical terms, this means you can easily open a half a dozen or more applications, some of which may have multiple open windows. To help locate and navigate to the window you need, use the Mission Control feature.

View Running Applications with Mission Control

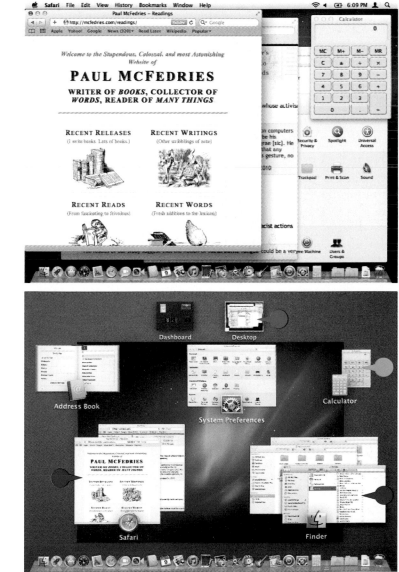

1 Place three fingers on your Mac's trackpad and then swipe up.

Note: You can also invoke Mission Control by pressing `F9` or, depending on how your keyboard is configured, `Fn`+`F9`.

● Mission Control displays each open window.

● Mission Control groups windows from the same application.

To switch to a particular window, click it.

● To close Mission Control without selecting a window, click **Desktop** or press `Esc`.

Tour an Application Window

When you start an application, it appears on the Mac OS X desktop in its own window. Each application has a unique window layout, but almost all application windows have a few features in common.

To get the most out of your applications and to start working quickly and efficiently in an application, you need to know what these common features are and where to find them within the application window.

Close Button

Click the **Close** button (●) to remove the application window from the desktop, usually without exiting the application.

Minimize Button

Click the **Minimize** button (●) to remove the window from the desktop and display an icon for the currently open document in the right side of the Dock. The window is still open, but not active.

Zoom Button

Click the **Zoom** button (●) to enlarge the window so that it can display all of its content, or as much of its content as can fit the screen.

Toolbar

The toolbar contains buttons that offer easy access to common application commands and features, although not all applications have toolbars. To move the window, click and drag the toolbar.

Status Bar

The status bar displays information about the current state of the application or document.

Vertical Scrollbar

Use the vertical scrollbar to navigate up and down in a document. Click **Scroll Up** (▲) to navigate up; click **Scroll Down** (▼) to navigate down.

Horizontal Scrollbar

Use the horizontal scrollbar to navigate left and right in a document. Click **Scroll Left** (◄) to navigate left, and click **Scroll Right** (►) to navigate right.

Resize Control

Click and drag ▨ in the lower right corner of the window to make the window larger or smaller.

Run an Application Full Screen

You can maximize the viewing and working areas of an application by running that application in full-screen mode. When you switch to full-screen mode, Mac OS X hides the menu bar, the application's status bar, the Dock, and the top section of the application window (the section that includes the Close, Minimize, and Zoom icons). Mac OS X then expands the rest of the application window so that it takes up the entire screen.

You must be running Mac OS X Lion to use full-screen mode. Note, too, that not all programs are capable of switching to full-screen mode.

Run an Application Full Screen

1 Click **View**.

2 Click **Enter Full Screen**.

● You can also hold down
Option and click 🔲 .

Mac OS X expands the application window to take up the entire screen.

Note: To exit full-screen mode, move the mouse ▸ up to the top of the screen to reveal the menu bar, click **View**, and then click **Exit Full Screen**.

Select a Command from a Pull-Down Menu

When you are working in an application, you can use the menu bar to access the application's commands and features. Each item in the menu bar represents a *pull-down menu*, a collection of commands usually related to each other in some way. For example, the File menu commands usually deal with file-related tasks such as opening and closing documents.

The items in a menu are either commands that execute an action in the application, or features that you can turn on and off.

Select a Command from a Pull-Down Menu

Execute Commands

1 Click the name of the menu that you want to display.

● The application displays the menu.

2 Click the command that you want to execute.

The application executes the command.

● If a command is followed by an ellipsis (...), it means the command displays a dialog.

● If a command is followed by an arrow (▶), it means the command displays a submenu. Click the command to open the submenu and then click the command that you want to run.

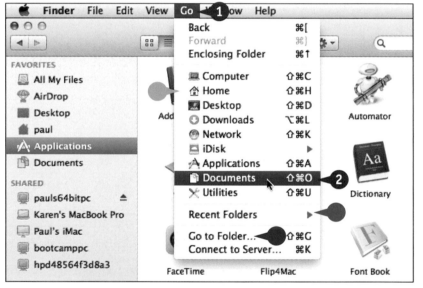

Turn Features On and Off

1 Click the name of the menu that you want to display.

● The application displays the menu.

2 Click the menu item.

You may have to click for a submenu if your command is not on the main menu.

The application turns the feature either on (a check mark (✓) appears the next time you open the menu) or off (no check mark appears the next time you open the menu).

Select a Command Using a Toolbar

Y ou can access many application commands faster by using the toolbar. Many applications come with a toolbar, which is a collection of buttons, lists, and other controls displayed in a strip, usually across the top of the application window. Because the toolbar is always visible, you can always use it to select commands, which means that the toolbar often gives you one-click access to the application's most common features. This is faster than using the menu bar method, which often takes several clicks, depending on the command.

Select a Command Using a Toolbar

Turn Features On and Off

1 Click the toolbar button that represents the feature you want to turn on.

● The application turns the feature on and indicates this state by highlighting the toolbar button.

● When a feature is turned off, the application does not highlight the button.

Execute Commands

1 Click the toolbar button that represents the command that you want.

2 If the button displays a menu, click the command on the menu.

● The application executes the command.

Select Options with Dialog Controls

You often interact with an application by selecting options or typing text using a dialog.

A *dialog* is a small window that appears when an application has information for you, or needs you to provide information. For example, when you select the File menu's Print command to print a document, you use the Print dialog to specify the number of copies that you want to print.

You provide that and other information by accessing various types of dialog controls. To provide information to an application quickly and accurately, you need to know what these dialog controls look like and how they work.

Command Button

Clicking a command button executes the command written on the button face. For example, you can click **OK** to apply settings that you have chosen in a dialog, or you can click **Cancel** to close the dialog without changing the settings.

Enter the URL of the calendar you want to subscribe to.

Calendar URL: `http://ical.me.com/mycalendar.ics`

Cancel   Subscribe

Text Box

A text box enables you to enter typed text. Use the **Del** key to delete any existing characters, and then type your text.

List Box

A list box displays a list of choices from which you select the item you want. Use the vertical scrollbar to bring the item you want into view, and then click the item to select it.

Spelling and Grammar

fleet

Change
Find Next

glee
glees
Glenn
glen
fleet
gleed

Ignore
Learn
Define
Guess

Automatic by Language
Check grammar

Tabs

Many dialogs offer a large number of controls, so related controls appear on different tabs, and the tab names and icons appear across the top of the dialog. Click a tab to see its controls.

Pop-Up Menu

A pop-up menu displays a list of choices from which you select the item you want. Click ⬍ to pop up the menu, and then click the item that you want to select.

Check Box

Clicking a check box toggles an application feature on and off. If you are turning on a feature, the check box changes from ☐ to ☑; if you are turning off the feature, the check box changes from ☑ to ☐.

Radio Button

Clicking a radio button turns on an application feature. Only one radio button in a group can be turned on at a time. When you click a radio button that is currently off, it changes from ○ to ◉; a radio button that is on changes from ◉ to ○.

CHAPTER 3

Learning Basic Mac OS X Document Tasks

Much of the work you do in Mac OS X will involve documents, which are files that contain text, images, and other data. These tasks include saving, opening, printing, and editing documents, as well as copying and renaming files.

Save a Document

After you create a document and make changes to it, you can save the document to preserve your work.

When you work on a document, Mac OS X stores the changes in your computer's memory. However, Mac OS X erases the contents of the Mac's memory each time you shut down or restart the computer. This means that the changes you have made to your document are lost when you turn off or restart your Mac.

However, saving the document preserves your changes on your Mac's hard disk.

Save a Document

1 Click **File**.

2 Click **Save**.

In most applications, you can also press ⌘+S.

If you have saved the document previously, your changes are now preserved, and you do not need to follow the rest of the steps in this section.

If this is a new document that you have never saved before, the Save dialog appears.

3 Use the Save As text box to type the filename you want to use.

● To store the file in a different folder, you can click ⁝ in the Where list and then click the location that you prefer.

4 Click **Save**.

The application saves the file.

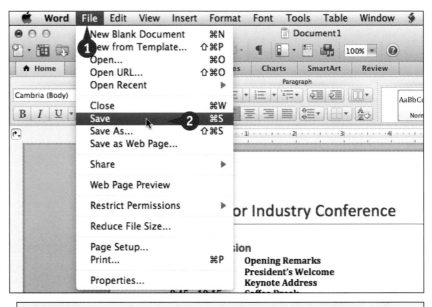

Open a Document

To work with a document that you have saved in the past, you can open it in the application that you used to create it.

When you save a document, you save its contents to your Mac's hard disk, and those contents are stored in a separate file. When you open the document using the same application that you used to save it, Mac OS X loads the file's contents into memory and displays the document in the application. You can then view or edit the document as needed.

Open a Document

1 Start the application that you want to work with.

2 Click **File**.

3 Click **Open**.

In most applications, you can also press ⌘+O.

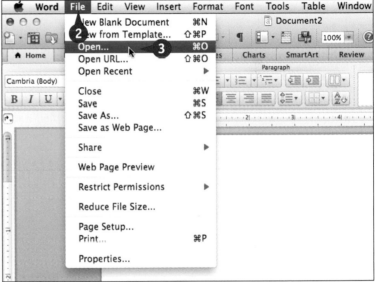

The Open dialog appears.

● To select a different folder from which to open the file, you can click ⁑ and then click the location that you prefer.

4 Click the document.

5 Click **Open**.

The document appears in the application window.

Print a Document

When you need a hard copy of your document, either for your files or to distribute to someone else, you can send the document to your printer.

Most applications that deal with documents also come with a Print command. When you run this command, the Print dialog appears. You use the Print dialog to choose the printer you want to use as well as to specify how many copies you want to print. Many Print dialogs also enable you to see a preview of your document before printing it.

Print a Document

1 Turn on your printer.

2 Open the document that you want to print.

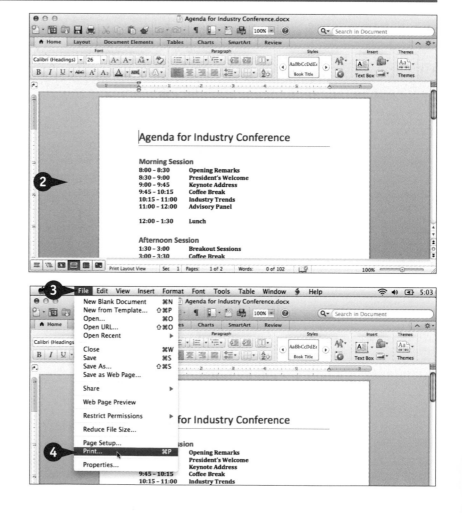

3 Click **File**.

4 Click **Print**.

In many applications, you can select the Print command by pressing ⌘+P.

The Print dialog appears.

The layout of the Print dialog varies from application to application. The version shown here is a typical example.

5 If you have more than one printer, click ⁝ in the Printer list to select the printer that you want to use.

● To print more than one copy, click **Show Details** (in some cases, you click ⊡ to expand the dialog instead) and then use the Copies text box to type the number of copies to print.

6 Click **Print**.

● Mac OS X prints the document. The printer's icon appears in the Dock while the document prints.

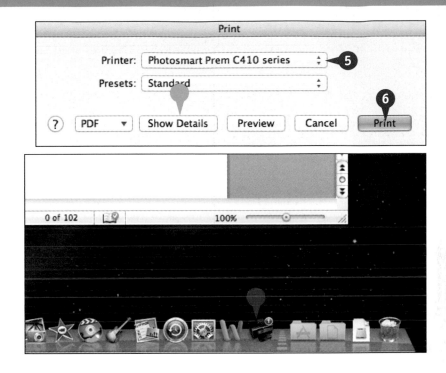

Can I preview my document before I print it?
Yes. It is a good idea to preview the document before printing it to ensure that the document layout looks the way you want. To preview the document, follow Steps **1** to **4** in this section to display the Print dialog. Click **Preview** to display the document in the Preview application. When you are done, click **Preview** and then click **Quit Preview**.

Edit Document Text

When you work with a character-based file, such as a text or word processing document or an e-mail message, you need to know the basic techniques for editing, selecting, copying, and moving text.

It is rare that any text you enter into a document is perfect the first time through. It is far more likely that the text contains errors that require correcting, or words, sentences, or paragraphs that appear in the wrong place.

To get your document text the way you want it, you need to know to edit text, including deleting characters, selecting the text you want to work with, and copying and moving text.

Edit Document Text

Delete Characters

1 In a text document, click immediately to the right of the last character that you want to delete.

● The cursor appears after the character.

Agenda for Industry Conference

Morning Session
8:00 – 8:30	Opening Remarks
8:30 – 9:00	President's Welcome
9:00 – 9:45	Keynote Address
9:45 – 10:15	Coffee Break
10:15 – 11:00	Industry Trends
11:00 – 12:00	Advisory Panel
12:00 – 1:30	Lunch

Afternoon Session
1:30 – 3:00	Breakout Sessions
3:00 – 3:30	Coffee Break
3:30 – 4:30	A Look at the Future of the Industry

2 Press Del until you have deleted all the characters you want.

If you make a mistake, immediately click **Edit**, and then click **Undo**. You can also press ⌘+Z.

Agenda for Industry Conference

Morning Session
8:00 – 8:30	Opening Remarks
8:30 – 9:00	President's Welcome
9:00 – 9:45	Keynote Address
9:45 – 10:15	Coffee Break
10:15 – 11:00	Industry Trends
11:00 – 12:00	Advisory Panel
12:00 – 1:30	Lunch

Afternoon Session
1:30 – 3:00	Breakout Sessions
3:00 – 3:30	Coffee Break
3:30 – 4:30	A Look at the Future

Select Text for Editing

1 Click and drag across the text that you want to select.

2 Release the mouse button.

● The application highlights the selected text.

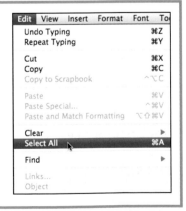

TIP

Are there any shortcut methods for selecting text?

Yes, most Mac OS X applications have shortcuts you can use. Here are the most useful ones:

- Double-click a word to select it.
- Hold down **Shift** and press → or ← to select entire words.
- Hold down **Shift** and **⌘** and press → to select to the end of the line, or ← to select to the beginning of the line.
- Triple-click inside a paragraph to select it.
- Click **Edit** and then click **Select All**, or press **⌘**+**A** to select the entire document.

continued ►

O nce you select text, you can then copy or move the text to another location in your document. Copying text is often a useful way to save work. For example, if you want to use the same passage of text elsewhere in the document, you can copy it instead of typing it from scratch. Similarly, if you need a similar passage in another part of the document, copy the original and then edit the copy as needed.

If you entered a passage of text in the wrong position within the document, you can fix that by moving the text to the correct location.

Edit Document Text (continued)

Copy Text

1 Select the text that you want to copy.

2 Click **Edit**.

3 Click **Copy**.

In most applications, you can also press ⌘+C.

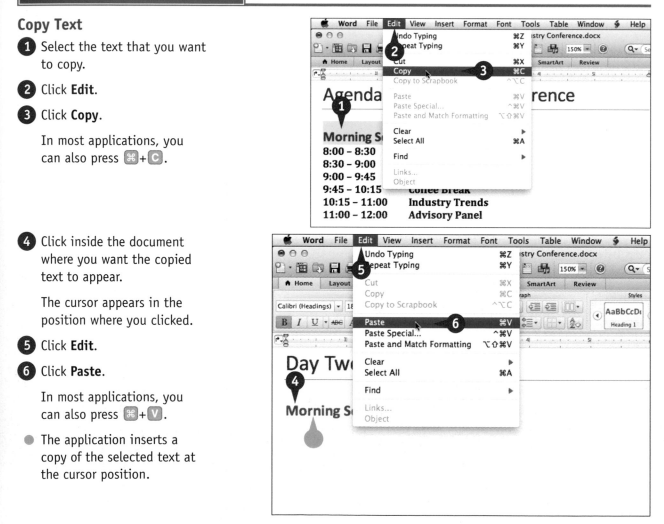

4 Click inside the document where you want the copied text to appear.

The cursor appears in the position where you clicked.

5 Click **Edit**.

6 Click **Paste**.

In most applications, you can also press ⌘+V.

● The application inserts a copy of the selected text at the cursor position.

Move Text

1 Select the text that you want to move.

2 Click **Edit**.

3 Click **Cut**.

In most applications, you can also press ⌘+X.

The application removes the text from the document.

4 Click inside the document where you want to move the text.

The cursor appears at the position where you clicked.

5 Click **Edit**.

6 Click **Paste**.

In most applications, you can also press ⌘+.

● The application inserts the text at the cursor position.

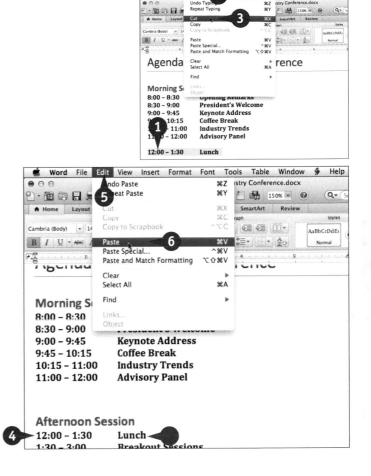

TIP

How do I move and copy text with my mouse?

First, select the text that you want to move or copy. To move the selected text, position the mouse pointer over the selection and then click and drag the text to the new position within the document.

To copy the selected text, position the mouse pointer over the selection, press and hold the **Option** key, and then click and drag the text (the mouse ➤ changes to ➤) to the new position within the document.

Afternoon Session
12:00 – 1:30	Lunch
1:30 – 3:00	Breakout Sessions
3:00 – 3:30	Coffee Break
3:30 – 4:30	A Look at the Future

Day Two

Morning Session

Afternoon Session
8:00 – 1:30	Lunch
1:30 – 3:00	Breakout Sessions
3:00 – 3:30	Coffee Break
3:30 – 4:30	A Look at the Future

Copy a File

You can use Mac OS X to make an exact copy of a file. This is useful when you want to make an extra copy of an important file to use as a backup. Similarly, you might require a copy of a file if you want to send the copy on a disk to another person. Finally, copying a file is also a real timesaver if you need a new file very similar to an existing file: You copy the original file and then make the required changes to the copy.

You can copy either a single file or multiple files. You can also use this technique to copy a folder.

Copy a File

1 Locate the file that you want to copy.

2 Open the folder to which you want to copy the file.

To open a second folder window, click **File** and then click **New Finder Window**, or press ⌘+N.

3 Press and hold the Option key, and then click and drag the file and drop it inside the destination folder.

● The original file remains in its folder.

● A copy of the original file appears in the destination folder.

You can also make a copy of a file in the same folder, which is useful if you want to make major changes to the file and you would like to preserve a copy of the original. Click the file, click **File**, and then click **Duplicate**, or press ⌘+D. Mac OS X creates a copy with the word "copy" added to the filename.

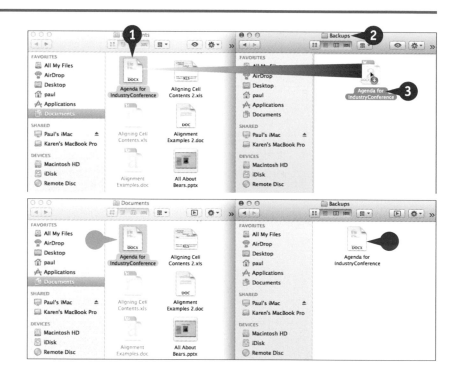

Move a File

When you need to store a file in a new location, the easiest way is to move the file from its current folder to another folder on your Mac.

When you save a file for the first time, you specify a folder on your Mac's hard disk. This original location is not permanent, however. Using the technique in this section, you can move the file to another location on your Mac's hard disk.

You can use this technique to move a single file, multiple files, and even a folder.

Move a File

1 Locate the file that you want to move.

2 Open the folder to which you want to move the file.

To create a new destination folder in the current folder, click **File** and then click **New Folder**, or press Shift | ⌘ | N.

3 Click and drag the file and drop it inside the destination folder.

Note: If you are moving the file to another disk drive, you must hold down ⌘ while you click and drag the file.

● The file disappears from its original folder.

● The file moves to the destination folder.

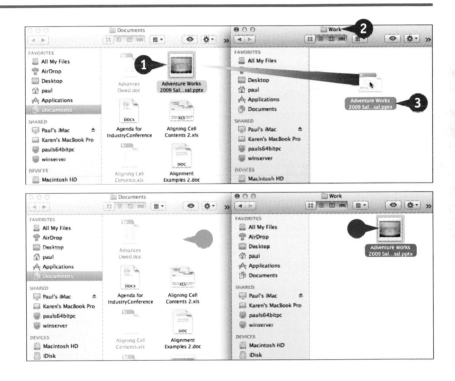

Rename a File

You can change the name of a file, which is useful if the current filename does not accurately describe the contents of the file. By giving your document a descriptive name, you make it easier to find the file later.

You should rename only those documents that you have created or that have been given to you by someone else. Do not try to rename any of the Mac OS X system files or any files associated with your applications, or your computer may behave erratically, or even crash.

Rename a File

1 Open the folder containing the file that you want to rename.

2 Click the file.

3 Press **Return**.

● A text box appears around the filename.

You can also rename any folders that you have created.

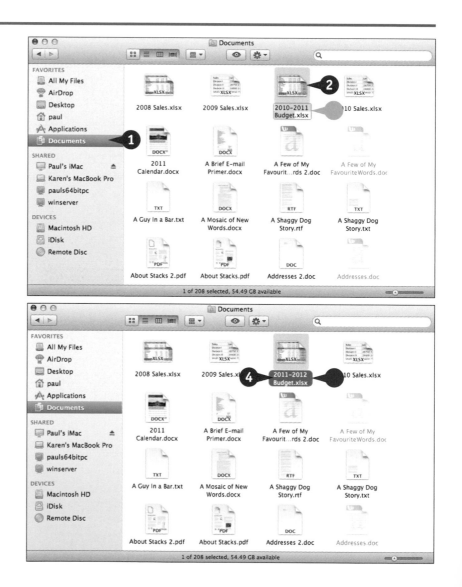

4 Edit the existing name or type a new name that you want to use for the file.

If you decide that you do not want to rename the file after all, you can press **Esc** to cancel the operation.

5 Press **Return** or click an empty section of the folder.

● The new name appears under the file icon.

Delete a File

When you no longer need a file, you can delete it. This helps to prevent your hard drive from becoming cluttered with unnecessary files.

You should ensure that you delete only those documents that you have created or that have been given to you by someone else. Do not delete any of the Mac OS X system files or any files associated with your applications, or your computer may behave erratically, or even crash.

Delete a File

1 Locate the file that you want to delete.

2 Click and drag the file and drop it on the Trash icon in the Dock.

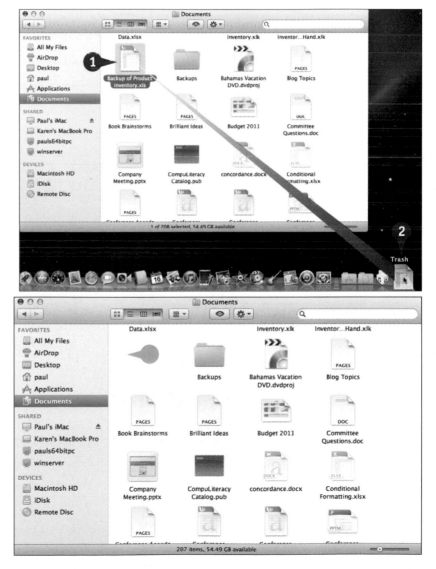

● The file disappears from the folder.

You can also delete a file by clicking it and then pressing ⌘+Del.

If you delete a file accidentally, you can restore it. Simply click the Dock's Trash icon to open the Trash window. Click and drag the file from the Trash window and drop it back in its original folder.

CHAPTER 4

Surfing the World Wide Web

The *World Wide Web*, or simply, the web, is a massive storehouse of information that resides on computers, called web servers, located all over the world. Information is presented on web pages that you download to your computer using a web browser program, such the Mac OS X Safari application. Each web page can combine text with images, sounds, music, and even videos to present information on a particular subject.

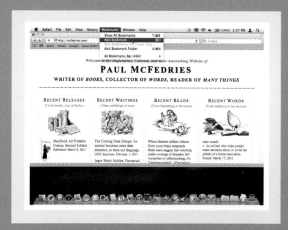

Open and Close Safari

To access websites and view web pages, you must use a web browser program. In Mac OS X, the default web browser is Safari, which you can use to surf websites when your Mac is connected to the Internet.

The Safari application offers a number of features that make it easier to browse the web. For example, you can open multiple pages in a single Safari window, you can save your favorite sites for easier access, and you can perform Internet searches from the Safari window.

To use these features, you must know how to start the Safari application. When you have finished surfing the web, you also need to know how to shut down Safari to save system resources on your Mac.

Open and Close Safari

Open Safari

1 In the Dock, click the **Safari** icon (●).

The Safari window appears.

Note: The initial web page you see depends on how your version of Safari has been configured. In most cases, you see the Apple.com Start page.

Close Safari

1 Click **Safari**.

2 Click **Quit Safari**.

TIPS

Are there other methods I can use to open Safari?

If you have removed the ◎ icon from the Dock, there are a couple of other quick methods you can use to start Safari. If you have used Safari recently, click ⬥, click **Recent Items**, and then click **Safari**. You can also click **Spotlight** (🔍), type **Safari**, and then click **Safari** in the search results.

Are there faster methods I can use to close Safari?

Probably the fastest method you can use to quit Safari is to right-click its icon (◎) and then click **Quit**. If your hands are closer to the keyboard than to the mouse, you can quit Safari by switching to the application and then pressing ⌘+Q.

Select a Link

Almost all web pages include links to other pages that contain related information. When you select a link, your web browser loads the other page.

Web page links come in two forms: text and images. Text links consist of a word or phrase that usually appears underlined and in a different color from the rest of the page text. However, web page designers can control the look of their links, so text links may not always stand out in this way. Therefore, knowing which words, phrases, or images are links is not always obvious. The only way to tell for sure is to position the mouse ( ) over the text or image; if the changes to , you know the item is a link.

Select a Link

1 Position over the link (changes to).

2 Click the text or image.

● The status bar shows the address of the linked page.

Note: The address shown in the status bar when you point at a link may be different from the one shown when the page is downloading. This occurs when the website "redirects" the link.

Note: If you do not see the status bar, click **View** then click **Show Status Bar**.

The linked web page appears.

● The status bar shows the current download status.

● The web page title and address change after the linked page is loaded.

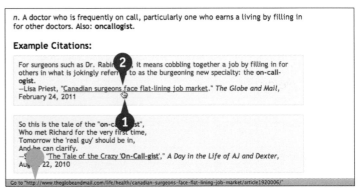

Enter a Web Page Address

If you know the address of a specific web page, you can type it into the web browser to display the page. Every web page is uniquely identified by an address called the Uniform Resource Locator, or URL (pronounced *yoo-ar-ell* or *erl*).

The URL is composed of four basic parts: the *transfer method* (usually HTTP, which stands for Hypertext Transfer Protocol), the website *domain name*, the *directory* where the web page is located on the server, and the *web page filename*.

The website domain name suffix most often used is .com (commercial), but other common suffixes include .gov (government), .org (nonprofit organization), .edu (education), and country domains such as .ca (Canada).

Enter a Web Page Address

1 Click inside the address bar.

2 Press **Del** to delete the existing address.

3 Type the address of the web page you want to visit.

4 Press **Return**.

The web page appears.

● The web page title changes after the page is loaded.

Open a Web Page in a Tab

You can make it easier to work with multiple web pages and sites simultaneously by opening each page in its own tab. As you surf the web, you may come upon a page that you want to keep available while you visit other sites. That page may contain important information that you need to reference, or it might be a page that you want to read later on.

Instead of leaving the page and trying to find it again when you need it, Safari lets you leave the page open in a special section of the browser window called a *tab*. You can then use a second tab to visit your other sites, and to resume viewing the first site, you need only click its tab.

Open a Web Page in a Tab

Open a Link in a New Tab

1 Right-click the link you want to open.

2 Click **Open Link in New Tab**.

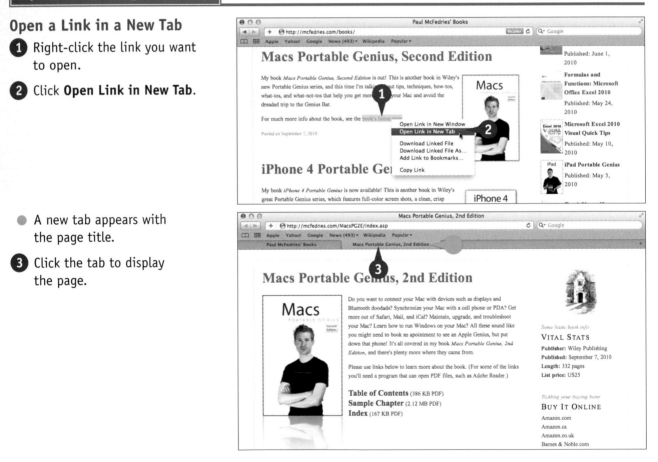

● A new tab appears with the page title.

3 Click the tab to display the page.

Create a New Tab

1 Click **File**.

2 Click **New Tab**.

● If you already have two or more tabs open, you can also click the **Create a new tab** icon (+).

● Safari creates a new tab.

3 Type the address of the page you want to load into the new tab.

4 Press **Return**.

● Safari displays the page in the tab.

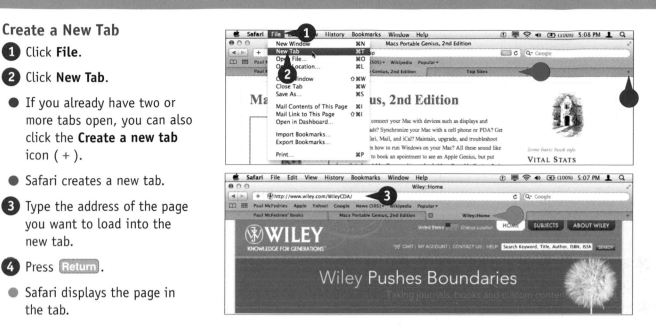

TIP

Are there any shortcuts I can use to open web pages in tabs?

Here are some useful keyboard techniques:

• Press and hold ⌘ and click a link to open the page in a tab.

• Press and hold ⌘+Shift and click a link to open the page in a tab and display the tab.

• Type an address and then press ⌘+Return to open the page in a new tab.

• Type an address and then press Shift+⌘+Return to open the page in a new foreground tab.

• Press Shift+⌘+] or Shift+⌘+[to cycle through the tabs.

• Press ⌘+W to close the current tab.

• Press Option and click ⊠ to close every tab but the one you clicked.

Navigate Web Pages

After you have visited several pages, you can return to a page you visited earlier. Instead of retyping the address or looking for the link, Safari gives you some easier methods.

When you navigate from page to page, you create a kind of "path" through the web. Safari keeps track of this path by maintaining a list of the pages you have visited. You can use that list to go back to a page you have visited.

After you have gone back to a page you have visited, you can also use the same list of pages to go forward through the pages again.

Navigate Web Pages

Go Back One Page

1 Click the **Previous Page** icon (◀).

The previous page you visited appears.

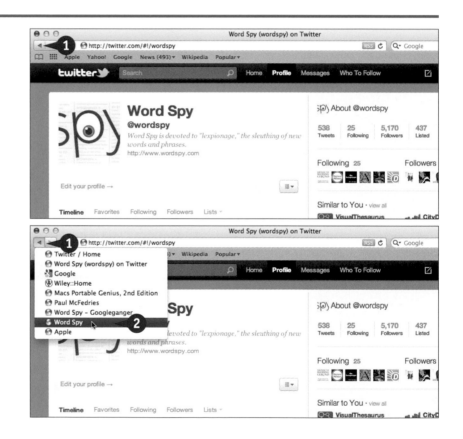

Go Back Several Pages

1 Click and hold down ▸ on ◀.

Note: The list of visited pages is different for each tab that you have open. If you do not see the page you want, you may need to click a different tab.

A list of the pages you have visited appears.

2 Click the page you want to revisit.

The page appears.

Go Forward One Page

1 Click the **Next Page** icon (▶).

The next page appears.

Note: If you are at the last page viewed up to that point, ▶ is not active.

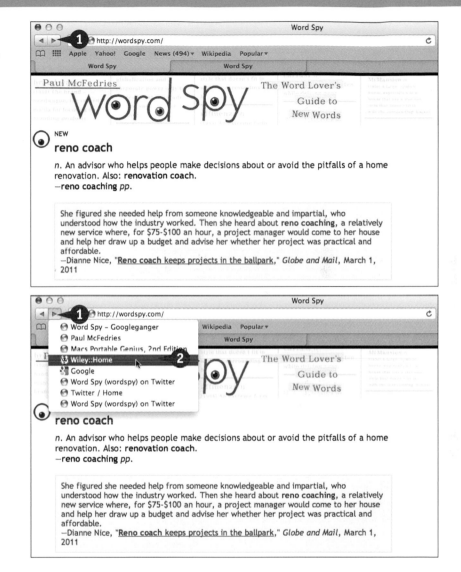

Go Forward Several Pages

1 Click and hold down ⬉ on ▶.

A list of the pages you have visited appears.

Note: The list of visited pages is different for each tab that you have open. If you do not see the page you want, you may need to click a different tab.

2 Click the page you want to revisit.

The page appears.

TIP

Are there any shortcuts I can use to navigate web pages?

Yes, there are a few useful keyboard shortcuts you can use:

- Press ⌘+[to go back one page.
- Press ⌘+] to go forward one page.
- Press Shift+⌘+H to return to the Safari home page (the first page you see when you open Safari).

Navigate with the History List

The Previous Page and Next Page buttons (◄ and ►) enable you to navigate pages in the current browser session. To redisplay sites that you have visited in the past few days or weeks, you need to use the History list, which is a collection of the websites and pages you have visited over the past month.

If you visit sensitive places such as an Internet banking site or your corporate site, you can increase security by clearing the history list so that other people cannot see where you have been.

Navigate with the History List

Load a Page from the History List

1 Click **History**.

2 Click the date when you visited the page.

A submenu of pages that you visited during that day appears.

3 Click the page you want to revisit.

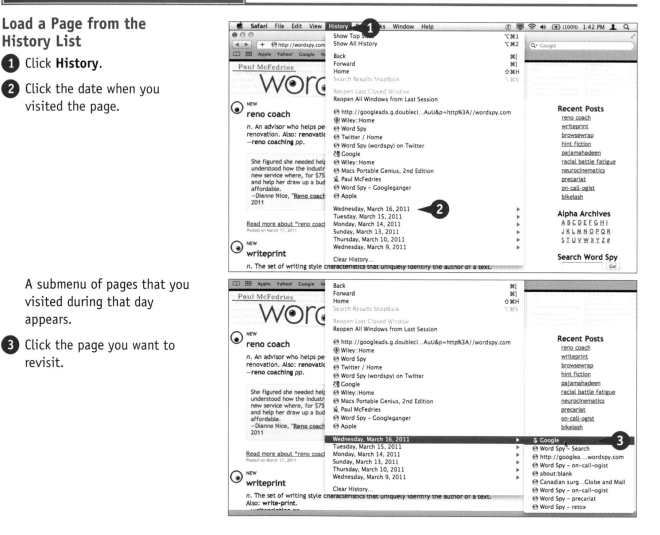

● The page appears.

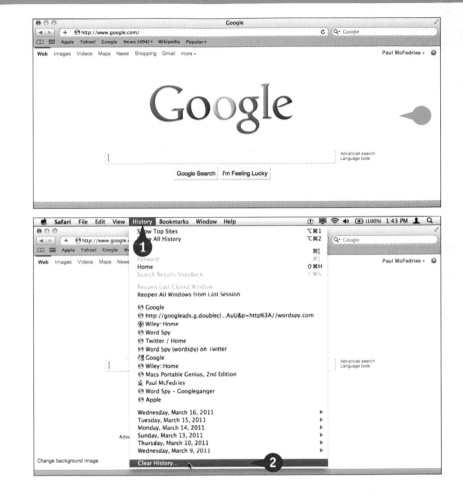

Clear the History List

1 Click **History**.

2 Click **Clear History**.

Safari deletes all the pages from the history list.

TIP

Can I control the length of time that Safari keeps track of the pages I visit?

Yes, by following these steps:

1 In the menu bar, click **Safari**.

2 Click **Preferences**.

3 Click **General**.

4 In the Remove history items pop-up menu, click and then click the amount of time you want Safari to track your history.

5 Click .

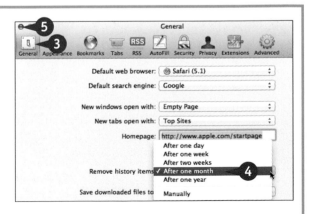

Change Your Home Page

Your home page is the web page that appears when you first start Safari. The default home page is usually the Apple.com Start page, but you can change that to any other page you want, or even to an empty page. This is useful if you do not use the Apple.com Start page, or if there is another page that you always visit at the start of your browsing session. For example, if you have your own website, it might make sense to always begin there.

Safari also comes with a command that enables you to view the home page at any time during your browsing session.

Change Your Home Page

Change the Home Page

1 Display the web page that you want to use as your home page.

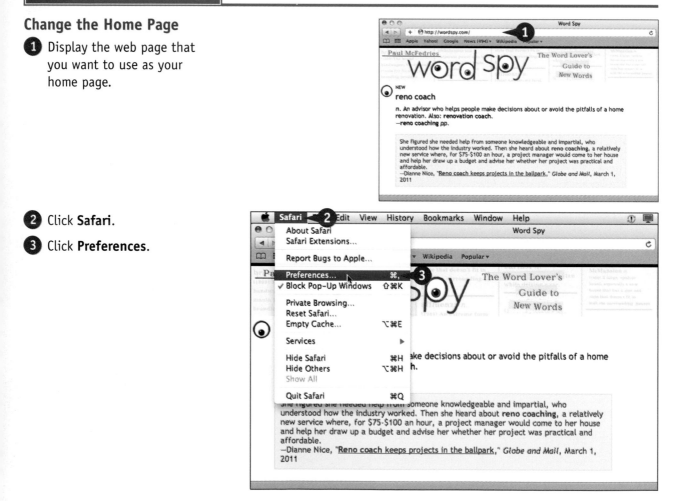

2 Click **Safari**.

3 Click **Preferences**.

④ Click **General**.

⑤ Click **Set to Current Page**.

● Safari inserts the address of the current page in the Homepage text box.

Note: If your Mac is not currently connected to the Internet, you can also type the new home page address manually using the Homepage text box.

⑥ Click .

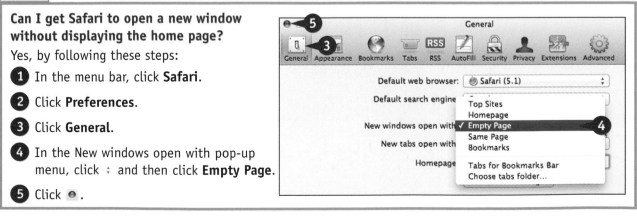

View the Home Page

① Click **History**.

② Click **Home**.

Note: You can also display the home page by pressing Shift + ⌘ + H.

Safari displays the home page.

TIP

Can I get Safari to open a new window without displaying the home page?
Yes, by following these steps:

① In the menu bar, click **Safari**.

② Click **Preferences**.

③ Click **General**.

④ In the New windows open with pop-up menu, click ⁝ and then click **Empty Page**.

⑤ Click ●.

Bookmark Web Pages

If you have web pages that you visit frequently, you can save yourself time by storing those pages as bookmarks within Safari. This enables you to display the pages with just a couple of mouse clicks.

The bookmark stores the name of the page as well as the address of the page. Most bookmarks are stored on Safari's Bookmarks menu. However, Safari also offers the Bookmarks bar, which appears just below the address bar. You can put your favorite sites on the Bookmarks bar for easiest access.

Bookmark Web Pages

Bookmark a Web Page

1 Display the web page you want to save as a bookmark.

2 Click **Bookmarks**.

3 Click **Add Bookmark**.

● You can also run the Add Bookmark command by clicking **Add a bookmark** (+).

The Add Bookmark dialog appears.

Note: You can also display the Add Bookmark dialog by pressing ⌘+D.

4 Edit the page name, if necessary.

5 Click ⁝ and then click the location where you want to store the bookmark.

6 Click **Add**.

Safari adds a bookmark for the page.

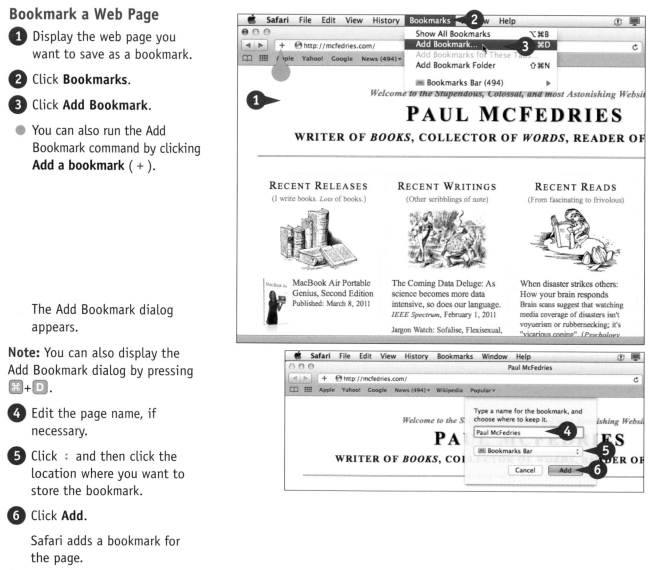

Display a Bookmarked Web Page

1 Click the **Show all bookmarks** button (📖).

● If you added the bookmark to the Bookmarks bar, click the page name.

● If you added the bookmark to a folder, click the folder and then click the page name.

The Bookmarks window appears.

2 Click ▸ to open the folder that contains the bookmark you want (▸ changes to ▾).

3 Double-click the bookmark.

The web page appears.

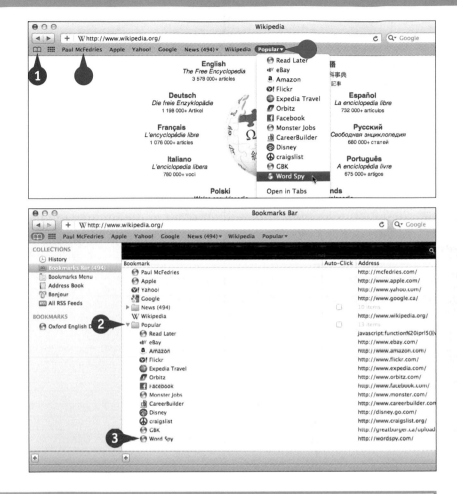

TIPS

I use my Bookmarks bar a lot. Is there an easier way to display these pages?

Yes. Safari automatically assigns keyboard shortcuts to the first nine bookmarks, counting from left to right and not including folders. For example, you display the left-most bookmark by pressing ⌘+1. Moving to the right, the shortcuts are ⌘+2, ⌘+3, and so on.

How do I delete a bookmark?

If the site is on the Bookmarks bar, right-click the bookmark and then click **Delete**, or hold down ⌘ and drag it off the bar. For all other bookmarks, click 📖 to display the Bookmarks window. Locate the bookmark you want to remove, right-click the bookmark, and then click **Delete**. You can also click the bookmark and then press Del.

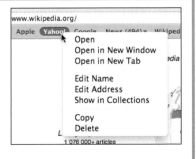

Search for Sites

I f you need information on a specific topic, Safari has a built-in feature that enables you to quickly search the web for sites that have the information you require.

The web has a number of sites called *search engines* that enable you to find what you are looking for. By default, Safari uses the Google search site (www.google.com). Simple, one-word searches often return tens of thousands of *hits*, or matching sites. To improve your searching, type multiple search terms that define what you are looking for. To search for a phrase, enclose the words in quotation marks.

Search for Sites

1 Click in the search box.

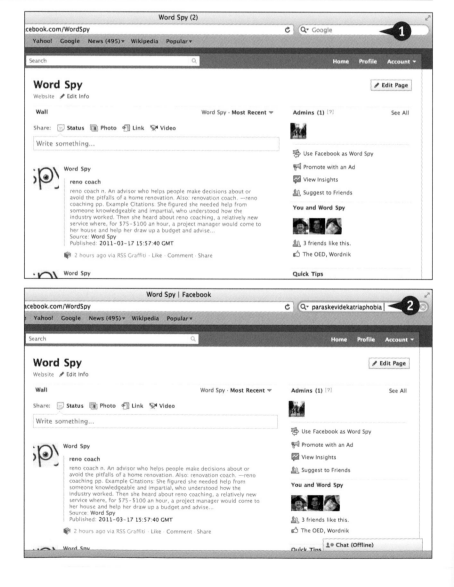

2 Type a word, phrase, or question that represents the information you want to find.

3 Press Return.

● A list of pages that match your search text appears.

④ Click a web page.

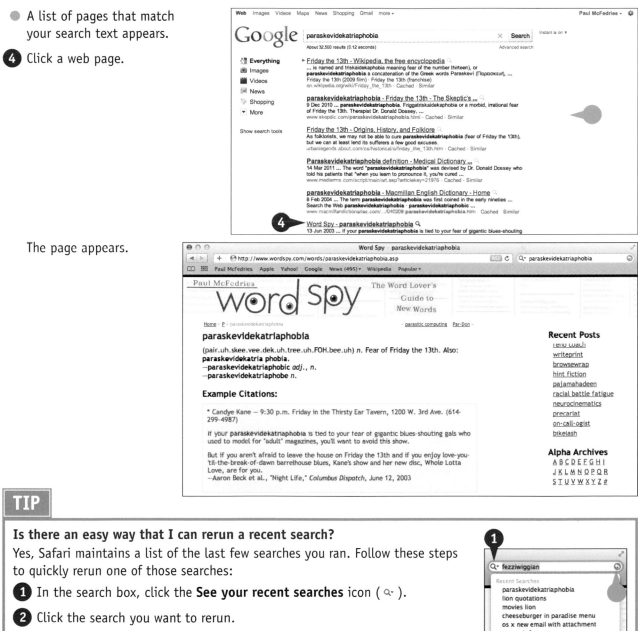

The page appears.

Is there an easy way that I can rerun a recent search?

Yes, Safari maintains a list of the last few searches you ran. Follow these steps to quickly rerun one of those searches:

① In the search box, click the **See your recent searches** icon (⌁).

② Click the search you want to rerun.

● In many cases you can also click the **Snapback** icon (⌁) to rerun the most recent search.

Safari sends the search text to Google again.

Download a File

Some websites make files available for you to open on your Mac. To use these files, you can download them to your Mac using Safari. Saving data from the Internet to your computer is called *downloading*.

For certain types of files, Safari may display the content right away instead of letting you download it. This happens for files such as text documents and PDF files. In any case, to use a file from a website, you must have an application designed to work with that particular file type. For example, if the file is an Excel workbook, you need either Excel for the Mac or a compatible program.

Download a File

1 Navigate to the page that contains the link to the file.

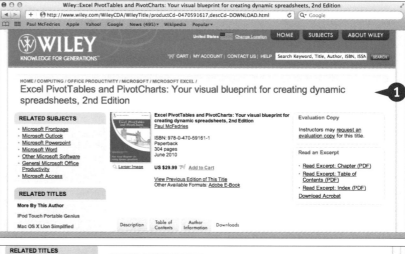

2 Click the link to the file.

Safari downloads the file to your Mac.

- The Show Downloads button shows the progress of the download.

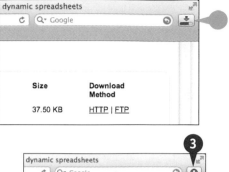

③ When the download is complete, Click the Show Downloads button (⊙).

④ Right-click the file.

- You can also double-click the icon to the left of the file.

- If you want to access the downloaded file itself, click **Show in Finder** (🔍) to view the file in the Downloads folder.

⑤ Click **Open**.

The file opens in the corresponding application.

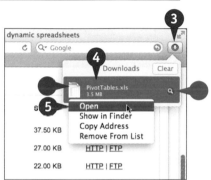

TIPS

If Safari displays the file instead of downloading it, how do I save the file to my Mac?
Click **File** and then click **Save As**. Type a name for the new file, choose a folder, and then click **Save**.

Is it safe to download files from the web?
Yes, as long as you only download files from sites you trust. If you notice that Safari is attempting to download a file without your permission, cancel the download immediately because it is likely the file contains a virus or other malware. If you do not completely trust a file you have downloaded, use an antivirus program — such as ClamXav; see www.clamxav.com — to scan the file before you open it.

CHAPTER 5

Communicating via E-mail and FaceTime

Mac OS X comes with the Apple Mail application, which you can use to exchange e-mail messages and attach documents, images, and other types of files to your e-mail messages. The FaceTime application allows you to make video calls to other people.

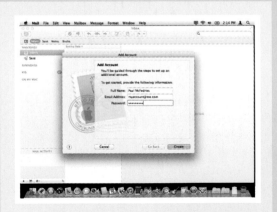

Open and Close Mail

Mac OS X includes the Apple Mail application to enable you to use an e-mail account to exchange and manage e-mail messages. E-mail is one of the most popular Internet services because it offers three main advantages: It is universal, fast, and convenient.

E-mail is universal because nearly anyone who can access the Internet has an e-mail address. E-mail is fast because messages are generally delivered within a few minutes. E-mail is convenient because you can send messages at any time of day, and your recipient does not need to be at the computer or connected to the Internet.

Before you can send or receive e-mail messages, you must know how to start the Mail application.

Open and Close Mail

Open Mail

1 In the Dock, click the **Mail** icon (■).

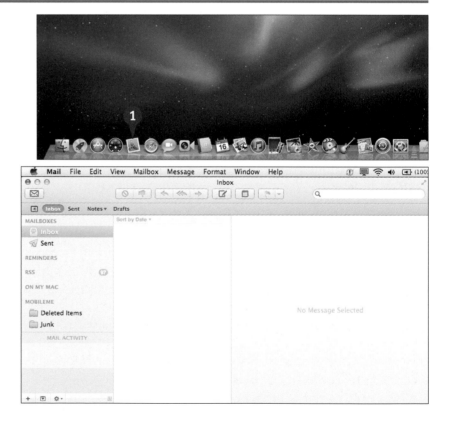

Note: If the Welcome to Mail dialog appears, see the next section to learn how to set up your first e-mail account in Mail.

The Mail window appears.

Close Mail

1 Click **Mail**.

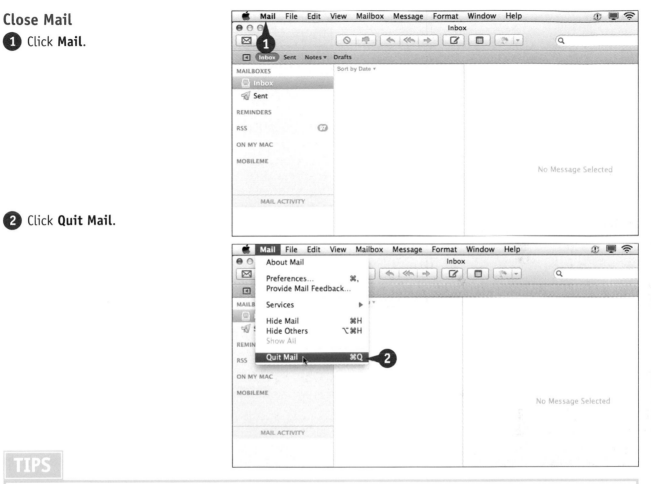

2 Click **Quit Mail**.

TIPS

Are there other methods I can use to open Mail?
If you have removed the ☒ icon from the Dock, there are a couple of other quick methods you can use to start Mail. If you have used Mail recently, click 🍎, click **Recent Items**, and then click **Safari**. You can also click **Spotlight** (🔍), type **Mail**, and then click **Mail** in the search results.

Are there faster methods I can use to close Mail?
Probably the fastest method you can use to quit Mail is to right-click its icon (☒) in the Dock and then click **Quit**. If your hands are closer to the keyboard than to the mouse, you can quit Mail by switching to the application and then pressing ⌘+Q.

Add an E-mail Account

Before you can send and receive e-mail messages, you must add your e-mail account to the Mail application. Your e-mail account is usually a POP (Post Office Protocol) account supplied by your Internet service provider, which should have supplied you with the POP account details. You can also set up web-based e-mail accounts with services such as Hotmail and Gmail. A web-based account is convenient because it enables you to send and receive messages from any computer.

If you have an Apple e-mail account, you can also set up Mail with your Apple account details.

Add an E-mail Account

Get Started Adding an Account

1 Click **File**.

2 Click **Add Account**.

Note: If you are just starting Mail and the Welcome to Mail dialog is on-screen, you can skip Steps **1** and **2**.

The Add Account dialog appears. If you are starting Mail for the first time, the Welcome to Mail dialog is identical.

Add an Apple Account

1 Type your name.

2 Type your Apple account address.

3 Type your Apple account password.

4 Click **Create**.

Mail adds your Apple account.

Add a POP Account

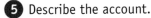

1 Type your name.

2 Type your POP account address.

3 Type your POP account password and click **Continue**.

4 Click ⁝ and then click POP.

5 Describe the account.

6 Type the address of the account's incoming mail server, which may be called the POP or POPD server.

7 Edit the User Name text as required and click **Continue**.

8 Type a description of the outgoing mail server.

9 Type the address of the outgoing mail server, which is sometimes called the SMTP server.

● If your ISP requires authentication, click **Use Authentication** (☐ changes to ☑).

10 Click **Continue**, click **Continue** again, and then click **Create**.

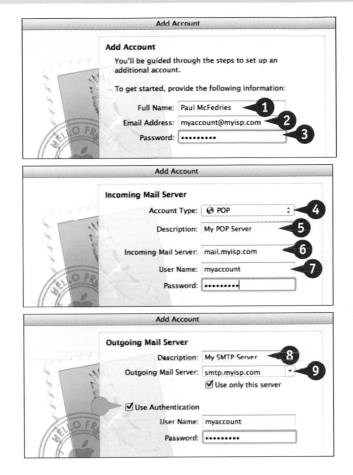

TIP

My e-mail account requires me to use a nonstandard outgoing mail port. How do I set this up?

1 In the menu bar, click **Mail**.

2 Click **Preferences**.

3 Click **Accounts**.

4 In the Outgoing Mail Server (SMTP) list, click ⁝ and then click **Edit SMTP Server List**.

5 Click the outgoing mail server.

6 Click **Advanced**.

7 Click **Use custom port** (○ changes to ⊙).

8 Type the nonstandard port number.

9 Click **OK**.

10 Click ⊙ .

11 Click **Save**.

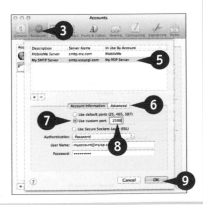

Send an E-mail Message

If you know the e-mail address of a person or organization, you can send an e-mail message to that address. An e-mail address is a set of characters that uniquely identifies the location of an Internet mailbox. Each e-mail address takes the form *username@domain*, where *username* is the name of the person's account with the ISP or within his or her organization, and *domain* is the Internet name of the company that provides the person's e-mail account.

When you send an e-mail message, it travels through your ISP's outgoing mail server. This server routes the messages to the recipient's incoming mail server, which then stores the message in the recipient's mailbox.

Send an E-mail Message

1 Click **New Message** (icon).

Note: You can also start a new message by pressing ⌘+N.

A message window appears.

2 Use the To field to type the e-mail address of the person to whom you are sending the message.

3 To send a copy of the message to another person, use the Cc field to type that person's e-mail address.

Note: You can add multiple e-mail addresses in both the To line and the Cc line. Separate each address with a comma (,).

4 Use the Subject field to type a title or short description for the message.

5 Type the message.

● To change the message font, click **Fonts** ( ) to display the Font dialog.

● To change the text colors, click **Colors** (🎨) to display the Color Picker.

● To change the overall look of the message, click **Show Stationery** (▦) and then click a theme.

Note: Many people use e-mail programs that cannot process text formatting. Unless you are sure your recipient's program supports formatting, it is best to send plain-text messages. To do this, click **Format** and then click **Make Plain Text**.

6 Click **Send** (✈).

Mail sends your message.

Note: Mail stores a copy of your message in the Sent folder.

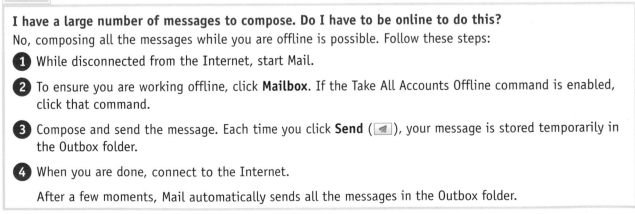

TIP

I have a large number of messages to compose. Do I have to be online to do this?

No, composing all the messages while you are offline is possible. Follow these steps:

1 While disconnected from the Internet, start Mail.

2 To ensure you are working offline, click **Mailbox**. If the Take All Accounts Offline command is enabled, click that command.

3 Compose and send the message. Each time you click **Send** (✈), your message is stored temporarily in the Outbox folder.

4 When you are done, connect to the Internet.

After a few moments, Mail automatically sends all the messages in the Outbox folder.

Add a File Attachment

If you have a document that you want to send to another person, you can attach the document to an e-mail message. A typical e-mail message is fine for short notes, but you may have something more complex to communicate, such as budget numbers or a slide show, or some form of media that you want to share, such as an image or a song.

Because these more complex types of data usually come in a separate file — such as a spreadsheet, presentation file, or picture file — it makes sense to send that file to your recipient. You do this by attaching the file to an e-mail message.

Add a File Attachment

1 Click **New Message** (□).

A message window appears.

2 Fill in the recipients, subject, and message text as described in the previous section.

3 Press Return two or three times to move the cursor a few lines below your message.

4 Click **Attach** (□).

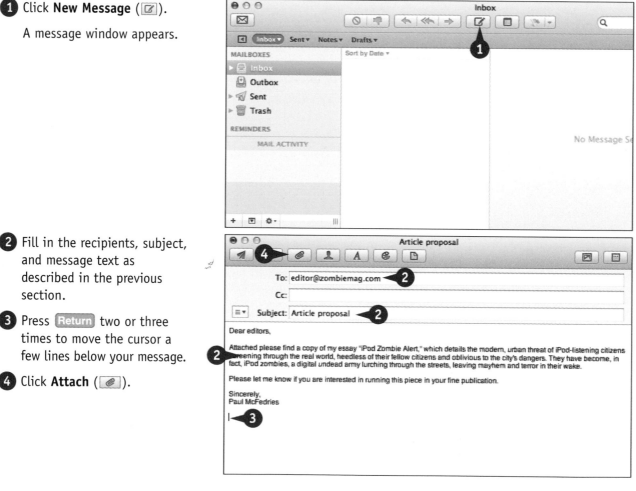

A file selection dialog appears.

5 Click the file you want to attach.

6 Click **Choose File**.

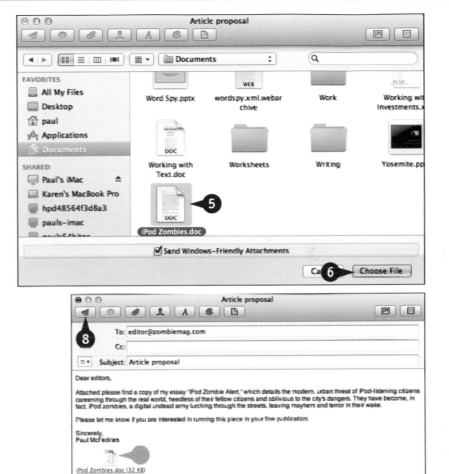

● Mail attaches the file to the message.

Note: Another way to attach a file to a message is to click and drag the file from Finder and drop it inside the message.

7 Repeat Steps **4** to **6** to attach additional files to the message.

8 Click **Send** ().

Mail sends your message.

TIP

Is there a limit to the number of files I can attach to a message?

The number of files you can attach to the message has no practical limit. However, you should be careful with the total *size* of the files you send. If you or the recipient has a slow Internet connection, sending or receiving the message can take an extremely long time. Also, many ISPs place a limit on the size of a message's attachments, which is usually between 2MB and 5MB. In general, use e-mail to send only a few small files at a time.

Add a Signature

I n an e-mail message, a *signature* is a small amount of text that appears at the bottom of the message. Instead of typing this information manually in each message, you can save the signature in your Mail preferences. When you compose a new e-mail message, reply to an existing message, or forward a message, you can click a button to have Mail add the signature to your outgoing message.

Signatures usually contain personal contact information, such as your phone numbers, business address, and e-mail and website addresses. Mail supports multiple signatures, which is useful if you use Mail with multiple accounts or for different purposes such as business and personal.

Add a Signature

Create a Signature

1 Click **Mail**.

2 Click **Preferences**.

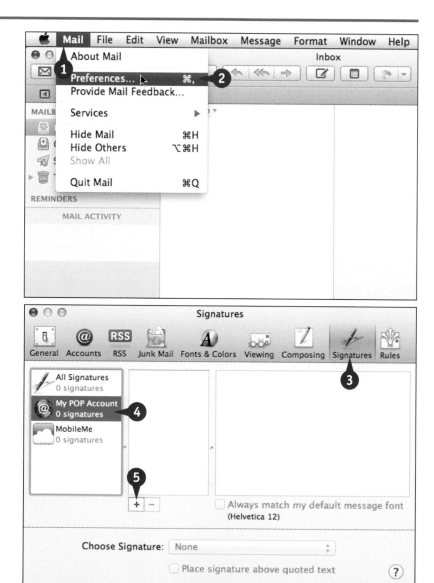

The Mail preferences appear.

3 Click **Signatures**.

4 Click the account for which you want to use the signature.

5 Click **Create a signature** (+).

Mail adds a new signature.

6 Type a name for the signature.

7 Type the signature text.

8 Repeat Steps **4** to **7** to add other signatures, if required.

Note: You can add as many signatures as you want. For example, you may want to have one signature for business use and another for personal use.

9 Click ⊖.

Insert the Signature

1 Click **New Message** (✉) to start a new message.

Note: To start a new message, see the section "Send an E-mail Message."

2 In the message text area, move the insertion point to the location where you want the signature to appear.

3 Click ⫶ and then click the signature you want to insert.

● The signature appears in the message.

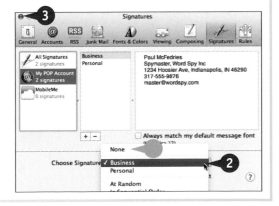

TIP

When I have multiple signatures, how can I choose which of them Mail adds automatically?

1 Follow Steps **1** to **4** to display the signature preferences and choose an account.

2 Click ⫶ and then click the signature you want to insert automatically into each message.

● If you prefer to add a signature manually, click **None** instead of a signature.

3 Click ⊖.

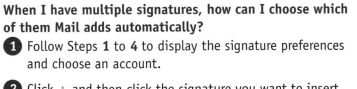

Receive and Read E-mail Messages

You must connect to your mail provider's incoming mail server to retrieve and read messages sent to you.

When another person sends you an e-mail message, that message ends up in your e-mail account's mailbox on the incoming mail server maintained by your ISP or e-mail provider. However, that company does not automatically pass along that message to you. Instead, you must use Mail to connect to your mailbox on the incoming mail server and then retrieve any messages waiting for you.

By default, Mail automatically checks for new messages every 5 minutes while you are online, but you can also check for new messages at any time.

Receive and Read E-mail Messages

Receive E-mail Messages

1 Click **Get Mail** (✉).

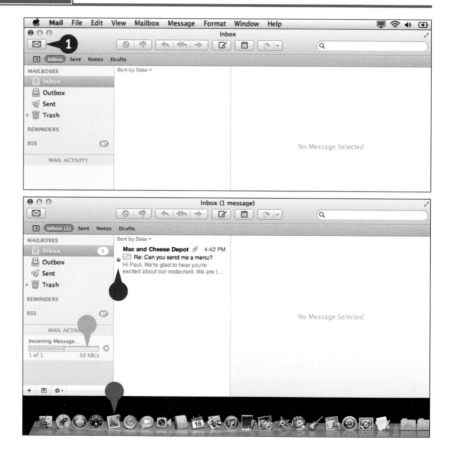

● The Mail Activity area lets you know if you have any incoming messages.

● If you have new messages, they appear in your Inbox folder with a blue dot in this column.

● The 🖼 icon in the Dock shows the number of unread messages in the Inbox folder.

Read a Message

1 Click the message.

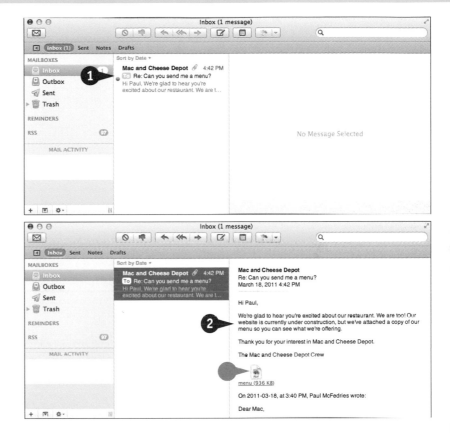

2 Read the message text in the preview pane.

● If the message comes with an attached file, double-click the file icon to open it.

Note: If you want to open the message in its own window, double-click the message.

Can I change how often Mail automatically checks for messages?

Yes, by following these steps:

1 Click **Mail**.

2 Click **Preferences**.

The Mail preferences appear.

3 Click the **General** tab.

4 In the Check for new messages pop-up menu, click ⁝ and then click the time interval that you want Mail to use when checking for new messages automatically.

● If you do not want Mail to check for messages automatically, click **Manually** instead.

5 Click ●.

Reply to a Message

When a message you receive requires some kind of response — whether it is answering a question, supplying information, or providing comments — you can reply to that message.

Most replies go only to the person who sent the original message. However, it is also possible to send the reply to all the people who were included in the original message's To and Cc lines.

Mail includes the text of the original message in the reply, but you should edit the original message text to include only enough of the original message to put your reply into context.

Reply to a Message

① Click the message to which you want to reply.

② Click the reply type you want to use.

Click **Reply** (◄) to respond only to the person who sent the message.

Click **Reply All** (◄◄) to respond to all the addresses in the message's From, To, and Cc lines.

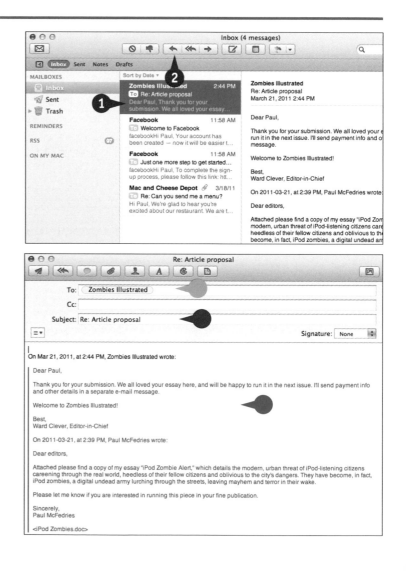

A message window appears.

● Mail automatically inserts the recipient addresses.

● Mail also inserts the subject line, preceded by Re:.

● Mail includes the original message text at the bottom of the reply.

③ Edit the original message to include only the text relevant to your reply.

④ Click the area above the original message text and type your reply.

⑤ Click **Send** (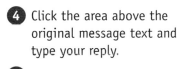).

Mail sends your reply.

Note: Mail stores a copy of your reply in the Sent folder.

TIPS

I received a message inadvertently. Is there a way that I can pass it along to the correct recipient?
Yes. Mail comes with a feature that enables you to pass along inadvertent messages to the correct recipient. Click the message that you received inadvertently, click **Message**, and then click **Redirect** (or press Shift+⌘+E). Type the recipient's address and then click **Send**. Replies to this message will be sent to the original sender, not to you.

How much of the original message should I include in my reply?
If the original message is fairly short, you usually do not need to edit the text. However, if the original message is long, and your response deals only with part of that message, you will save the recipient time and confusion by deleting everything except the relevant portion of the text. Also, rather than editing the original text within the reply, first select the text you want to keep and then click **Reply** (or **Reply All**), which tells Mail to only include the selected text in the reply.

Forward a Message

If a message has information relevant to or that concerns another person, you can forward a copy of the message to that person. You can also include your own comments in the forward.

In the body of the forward, Mail includes the original message's addresses, date, and subject line. Below this information Mail also includes the text of the original message. In most cases you will leave the entire message intact so your recipient can see it. However, if only part of the message is relevant to the recipient, you should edit the original message accordingly.

Forward a Message

1 Click the message that you want to forward.

2 Click **Forward** (➡).

Note: You can also press Shift + ⌘ + F.

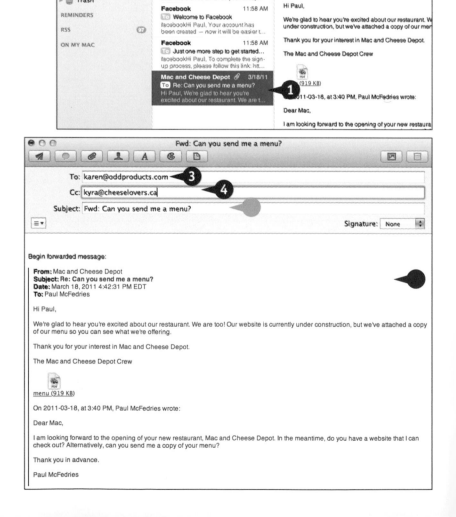

A message window appears.

● Mail inserts the subject line, preceded by Fwd:.

● The original message's addressees (To and From), date, subject, and text are included at the top of the forward.

3 Type the e-mail address of the person to whom you are forwarding the message.

4 To send a copy of the forward to another person, type that person's e-mail address in the Cc line.

5 Edit the original message to include only the text relevant to your forward.

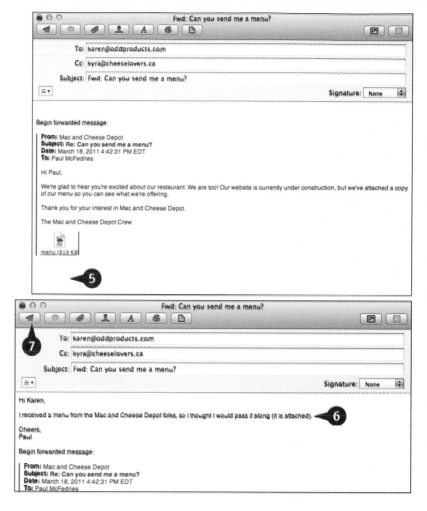

6 Click the area above the original message text and type your comments.

7 Click **Send** (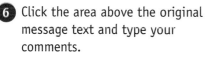).

Mail sends your forward.

Note: Mail stores a copy of your forward in the Sent folder.

Note: You can forward someone a copy of the actual message instead of just a copy of the message text. Click the message, click **Message**, and then click **Forward As Attachment**. Mail creates a new message and includes the original message as an attachment.

 TIP

Mail always formats my replies as rich text, even when the original message is plain text. How can I fix this problem?
You can configure Mail to always reply using the same format as the original message. Follow these steps:

1 Click **Mail**.

2 Click **Preferences**.

The Mail preferences appear.

3 Click the **Composing** tab.

4 Click the **Use the same message format as the original message** check box (☐ changes to ☑).

5 Click ●.

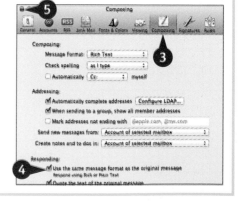

Sign in to FaceTime

M ac OS X Lion comes with a video chat feature called FaceTime that enables you to see and speak to another person over the Internet.

To use FaceTime, you and your friend must have the right type of equipment. If either or both of you are using a Mac, you must have a web camera attached to the computer, such as the iSight camera that comes with many Macs, and you must have a microphone attached to the computer, such as the built-in microphone that is part of the iSight camera.

Once you have all the necessary equipment, you must first sign in to FaceTime using an Apple ID.

Sign in to FaceTime

1 In the Dock, click **FaceTime** (▣).

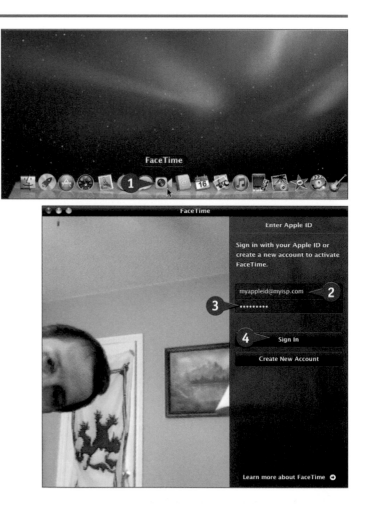

The FaceTime window appears.

2 Type your Apple ID e-mail address.

3 Type your Apple ID password.

4 Click **Sign In**.

FaceTime prompts you to specify an e-mail address that people can use to contact you via FaceTime.

⑤ If the address you prefer to use is different than your Apple ID, type the address you want to use.

⑥ Click **Next**.

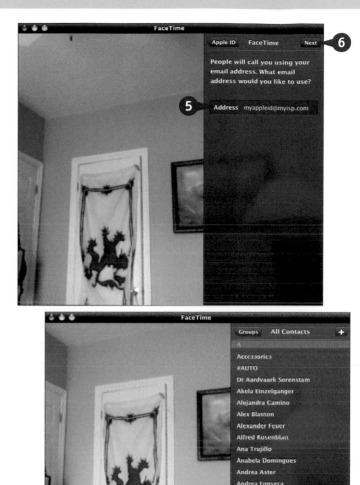

FaceTime verifies your Apple ID and then displays a list of contacts.

TIPS

Which devices support FaceTime?
You can use the FaceTime application on any Mac that is running Mac OS X 10.6.6 or later. For Mac OS X Snow Leopard (10.6.6), FaceTime is available through the App Store for 99 cents. For Mac OS X Lion (10.7), FaceTime is installed by default. The FaceTime software is also available as an app that runs on the iPhone 4, the iPad 2, and the iPod touch.

Can I use FaceTime if I do not have an Apple ID?
No, FaceTime requires an ID that has been registered with Apple. It does not cost anything to register, and you can use an existing e-mail address. To create a new account with Apple, click to open FaceTime, and then click **Create New Account**. In the New Account screen, fill in your name, the e-mail address and password you would like to use, and so on.

Connect Through FaceTime

Once you have signed in with your Apple ID, you can use the FaceTime application to connect with another person and conduct a video chat.

How you connect with the other person depends on what device he or she is using for FaceTime. If the person is using a Mac, an iPad 2, or an iPod touch, you would use whatever e-mail address the person has designated as his or her FaceTime contact address, as described in the previous section. If the person is using an iPhone 4, you would use that person's mobile number to make the connection.

Connect Through FaceTime

① Click **Contacts**.

② Click the contact you want to call.

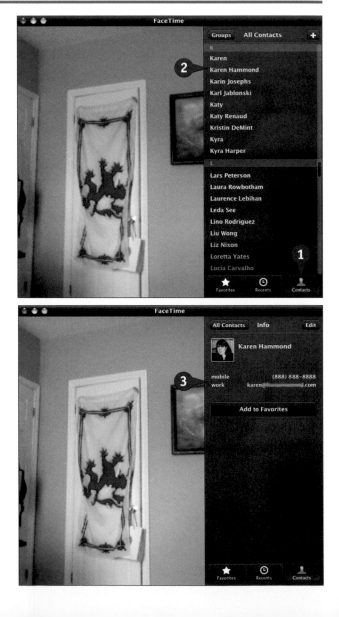

FaceTime displays the contact's data.

③ Click the phone number (for an iPhone) or e-mail address (for a Mac, iPad 2, or iPod touch) that you want to use to connect to the contact.

FaceTime sends a message to the contact asking if he or she would like a FaceTime connection.

④ The other person must click or tap **Accept** to complete the connection.

FaceTime connects with the other person.

● The other person's video takes up the bulk of the FaceTime screen.

● Your video appears in the picture-in-picture (PiP) window.

Note: You can click and drag the PiP to a different location within the FaceTime window.

⑤ When you have finished your FaceTime call, click **End**.

Are there easier ways to connect to someone through FaceTime?

Yes, FaceTime offers a couple of methods that you might find faster. If you have connected with a person through FaceTime recently, that person may appear in the FaceTime Recents list. In the FaceTime window, click **Recents** and then click the person you want to contact.

Alternatively, if you have someone you connect with frequently, you can add that person to the FaceTime Favorites list. Use the Contacts list to click the person, and then click **Add to Favorites**. To connect with a favorite, click **Favorites** and then click the person.

CHAPTER 6

Tracking Your Contacts and Events

Mac OS X comes with two applications that help you manage your busy life. You use the Address Book application to manage your contacts by storing information such as phone numbers and e-mail addresses. You use the iCal application to enter and track events and to-do items.

Open and Close Address Book

M ac OS X includes the Address Book application to enable you to manage information about the people you know, whether they are colleagues, friends, or family members. Address Book refers to these people as *contacts*, and you store each person's data in an object called a *card*.

Before you can add or work with contacts, you must know how to start the Address Book application. When you are finished with Address Book, you should close it to reduce desktop clutter and save system resources.

Open and Close Address Book

Open Address Book

1 In the Dock, click **Address Book** (⬛).

The Address Book window appears.

Close Address Book

1 Click **Address Book**.

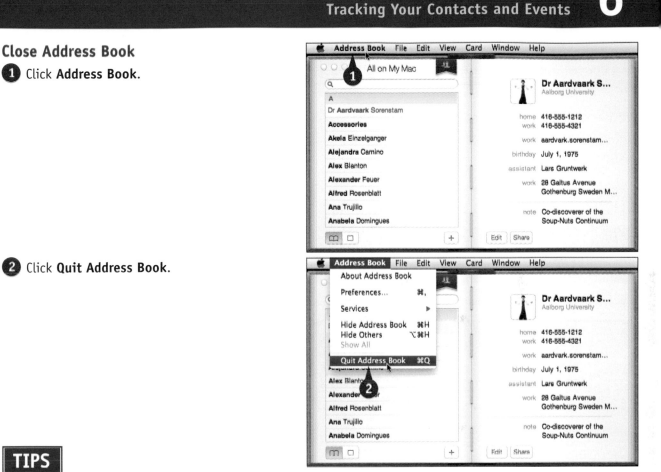

2 Click **Quit Address Book**.

TIPS

Are there other methods I can use to open Address Book?

If you have removed the 🔲 icon from the Dock, there are a couple of other quick methods you can use to start Address Book. If you have used Address Book recently, a reasonably fast method is to click ,, click **Recent Items**, and then click **Address Book**. You can also click **Spotlight** (🔍), type **Address**, and then click **Address Book** in the search results.

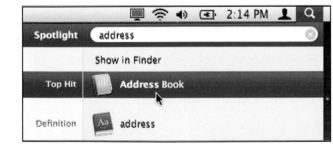

Are there faster methods I can use to close Address Book?

Probably the fastest method you can use to quit Address Book is to right-click its icon (🔲) and then click **Quit**. If your hands are closer to the keyboard than to the mouse, you can quit Address Book by switching to the application and then pressing ⌘+Q.

Add a New Contact

To store contact information for a particular person, you first need to create a new contact within Address Book. You do that by creating a new card, which is an Address Book item that stores data about a person or company.

Each card can store a wide variety of information. For example, you can store a person's name, company name, phone numbers, e-mail address and instant messaging data, street address, notes, and much more.

Although you will mostly use Address Book cards to store data about people, you can also use a card to keep information about companies.

Add a New Contact

1 Click **File**.

2 Click **New Card**.

● You can also begin a new contact by clicking +.

Note: You can also run the New Card command by pressing ⌘+N.

● Address Book adds a new card.

3 Use the First field to type the contact's first name.

4 Use the Last field to type the contact's last name.

5 Use the Company field to type the contact's company name.

6 If the contact is a company, click **Company** (☐ changes to ☑).

7 In the first Phone field, click ‡ and then click the category you want to use.

8 Type the phone number.

9 Repeat Steps **7** and **8** to enter data in some or all of the other fields.

Note: See the next section to learn how to add more fields to the card.

10 Click **Done**.

Address Book saves the new card.

TIP

If I include a contact's e-mail address, is there a way to send that person a message without having to type the address?

Yes. You can follow these steps:

1 Click the contact's card.

2 Click the e-mail address category.

3 Click **Send Email**.

Apple Mail displays a new e-mail message with the contact already added in the To line.

4 Fill in the rest of the message as required.

5 Click **Send**.

Note: Alternatively, start a new message in Mail, click **Address**, click the contact, and then click **To:** (or **Cc:** or **Bcc:**).

Edit a Contact

If you need to make changes to the information already in a contact's card, or if you need to add new information to a card, you can edit the card from within Address Book.

The default fields you see in a card are not the only types of data you can store for a contact. Address Book offers a large number of extra fields. These include useful fields such as Middle Name, Nickname, Job Title, Department, URL (web address), and Birthday. You can also add extra fields for common data items such as phone numbers, e-mail addresses, and dates.

Edit a Contact

1 Click the card you want to edit.

2 Click **Edit**.

● Address Book makes the card's fields available for editing.

3 Edit the existing fields as required.

4 To add a field, click an empty placeholder and then type the field data.

5 To remove a field, click ⊖.

6 To add a new field type, click **Card**.

7 Click **Add Field**.

8 Click the type of field you want.

● Address Book adds the field to the card.

9 When you have completed your edits, click **Done**.

Address Book saves the edited card.

TIP

How do I add a picture for the new contact?
Follow these steps:

1 Click the contact's card.

2 Click **Edit**.

3 Double-click the picture box.

4 Click **Choose** and choose the picture you want to use.

5 Click **Open**.

6 Click and drag the picture to the position you want.

7 Click **Set**.

8 Click **Done**.

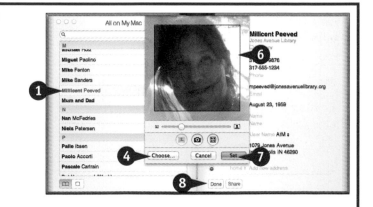

Create a Contact Group

You can organize your contacts into one or more groups, which is useful if you want to view just a subset of your contacts. For example, you could create separate groups for friends, family members, work colleagues, or business clients.

Groups are particularly handy if you have a large number of contacts in Address Book. By creating and maintaining groups, you can navigate your contacts more easily. You can also perform groupwide tasks, such as sending a single e-mail message to everyone in the group. You can create a group first and then add members, or you can select members in advance and then create the group.

Create a Contact Group

Create a Contact Group

1 Click **File**.

2 Click **New Group**.

Note: You can also run the New Group command by pressing `Shift` + `⌘` + `N`.

● Address Book adds a new group.

3 Type a name for the group.

4 Press `Return`.

5 Click **All on My Mac**.

6 Click and drag a contact to the group.

Address Book adds the contact to the group.

7 Repeat Step **6** for the other contacts you want to add to the group.

Create a Group of Selected Contacts

① Select the contacts you want to include in the new group.

Note: To select multiple contacts, press and hold ⌘ and click each card.

② Click **File**.

③ Click **New Group From Selection**.

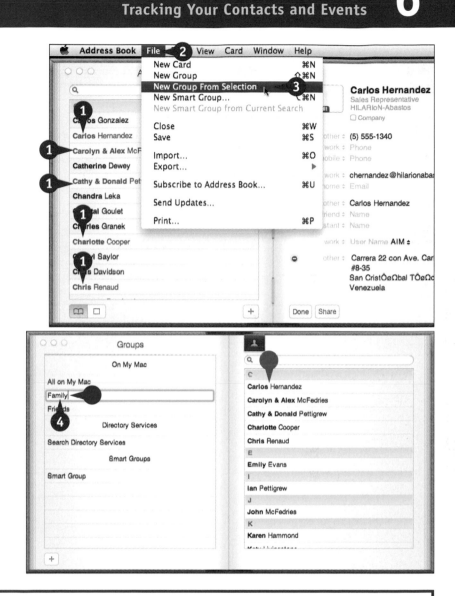

● Address Book adds a new group.

● Address Book adds the selected contacts as group members.

④ Type a name for the group.

⑤ Press **Return**.

TIPS

Can I send an e-mail message to the group?
Yes, this is one of the best reasons to create a group. Normally, sending an e-mail message to multiple contacts involves typing or selecting multiple addresses. With a group, however, you send a single message to the group, and Mail automatically sends a copy to each member. Right-click the group and then click **Send Email to "Group"**, where *Group* is the name of the group.

What is a smart group?
A *smart group* is a special group where each member has one or more fields in common, such as the company name, department name, city, or state. When you create the smart group, you specify one or more criteria, and then Address Book automatically adds members to the group if they meet those criteria. To create a smart group, click **File**, click **New Smart Group**, and then enter your group criteria.

Open and Close iCal

Your Mac comes with the iCal application to enable you to manage your schedule. iCal enables you to create and work with events, which are either scheduled appointments such as meetings, lunches, or visits to the dentist; or all-day activities, such as birthdays, anniversaries, or vacations. You can also use iCal to keep track of to-do items, which are tasks that you have to perform.

Before you can add or work with events (appointments, meetings, all-day activities, and so on), and to-do items (tasks), you must know how to start the iCal application.

Open and Close iCal

Open iCal

1 In the Dock, click **iCal** (icon).

iCal

The iCal window appears.

Close iCal

1 Click **iCal**.

2 Click **Quit iCal**.

TIPS

Are there other methods I can use to open iCal?

If you have removed the 🗓 icon from the Dock, there are a couple of other quick methods you can use to start iCal. If you have used iCal recently, a reasonably fast method is to click , click **Recent Items**, and then click **iCal**. You can also click **Spotlight** (Q), type **ical**, and then click **iCal** in the search results.

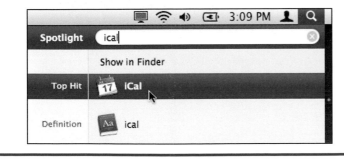

Are there faster methods I can use to close iCal?

Probably the fastest method you can use to quit iCal is to right-click its icon (🗓) and then click **Quit**. If your hands are closer to the keyboard than to the mouse, you can quit iCal by switching to the application and pressing ⌘+Q .

Navigate the Calendar

Before you create an event such as an appointment or meeting, or an all-day event such as a conference or trip, you must first select the date on which the event occurs. You do that in iCal by navigating the built-in calendar or by specifying the date you want.

iCal also lets you change the calendar view to suit your needs. For example, you can show just a single day's worth of events if you want to concentrate on that day's activities. Similarly, you can view a week's worth of events if you want to get a larger sense of what your overall schedule looks like.

Navigate the Calendar

Use the Calendar

① Click **Month**.

② Click the **Next** button (▶)
    until the month of your event
    appears.

● If you go too far, click the
    Previous button (◀) to move
    back to the month you want.

● To see a specific date, click
    the day and then click **Day**
    (or press ⌘+①).

● To see a specific week, click
    any day within the week
    and then click **Week** (or
    press ⌘+②).

● To return to viewing the entire
    month, click **Month** (or press
    ⌘+③).

● If you want to return to
    today's date, click **Today**
    (or press ⌘+T).

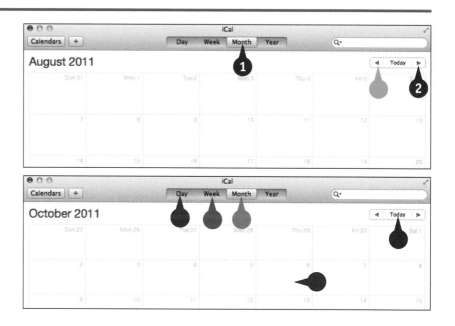

Go to a Specific Date

1 Click **View**.

2 Click **Go to Date**.

Note: You can also select the Go to Date command by pressing Shift + ⌘ + T.

The Go to date dialog appears.

3 Use the Date text box to type the date you want using the format mm/dd/yyyy.

● You can also click the day, month, or year and then click ⊟ to increase or decrease the value.

4 Click **Show**.

5 Click **Day**.

● iCal displays the date.

TIP

In the Week view, the week begins on Sunday. How can I change this to Monday?

iCal's default Week view has Sunday on the left and Saturday on the right. Many people prefer to display the weekend days together, with Monday on the left signaling the start of the week. To set this up, follow these steps:

1 Click **iCal** in the menu bar.

2 Click **Preferences**.

3 Click the **General** tab.

4 In the Start week on pop-up menu, click ⁝ and then click **Monday**.

5 Click .

Create an Event

You can help organize your life by using iCal to record your events — such as appointments, meetings, phone calls, and dates — on the date and time they occur.

If the event has a set time and duration — for example, a meeting or a lunch date — you add the event directly to the calendar as a regular appointment. If the event has no set time — for example, a birthday, anniversary, or multiple-day event such as a convention or vacation — you can create an all-day event.

Create an Event

Create a Regular Event

1 Navigate to the date when the event occurs.

2 Click **Calendars**.

3 Click the calendar you want to use.

4 Double-click the time when the event starts.

● iCal adds a one-hour event.

Note: If the event is less than or more than an hour, you can also click and drag the mouse (↖) over the full event period.

5 Type the name of the event.

6 Press **Return**.

Create an All-Day Event

1 Click **Week**.

2 Navigate to the week that includes the date when the event occurs.

3 Click **Calendars**.

4 Click the calendar you want to use.

5 Double-click anywhere inside the event date's all-day section.

● iCal adds a new all-day event.

6 Type the name of the event.

7 Press **Return**.

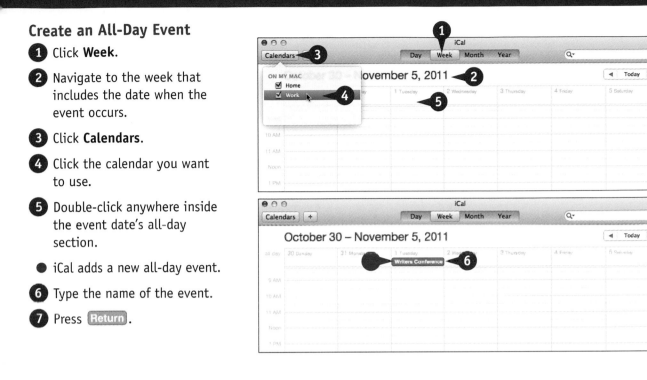

TIP

How can I specify event details such as the location and a reminder message?
Follow these steps:

1 Follow the steps in this section to create an event.

2 Double-click the event.

3 Click **Edit**.

4 Use the location text box to type the location of the event.

5 Use the alert pop-up menu to choose **Message**.

6 Choose the amount of time before the event that you want to receive the reminder.

7 Click **Done**.

iCal saves the new event configuration.

Create a Repeating Event

If you have an activity or event that recurs at a regular interval, you can create an event and configure it to automatically repeat in iCal. This saves you from having to repeatedly add the future events yourself because iCal adds them for you automatically.

You can repeat an event daily, weekly, monthly, or yearly. For even greater flexibility, you can set up a custom interval. For example, you could have an event repeat every five days, every second Friday, on the first Monday of every month, and so on.

Create a Repeating Event

1 Follow the steps in the previous section to create an event.

2 Double-click the event.

iCal displays information for the event.

3 Click **Edit**.

iCal opens the event for editing.

④ Beside the repeat label, click **None**.

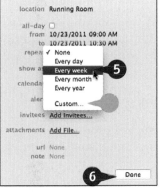

⑤ Click the interval you want to use.

● If you want to specify a custom interval such as every two weeks or the first Monday of every month, click **Custom** and configure your interval in the dialog that appears.

⑥ Click **Done**.

iCal adds the repeating events to the calendar.

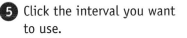

TIPS

How do I configure an event to stop after a certain number of occurrences?
Follow these steps:

❶ Follow Steps **1** to **5** to select a recurrence interval.

❷ Beside the end label, click **None** and then click **After**.

❸ Type the number of occurrences you want.

❹ Click **Done**.

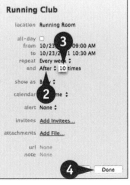

Is it possible to delete just a single occurrence out of a recurring series of events?
Yes, you can delete one occurrence from the calendar without affecting the rest of the series. Click the occurrence you want to delete, and then press ⟨Del⟩. iCal asks whether you want to delete all the occurrences or just the selected occurrence. Click **Delete Only This Event**.

Create a To-Do Item

You can also use iCal to create to-do items, which are current or future tasks that you need to track.

You can monitor to-do items — which can be tasks associated with large projects such as budgets, to basic chores such as returning phone calls — by using iCal to record these tasks. You can also help organize your life by giving each task a priority.

When the to-do item is done, you should mark it as complete so you can easily tell which items remain to be done.

Create a To-Do Item

Create a To-Do Item

1 Click **Calendars**.

2 Click the calendar you want to use.

3 Click **File**.

4 Click **New To Do**.

Note: You can also choose the New To Do command by pressing ⌘+K.

● iCal displays the To Do Items list.

● iCal adds a new to-do item to the list.

5 Type the name of the to-do item.

6 Press Return.

Set the Priority

1 Click the **Set Priority** icon ( ).

2 Click the priority you want to use.

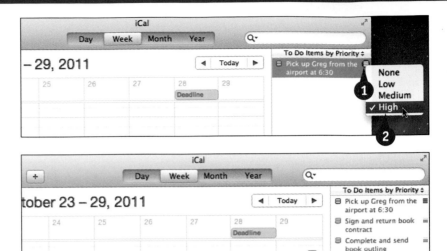

Mark a To-Do Item as Completed

1 Click the **Completed** check box (changes to).

TIP

How can I specify to-do item details such as the due date and a reminder message?

Follow these steps:

1 Follow the steps in this section to create a to-do item.

2 In the To Do Items list, double-click the to-do item.

3 Click **due date** (changes to).

4 Type the date the to-do item is due.

5 Use the alert pop-up menu to choose **Message**.

6 Choose when you want to receive the reminder.

7 Type the time you want the reminder to appear.

8 Click **Close**.

iCal saves the new to-do item configuration.

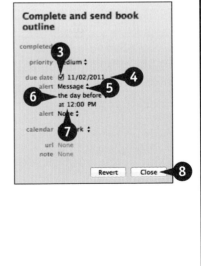

CHAPTER 7

Playing and Organizing Music

Using iTunes, you can create a library of music and use that library to play songs, albums, and collections of songs called playlists. You can also use iTunes to listen to music CDs, import tracks from music CDs, create your own CDs, and more.

Open and Close iTunes

Your Mac includes iTunes to enable you to play back and manage various types of audio files. iTunes also includes features for playing videos, watching movies and TV shows, and organizing eBooks, but this chapter focuses on iTunes's audio features.

To begin using the program, you must first learn how to find and open the iTunes window. When you finish using the program, you can close the iTunes window to free up computer processing power.

Open and Close iTunes

Open iTunes

1 In the Dock, click **iTunes** (icon).

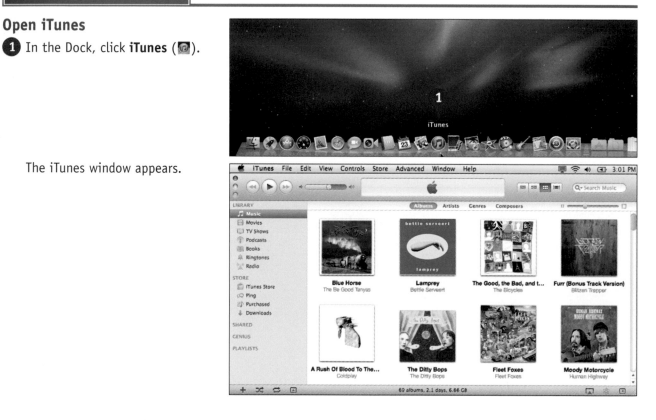

The iTunes window appears.

Close iTunes

1 Click **iTunes**.

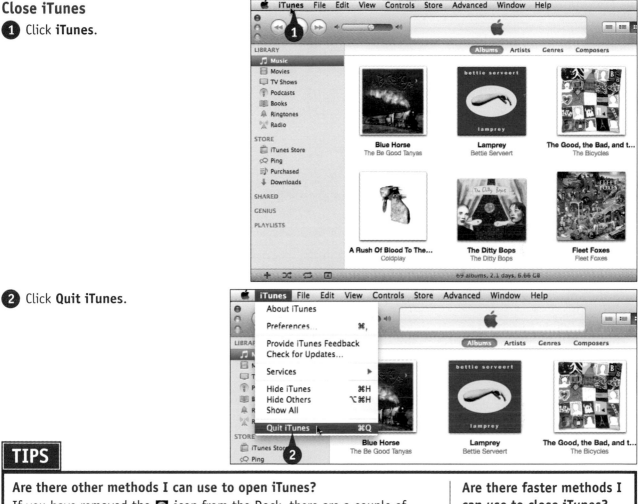

2 Click **Quit iTunes**.

TIPS

Are there other methods I can use to open iTunes?
If you have removed the 🎵 icon from the Dock, there are a couple of other quick methods you can use to start iTunes. If you have used iTunes recently, a reasonably fast method is to click the Apple icon (), click **Recent Items**, and then click **iTunes**. You can also click **Spotlight** (Q), type **itunes**, and then click **iTunes** in the search results.

Are there faster methods I can use to close iTunes?
Probably the fastest method you can use to quit iTunes is to click **Close** (●). Alternatively, right-click the iTunes icon (🎵) and then click **Quit**. Finally, if your hands are closer to the keyboard than to the mouse, you can quit iTunes by switching to the application and then pressing ⌘+Q.

Understanding the iTunes Library

Most of your iTunes time will be spent in the Library, so you need to understand what the Library is and how you work with it. In particular, you need to understand the various categories — such as music and audiobooks — that iTunes uses to organize the Library's audio content. Also, to make it easier to navigate the Library, you need to know how to configure the Library to show only the categories that you'll be working with.

The iTunes Library

The iTunes Library is where your Mac stores the files that you can play and work with in the iTunes application. Although iTunes has some video components, its focus is on audio features, so most of the Library sections are audio related. These sections enable you to work with music, podcasts, audiobooks, ringtones, and Internet radio.

Understanding Library Categories

The left side of the iTunes window is called the Source List and it displays the various categories that are available in the iTunes Library. In the Library list, the audio-related categories include Music, Podcasts, Books (for audiobooks), Ringtones, and Radio. The Store list includes items you've purchased from the iTunes Store.

Each category shows you the contents of that category and the details for each item. For example, in the Music category, you can see details such as the name of each album and the artist who recorded it.

Configuring the Library

You can configure which categories of the iTunes Library appear in the Library list on the left side of the iTunes window. Click **iTunes** and then click **Preferences** to open the iTunes preferences, and then click the **General** tab. In the Show section, click the check box for each type of content you want to work with (☐ changes to ☑), and then click **OK**.

Navigate the iTunes Window

Familiarizing yourself with the various elements of the iTunes window is a good idea so that you can easily navigate and activate elements when you are ready to play audio files, music CDs, or podcasts; import and burn audio CDs; create your own playlists; or listen to Internet radio.

In particular, you need to learn the iTunes playback controls because you will use them to control the playback of almost all music you work with in iTunes. It is also worthwhile learning the different View options because these often come in handy when navigating the iTunes Library.

Playback Controls

These buttons control media playback and enable you to adjust the volume.

Sort Buttons

These buttons sort the contents of the current iTunes category.

Status Area

This area displays information about the item that is currently playing or the action that iTunes is currently performing.

View Options

These buttons control how the contents of the current category appear. Click **List** (▤) to view the contents as a list by song; click **Album List** (▤) to view the contents as a list by album; click **Grid** (▦) to view the contents as thumbnails; click **Cover Flow** (▦) to view the contents as scrolling thumbnails.

Genius Sidebar

This area displays a list of songs, albums, or other iTunes Store content similar to the current item in the Library.

Contents

The contents of the current iTunes Library source appear here.

Categories

This area displays the iTunes Library categories that you can view.

Play a Song

You use the Music category of the iTunes Library to play a song that is stored on your computer. Although iTunes offers several methods to locate the song you want to play, the easiest method is to display the albums you have in your iTunes Library, and then open the album that contains the song you want to play.

While the song is playing, you can control the volume to suit the music or your current location. If you need to leave the room or take a call, you can also pause the currently playing song.

Play a Song

1 Click **Music**.

2 Click **Albums**.

3 Double-click the album that contains the song you want to play.

● If you want to play the entire album, click **Play Album**.

4 Click the song you want to play.

5 Click the **Play** button (▶).

iTunes begins playing the song.

● Information about the song playback appears here.

● iTunes displays a speaker icon (🔊) beside the currently playing song.

● If you need to stop the song temporarily, click the **Pause** button (⏸).

Note: You can also pause and restart a song by pressing the Spacebar.

● You can use the Volume slider to adjust the volume (see the Tip, below).

Note: See the "Play a Music CD" section to learn more about the playback buttons.

TIP

How do I adjust the volume?

To turn the volume up or down, click and drag the **Volume** slider to the left (to reduce the volume) or to the right (to increase the volume). You can also press ⌘+⬇ to reduce the volume, or ⌘+⬆ to increase the volume.

To mute the volume, either drag the **Volume** slider all the way to the left, or press Option+⌘+⬇. To restore the volume, adjust the **Volume** slider or press Option+⌘+⬇.

Play a Music CD

You can play your favorite music CDs in iTunes. When you insert an audio disc in your Mac's optical drive (that is, a drive capable of reading CDs and DVDs), the CD appears in the Devices section of the iTunes Library. When you click the CD, the iTunes contents area displays the individual tracks on the CD, and if you have an Internet connection you see the name of each track as well as other track data. During playback, you can skip tracks and pause and resume play.

To play a music CD, your Mac must have an optical drive.

Play a Music CD

Play a CD

1 Insert a music CD into your Mac's optical drive.

● The music CD appears in iTunes's Devices category.

iTunes asks if you want to import the CD.

2 Click **No**.

Note: To learn how to import a CD, see the section "Import Tracks from a Music CD."

● If you have an Internet connection, iTunes shows the contents of the CD.

Note: iTunes shows the contents for most CDs, but it may not show the correct information for some discs, particularly noncommercial mixed CDs.

3 Click ▶.

iTunes begins playing the CD from the first track.

Skip a Track

4 Click the **Next** button (⊙) to skip to the next track.

Note: You can also skip to the next track by pressing ⌘+→.

5 Click the **Previous** button (⊙) to skip to the beginning of the current track; click ⊙ again to skip to the previous track.

Note: You can also skip to the previous track by pressing ⌘+←.

Pause and Resume Play

6 Click ⊙ (⊙ changes to ⊙).

iTunes pauses playback.

7 Click ⊙.

iTunes resumes playback where you left off.

TIPS

Can I change the CD's audio levels?

Yes, iTunes has a graphic equalizer component that you can use to adjust the levels. To display the equalizer, click **Window** and then click **Equalizer** (or press Option+⌘+2). In the Equalizer window, use the sliders to set the audio levels, or click the pop-up menu (⬍) to choose an audio preset.

Can I display visualizations during playback?

Yes. You can click **View** and then click **Show Visualizer** (you can also press ⌘+T). To change the currently displayed visualizer, click **View**, click **Visualizer**, and then click the visualization you want to view.

continued ▶

iTunes gives you more options for controlling the CD playback. For example, you can easily switch from one song to another on the CD. You can also use the Repeat feature to tell iTunes to start the CD over from the beginning after it has finished playing the CD. iTunes also offers the Shuffle feature, which tells iTunes to play the CD's tracks in random order.

When the CD is done, you can use iTunes to eject it from your Mac.

If you want to learn how to import music from the CD to iTunes, see the section "Import Tracks from a Music CD."

Play a Music CD (continued)

Play Another Song

8 In the list of songs, double-click the song you want to play.

iTunes begins playing the song.

Repeat the CD

9 Click the **Repeat** button (🔁 changes to 🔁).

iTunes restarts the CD after the last track finishes playing.

To repeat just the current song, click 🔁 again (🔁 changes to 🔁).

Play Songs Randomly

10 Click the **Shuffle** button (🔀 changes to 🔀).

iTunes shuffles the order of play.

📺	TV Shows	3	✔ Arlington	4:54	The Wailin' Jennys	40 Days	Folk
🎙	Podcasts	4	✔ Beautiful Dawn	3:21	The Wailin' Jennys	40 Days	Folk
📚	Books	5 🔊	✔ Untitled ⊙	4:28	The Wailin' Jennys	40 Days	Folk
🔔	Ringtones	6	✔ This Is Where	5:08	The Wailin' Jennys	40 Days	Folk
📻	Radio	7	✔ Old Man	3:11	The Wailin' Jennys	40 Days	Folk
STORE		8	✔ Heaven When We're Home	4:25	The Wailin' Jennys	40 Days	Folk
🛒	iTunes Store	9	✔ Ten Mile Stilts	4:51	The Wailin' Jennys	40 Days	Folk
⊂Q	Ping	10	✔ Come All You Sailors	4:03	The Wailin' Jennys	40 Days	Folk
⊐	Purchased	11	✔ Take It Down	3:53	The Wailin' Jennys	40 Days	Folk
⬇	Downloads	12	✔ Something To Hold Onto	3:42	The Wailin' Jennys	40 Days	Folk
DEVICES		13	✔ The Parting Glass	2:20	The Wailin' Jennys	40 Days	Folk
💿	40 Days ⏏						
SHARED							
GENIUS							
PLAYLIS							Import S

13 songs, 50.8 minutes, 513.5 MB

Eject the CD

11 Click the **Eject** button (⏏) beside the CD.

Note: You can also eject the CD by pressing and holding the ⏏ key on the keyboard.

iTunes ejects the CD from your Mac's CD or DVD drive.

LIBRARY		▲	✔ Name	Time	Artist	Album	Genre
🎵	Music	1	✔ One Voice	3:24	The Wailin' Jennys	40 Days	Folk
🎬	Movies	2	✔ Saucy Sailor	3:11	The Wailin' Jennys	40 Days	Folk
📺	TV Shows	3	✔ Arlington	4:54	The Wailin' Jennys	40 Days	Folk
🎙	Podcasts	4	✔ Beautiful Dawn	3:21	The Wailin' Jennys	40 Days	Folk
📚	Books	5	✔ Untitled	4:28	The Wailin' Jennys	40 Days	Folk
🔔	Ringtones	6	✔ This Is Where	5:08	The Wailin' Jennys	40 Days	Folk
📻	Radio	7	✔ Old Man	3:11	The Wailin' Jennys	40 Days	Folk
		8	✔ Heaven When We're Home	4:25	The Wailin' Jennys	40 Days	Folk
STORE		9	✔ Ten Mile Stilts	4:51	The Wailin' Jennys	40 Days	Folk
🛒	iTunes Store	10	✔ Come All You Sailors	4:03	The Wailin' Jennys	40 Days	Folk
⊂Q	Ping	11	✔ Take It Down	3:53	The Wailin' Jennys	40 Days	Folk
⊐	Purchased	12	✔ Something To Hold Onto	3:42	The Wailin' Jennys	40 Days	Folk
⬇	Downloads	13	✔ The Parting Glass	2:20	The Wailin' Jennys	40 Days	Folk
DEVICES							
💿	40 Days ⏏						
SHARED							
GENIUS							

TIP

Why do I not see the song titles after I insert my music CD?

When you play a music CD, iTunes tries to gather information about the album from the Internet. If you still see only track numbers, it may be that you do not have an Internet connection established or that you inserted a noncommercial, mixed CD. Connect to the Internet, click **Advanced**, and then click **Get CD Track Names**.

Import Tracks from a Music CD

You can add tracks from a music CD to the iTunes Library. This enables you to listen to an album without having to put the CD into your Mac's optical drive each time. The process of adding tracks from a CD is called *importing,* or *ripping,* in Mac OS X.

After you import the tracks from a music CD, you can play those tracks from the Music category of the iTunes Library. You can also use the tracks to create your own playlists and to create your own custom CDs.

Import Tracks from a Music CD

① Insert a CD into your Mac's CD or DVD drive.

● The music CD appears in iTune's Devices category.

iTunes asks if you want to import the CD.

② Click **No.**

● If you want to import the entire CD, click **Yes** and skip the rest of the steps in this section.

● iTunes shows the contents of the CD.

③ Click the check box so it is unchecked next to each CD track that you do not want to copy (☑ changes to ☐).

④ Click **Import CD.**

iTunes begins importing the check-marked track or tracks.

● This area displays the copy progress for each track.

● When iTunes is importing a track, it displays ☼ beside the track number.

● When iTunes is finished importing a track, it displays ☑ beside the track number.

● When iTunes has completed the import, you see ☑ beside the track numbers of all the tracks you selected.

⑤ Click the **Eject** button (⏏) beside the CD, or press ⏏.

TIPS

I ripped a track by accident. How do I remove it from the Library?
Click the **Music** category, open the album you imported, right-click the track that you want to remove, and then click **Delete** from the shortcut menu. When iTunes asks you to confirm the deletion, click **Remove**. When iTunes asks if you want to keep the file, click **Move to Trash**.

Can I specify a different quality when importing?
Yes. You do that by changing the *bit rate*, which is a measure of how much of the CD's original data gets copied to your computer. This is measured in kilobits per second (Kbps): The higher the value, the higher the quality, but the more disk space each track takes up. Click **Import Settings** to open the Import Settings dialog. In the **Settings** pop-up menu, click ⁝, click **Custom**, and then use the Stereo Bit Rate pop-up to click the value you want.

Create a Playlist

A *playlist* is a collection of songs that are related in some way. Using your iTunes Library, you can create customized playlists that include only the songs that you want to hear.

For example, you might want to create a playlist of upbeat or festive songs to play during a party or celebration. Similarly, you might want to create a playlist of your current favorite songs to burn to a CD.

Create a Playlist

Create the Playlist

1 Click **File**.

2 Click **New Playlist**.

Note: You can also choose the New Playlist command by pressing ⌘+N.

● iTunes creates a new playlist.

3 Type a name for the new playlist.

4 Press Return.

Add Songs to the Playlist

1 Click **Music**.

2 Open an album that has one or more songs you want to add to the playlist.

3 Click a song that you want to add to the new playlist.

Note: If the album has multiple songs you want in the playlist, hold down ⌘ and click each of songs you want to add.

4 Drag the selected track (or tracks) and drop them on your playlist.

5 Repeat Steps **2** to **4** to add more songs to the playlist.

6 Click the playlist.

● iTunes displays the songs you added to the playlist.

● If you want to listen to the playlist, click ▶.

TIPS

Is there a faster way to create and populate a playlist?

Yes. First, click **Music** to open the Music category of the iTunes Library. Press and hold the ⌘ key and then click each song that you want to include in your playlist. When you are done, click **File** and then click **New Playlist from Selection**. (You can also press Shift + ⌘ + N.) Type the new playlist name and then press Return.

Is there any way to make iTunes add songs to a playlist automatically?

Yes, you can create a *smart playlist* where the songs that appear in the list have one or more properties in common, such as the genre, rating, artist, or text in the song title. Click **File** and then click **New Smart Playlist** (you can also press Option + ⌘ + N). Use the Smart Playlist dialog to create one or more rules that define which songs you want to appear in the playlist.

Burn Music Files to a CD

You can copy, or *burn*, music files from your Mac onto a CD. Burning CDs is a great way to create customized CDs that you can listen to on the computer or in a portable device that plays CDs.

You can burn music files from within the iTunes window. The easiest way to do this is to create a playlist of the songs you want to burn to the CD. You then organize the playlist by sorting the tracks in the order you want to hear them.

To burn music files to a CD, your Mac must have a recordable optical drive.

Burn Music Files to a CD

① Insert a blank CD into your Mac's recordable disc drive.

② If you already have iTunes running and your Mac asks you to choose an action, click **Ignore**.

● If you do not yet have iTunes running, use the Action menu to click ⁞, click **Open iTunes**, and then click **OK**.

③ Create a playlist for the songs you want to burn to the disc.

Note: See the section "Create a Playlist" to learn how to build an iTunes playlist.

④ Click the playlist that you want to burn.

5 To modify the play order, click and drag a song and drop it on a new position in the playlist.

6 Repeat Step **5** to get the songs in the order in which you want them to appear on the CD.

7 Click **File**.

8 Click **Burn Playlist to Disc**.

The Burn Settings dialog appears.

9 Click **Burn**.

iTunes burns the songs to the CD.

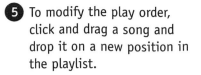

TIPS

Can I control the interval between songs on the CD?
Yes. By default, iTunes adds 2 seconds between each track on the CD. You can change that in the Burn Settings dialog. In the Gap Between Songs pop-up menu, click ⁝, and then click the interval you want to use: None, or any time between 1 second and 5 seconds.

What happens if I have more music than can fit on a single disc?
You can still add all the music you want to burn to the playlist. iTunes fills the first disc and then adds the remaining songs to a second disc. After iTunes finishes burning the first disc, it prompts you to insert the next one.

Edit Song Information

For each song in your Library or on a music CD, iTunes maintains a collection of information that includes the song title, artist, album title, genre, and more. If a song's information contains errors or omissions, you can edit the data. For example, it is common for an album to be categorized under the wrong music genre, so you can edit the album to give it the correct genre.

You can edit one song at a time, or you can edit multiple songs, such as an entire album or music CD.

Edit Song Information

Edit a Single Song

1 Click the song you want to edit.

2 Click **File**.

3 Click **Get Info**.

Note: You can also press ⌘+ⅈ. Alternatively, right-click the song and then click **Get Info**.

4 Click **Info**.

5 Edit or add information to the fields.

● If you want to edit a nearby song, click **Previous** or **Next** to display the song you want.

6 Click **OK**.

Edit Multiple Songs

1 Select all the songs that you want to edit.

Note: To select individual songs, press and hold ⌘ and click each song; to select all songs (on a music CD, for example), press ⌘+A.

2 Click **File**.

3 Click **Get Info**.

Note: You can also press ⌘+I. Alternatively, right-click any selected song and then click **Get Info**.

iTunes asks you to confirm that you want to edit multiple songs.

4 Click **Yes**.

The Multiple Item Information dialog appears.

5 Edit or add information to the fields.

● iTunes displays ☑ beside each modified field.

6 Click **OK**.

iTunes applies the edits to each selected song.

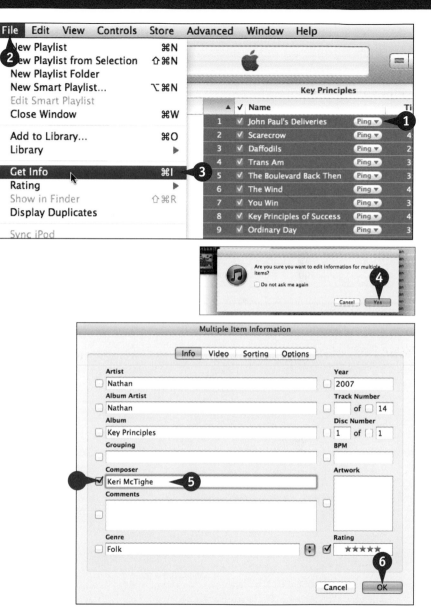

When I edit multiple songs, why do I not see all the fields in the Multiple Item Information dialog?
When you are editing multiple songs, you can only modify fields that contain data that is common to all the songs. This makes sense because any changes you make apply to all the selected songs. For example, each song usually has a different title, so you would not want to give every song the same title. This is why you do not see the Name field in the Multiple Item Information dialog. However, you do see fields that are common to all the selected songs. On a music CD, for example, data such as the artist, album title, and genre are usually the same for all the songs.

Purchase Music from the iTunes Store

You can add music to your iTunes Library by purchasing songs or albums from the iTunes Store. iTunes downloads the song or album to your computer and then adds it to both the Music category and the Purchased playlist. You can then play and manage the song or album just like any other content in the iTunes Library.

To purchase music from the iTunes Store, you must have an Apple account. This can either be an account on the Apple Store site or a MobileMe account. You can also use an AOL account, if you have one.

Purchase Music from the iTunes Store

1 Click **iTunes Store**.

2 Click **Music**.

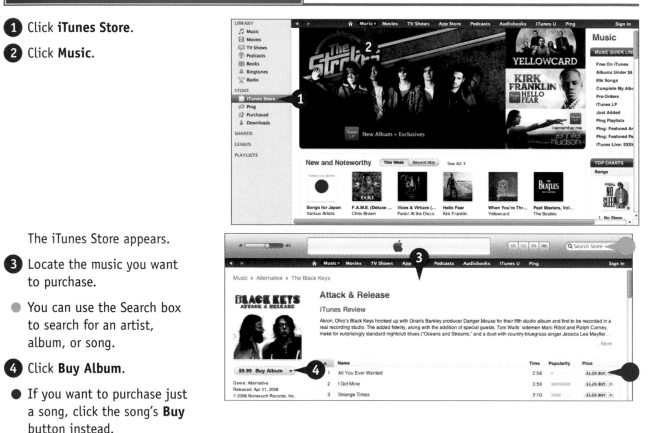

The iTunes Store appears.

3 Locate the music you want to purchase.

● You can use the Search box to search for an artist, album, or song.

4 Click **Buy Album**.

● If you want to purchase just a song, click the song's **Buy** button instead.

iTunes asks you to sign in to your iTunes store account.

5 If you have not signed in to your account, you must type your password.

6 Click **Buy**.

iTunes asks you to confirm your purchase.

7 Click **Buy**.

iTunes charges your credit card and begins downloading the music to your Mac.

● To watch the progress of the download, click **Downloads**.

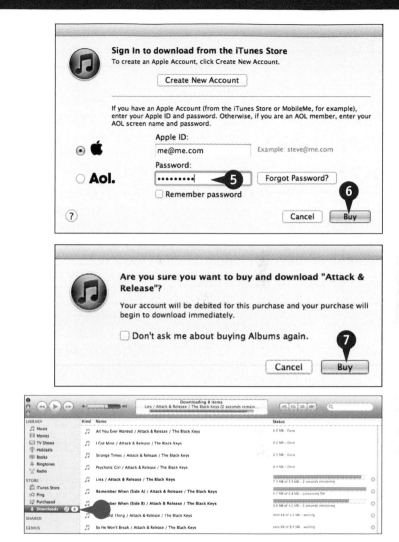

TIPS

Can I use my purchased music on other computers and devices?

Yes. Although many iTunes Store media — particularly movies and TV shows — have digital rights management (DRM) restrictions applied to prevent illegal copying, the songs and albums in the iTunes Store are DRM free, and so do not have these restrictions. This means you can play them on multiple computers and media devices (such as iPods, iPads, and iPhones), and burn them to multiple CDs.

If I want to purchase a number of songs, how do I avoid having many $0.99 charges on my credit card bill?

The easiest way to avoid lots of small iTunes charges is to purchase an iTunes gift card from an Apple Store or any retailer that sells gift cards. On the back of the card, scratch off the sticker that covers the redeem code. In iTunes, access the iTunes Store and click **Redeem** at the bottom of the store. Type in the redeem code, and then click **Redeem**.

Listen to an Internet Radio Station

The Internet offers a number of radio stations that you can listen to. iTunes maintains a list of many of these online radio stations, so it is often easier to use iTunes to listen to Internet radio.

Just like a regular radio station, an Internet radio station broadcasts a constant audio stream, except you access the audio over the Internet instead of over the air. iTunes offers several radio stations in each of its more than two dozen genres, which include Blues, Classic Rock, Classical, Folk, Hip Hop, Jazz, and Pop.

Listen to an Internet Radio Station

1 Click **Radio**.

Note: If you do not see the Radio category, see the first Tip on the next page.

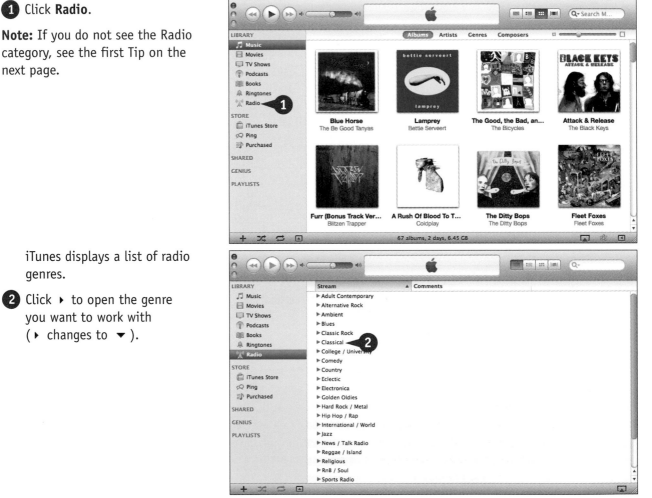

iTunes displays a list of radio genres.

2 Click ▶ to open the genre you want to work with (▶ changes to ▼).

iTunes displays a list of radio station streams in the genre.

③ Click the radio station stream you want to listen to.

④ Click ▶.

iTunes plays the radio station stream.

● The name of the station and the name of the currently playing track usually appear here.

TIPS

The Radio section of the iTunes Library does not appear. Can I still listen to Internet radio?
Yes. By default, iTunes does not show all of the available library categories and sources. To display the Radio source, click **iTunes** and then click **Preferences** to open the iTunes preferences. Click the **General** tab, click **Radio** (☐ changes to ☑), and then click **OK**.

Is it possible to use iTunes to save or record a song from a radio station stream?
No, an Internet radio stream is "listen only." iTunes does not give you any way to save the stream to your Mac hard disk or to record the stream as it plays.

Subscribe to a Podcast

You can use iTunes to locate, subscribe, manage, and listen to your favorite podcasts. A *podcast* is an audio feed — or sometimes a feed that combines both audio and video — that a publisher updates regularly with new episodes. The easiest way to get each episode is to subscribe to the podcast. This ensures that iTunes automatically downloads each new episode to your iTunes Library.

You can subscribe to podcasts either directly via the publisher's website, or via the iTunes Store.

Subscribe to a Podcast

Subscribe to a Podcast on the Web

1 Use your web browser to navigate to the podcast's home page.

2 Click the **Subscribe in iTunes** link.

Note: In some cases, the link is called **Add to iTunes** or simply **iTunes**.

Note: If after clicking the link you end up in the iTunes Store, see the steps on the following page.

● iTunes begins downloading the available episodes.

● The podcast subscription appears in the Library's Podcasts category.

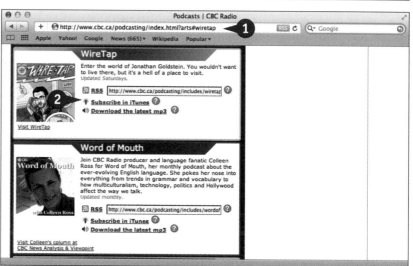

Subscribe to a Podcast Using the iTunes Store

1 Click **iTunes Store**.

2 Click **Podcasts**.

● You can also click here to display a list of podcast categories.

3 Locate the podcast you want to subscribe to.

4 Click **Subscribe Free**.

● If you just want to listen to one episode before subscribing, click the episode's **Free** button instead.

5 Click **Subscribe**.

iTunes begins downloading the podcast.

To listen to the podcast, click the subscription in the Podcasts category of the Library.

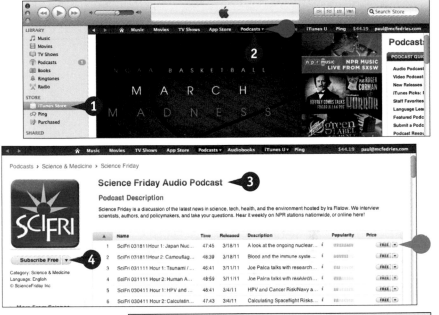

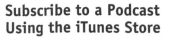

TIP

What do I do if the podcast website does not have an iTunes link?

In this case, you can subscribe to the podcast by telling iTunes the address of the podcast's feed. Follow these steps:

1 On the podcast website, copy the address of the podcast feed.

2 In iTunes, click **Advanced**.

3 Click **Subscribe to Podcast**.

The Subscribe to Podcast dialog appears.

4 Use the URL text box to paste (or type) the address of the podcast feed.

5 Click **OK**.

iTunes downloads the available episodes and adds the subscription to the Podcasts category of the Library.

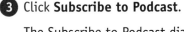

CHAPTER 8

Synchronizing an iPod, iPhone, or iPad

If you have an iPod, iPhone, or iPad, you can connect it to your Mac and keep the data on the two devices in sync. You can also learn how to synchronize various media, including music, photos, movies, and TV shows, between an iPhone or iPad and your Mac, as well as e-mail accounts, contacts, calendars, and apps.

Connect an iPod, iPhone, or iPad

Before you can synchronize data between Mac OS X and your iPod, iPhone, or iPad, you need to connect the device to your Mac.

To connect an iPod, iPhone, or iPad, you need the USB cable that came as part of the device package. You will connect one end of that cable to your Mac, so you need to make sure that your Mac has a free USB port for the connection. You can also connect an iPod, iPhone, or iPad using an optional dock.

Connect an iPod, iPhone, or iPad

Connect the iPod, iPhone, or iPad

1 Using the device cable, attach the USB connector to a free USB port on your Mac.

2 Attach the other end of the cable to the port on the device or dock.

Mac OS X launches iTunes and automatically begins synchronizing the device.

Note: Mac OS X usually also launches iPhoto to synchronize photos from the iPhone or iPad. See the section "Synchronize Photos from Your Device." For now, either quit iPhoto or switch to iTunes.

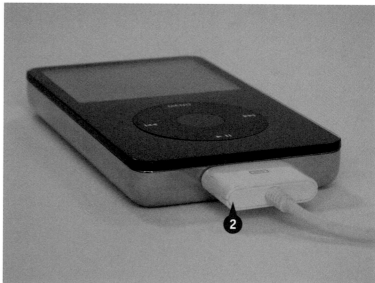

Disconnect the iPod, iPhone, or iPad

1 In iTunes, click the eject button ( ) beside your device's name.

iTunes begins releasing the iPod.

Note: See the second tip below to learn when it is safe to disconnect the cable from an iPod.

2 Pinch the sides of the connector and then pull the connector away from the device.

3 Disconnect the cable from the Mac's USB port.

Note: If your Mac has two or more free USB ports and you synchronize your device frequently, consider leaving the cable plugged into a USB port for easier connections in the future.

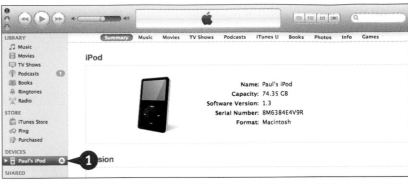

TIPS

Is there a way to prevent iTunes from starting the synchronization automatically when I connect my device?

Yes. In iTunes, click **iTunes** and then click **Preferences** to open the iTunes preferences window. Click the **Devices** tab and then click the **Prevent iPods, iPhones, and iPads from syncing automatically** check box (changes to). Click **OK**.

Do I always have to eject my iPod before disconnecting it?

No, not always. You must first eject the iPod if the iPod screen says "Do not disconnect," "Eject Before Disconnecting," or "Sync in Progress." You can safely disconnect the cable from your iPod if the iPod screen says "OK to disconnect," "Charging," "Charged," or you see the iPod main menu screen.

Synchronize Music

You can synchronize the music in your iTunes Library to your iPod, iPhone, or iPad. If your device has enough free storage space, you can synchronize all your music. However, if free space is limited on your device, you can synchronize just selected playlists to save space. Once the synchronization is complete and you have disconnected your iPod, iPhone, or iPad, you can then play the synced music on the device.

If you purchased music from the iTunes Store using your iPod touch, iPhone, or iPad, iTunes also synchronizes that music to your Mac.

Synchronize Music

1 Click your device in the iTunes Devices list.

2 Click the **Music** tab.

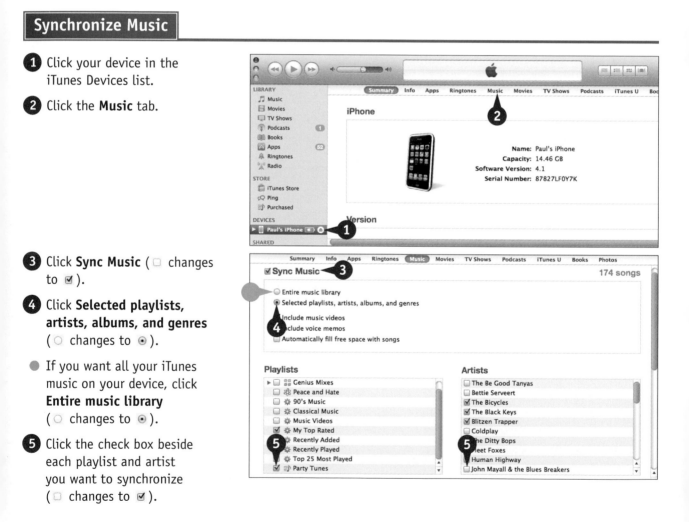

3 Click **Sync Music** (☐ changes to ☑).

4 Click **Selected playlists, artists, albums, and genres** (○ changes to ◉).

● If you want all your iTunes music on your device, click **Entire music library** (○ changes to ◉).

5 Click the check box beside each playlist and artist you want to synchronize (☐ changes to ☑).

Note: See the section "Create a Playlist" in Chapter 7 to learn how to add songs to an iTunes playlist.

6 Click the check box beside each album and genre you want to synchronize (☐ changes to ☑).

7 Click **Apply**.

iTunes synchronizes your music to your iPod, iPhone, or iPad.

● The progress of the synchronization appears here.

● When the synchronization is complete, you can disconnect your device.

TIPS

Is there any way to tell in advance how much storage space the music I am syncing will take up on my device?

Yes. If you are syncing a playlist, click the playlist in iTunes and then examine the status bar. In addition to telling you the number of songs in the playlist and its total duration, the status bar displays the total size of the playlist (●). If you are syncing all your music, click the **Music** category instead, and then note the total size displayed in the status bar.

Is there a way to control what music gets synchronized to my iPod Shuffle?

Yes. Although by default iTunes uses a feature called Autofill to send a selection of songs to the iPod Shuffle, you can configure iTunes to send a playlist instead. Connect your iPod Shuffle, click it in the Devices section, and then click the **Contents** tab. Click the **Autofill From** ↕, click the playlist you want to send to the device, and then click **Autofill**.

Synchronize Photos to Your Device

You can synchronize the photos on your Mac to your iPod, iPhone, or iPad. If your iPod or iPhone has enough storage capacity, you can synchronize all your photos. If you do not have much free space on your device, you can synchronize just selected albums and events instead. Once the synchronization is complete and you have disconnected your iPod, iPhone, or iPad, you can view the synced photos on the device.

To learn how to get photos taken with your iPod touch, iPhone, or iPad 2 onto your Mac, see the section "Synchronize Photos from Your Device."

Synchronize Photos to Your Device

1 Click your iPod, iPhone, or iPad in the iTunes Devices list.

2 Click the **Photos** tab.

3 Click **Sync Photos from** (☐ changes to ☑).

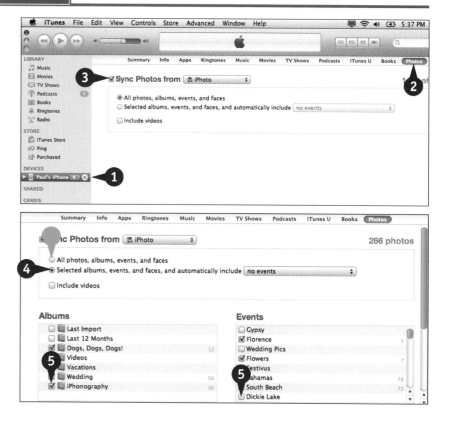

4 Click **Selected albums, events, and faces, and automatically include** (○ changes to ◉).

● If you want all your photos on your device, click **All photos, albums, events, and faces** (○ changes to ◉).

5 Click the check box beside each album and event you want to synchronize (☐ changes to ☑).

6 Click the check box beside faces you want to synchronize (☐ changes to ☑).

Note: See the section "Add Names to Faces in Your Photos" in Chapter 9 to learn how to apply faces.

7 Click **Apply**.

iTunes synchronizes your photos to your device.

● The progress of the synchronization appears here.

● When the synchronization is complete, you can disconnect your iPod or iPhone.

How do I sync a folder of photos?

Although it is easiest to sync based on iPhoto albums, events, and faces, you can also synchronize one or more folders.

1 Click the **Sync Photos from** ⁑ and then click **Pictures**.

You can also click **Choose folder**, use the dialog to open the folder, and then click **Choose**.

2 Click **Selected folders** (○ changes to ⊙).

● To synchronize the entire folder, click **All folders** (○ changes to ⊙) instead.

3 Click the check box beside each subfolder you want to synchronize.

Synchronize Photos from Your Device

Although you normally want to synchronize photos from your Mac to your iPhone, you can also perform the reverse procedure and sync your iPhone's photos to your Mac.

If you have received photos on your device, or used the built-in camera in a device such as the iPod touch, iPhone, or iPad 2 to take pictures, you may want to view and work with those pictures on your Mac. To do that, you must use iPhoto to synchronize the photos from your device.

To learn how to synchronize photos from your Mac to your iPod, iPhone, or iPad, see the section "Synchronize Photos to Your Device."

Synchronize Photos from Your Device

1 Connect your device to your Mac.

Note: See the section "Connect an iPod, iPhone, or iPad," earlier in this chapter.

Mac OS X automatically launches iPhoto.

● Your device appears in the iPhoto Devices list.

● iPhoto displays your device's Camera Roll photos.

2 Press and hold ⌘ and click each photo you want to import.

3 Use the Event Name text box to type a name for this event.

144

4 Click **Import Selected**.

● If you want to import every photo from your device, click **Import All** instead.

When the import is complete, iPhoto asks whether you want to keep the original photos on the device.

5 Click **Keep Photos**.

● If you are running out of storage space on your device or no longer need the photos on your device, click **Delete Photos** instead.

TIPS

I keep many photos on my device. Is there a way to make the importing process more manageable?
Yes. If you have imported some of your device photos in the past, you probably do not want to import them again. In that case, you should tell iPhoto to hide those photos that you have previously imported. To do that, click the **Hide photos already imported** check box (☐ changes to ☑).

Is there a way to prevent iPhoto from running every time I connect my device?
Yes. Click **Finder** (⬛), click **Applications** to open the Applications folder, and then double-click **Image Capture**. In the Image Capture application, click the **Connecting this iPhone opens** ⬦ and then click **No application**.

Synchronize Movies and TV Shows

If you have a video iPod, an iPhone, or an iPad, you can use iTunes to synchronize movies and TV show episodes to your device. Once the synchronization is complete and you have disconnected your device, you can play the synced movies or TV shows on the device.

Synchronize movies and TV shows with care. A single half-hour TV episode may be as large as 250MB, and full-length movies are several gigabytes, so even a modest video collection will consume lots of storage space on your device.

Synchronize Movies and TV Shows

1 Click your device.

2 Click **Movies**.

3 If you want to view a rented movie on your device, click **Move**.

4 Scroll down and click **Sync Movies** (☐ changes to ☑).

5 Click **Automatically include** (☑ changes to ☐).

6 Click each movie to synchronize (☐ changes to ☑).

Click **TV Shows.**

 Click **Sync TV Shows**
(☐ changes to ☑).

 Click **Automatically include**
(☑ changes to ☐).

 Click each TV show to
synchronize (☐ changes
to ☑).

 Click **Apply.**

iTunes synchronizes your
movies and TV shows to your
device.

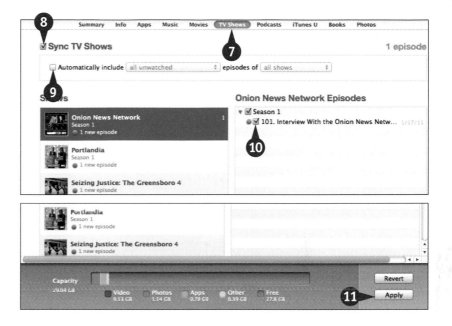

TIPS

Is there a way to synchronize just the TV shows that I have not watched yet?

Yes. Click **Automatically include** (☐ changes to ☑), click ⁝, and then click one of the "unwatched" options (such as **all unwatched**). A movie or TV episode is unwatched if you have not yet viewed it either in iTunes or your device. If you watch an episode on your device, the player sends this information to iTunes when you next sync.

Why does iTunes not sync some of my TV show episodes?

If you selected one of the "unwatched" options, then iTunes does not sync any episode marked as watched, which can occur even if you watch only a few seconds of an episode within iTunes. To mark a TV episode as unwatched, in iTunes choose the TV Shows library, right-click the episode, and then click **Mark as Unwatched.**

Synchronize Contacts, Calendars, and Mail

I f you will be away from your Mac, you can stay in touch by synchronizing your contacts, calendars, and e-mail accounts.

The iPod, iPhone, and iPad include both address book features and calendar tools, so you can ensure you are always dealing with the same data by synchronizing your Mac's Address Book contacts and iCal calendars to your iPod, iPhone, or iPad.

The iPod touch, iPhone, and iPad also support e-mail, so you can use the same e-mail on both your Mac and your device by synchronizing one or more e-mail accounts.

Synchronize Contacts, Calendars, and Mail

Synchronize Contacts and Calendars on Your Device

1 Click your device.

2 Click **Info**.

3 Click **Sync Address Book Contacts** (☐ changes to ☑).

4 Click **All contacts** (○ changes to ⊙).

5 Scroll down and click **Sync iCal Calendars** (☐ changes to ☑).

6 Click **All calendars** (○ changes to ⊙).

7 Click **Apply**.

iTunes synchronizes your contacts and calendars to your device.

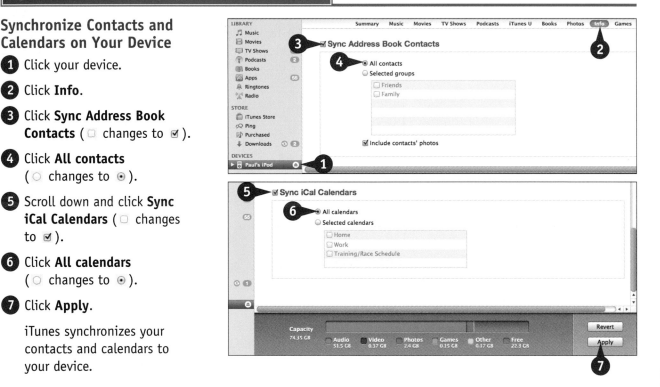

Synchronize E-mail Accounts on Your Device

1 Click your device.

2 Click **Info**.

3 Click **Sync Mail Accounts**
(☐ changes to ☑).

4 Click the check box beside each account you want to synchronize (☐ changes to ☑).

5 Click **Apply**.

iTunes synchronizes the selected e-mail accounts to your device.

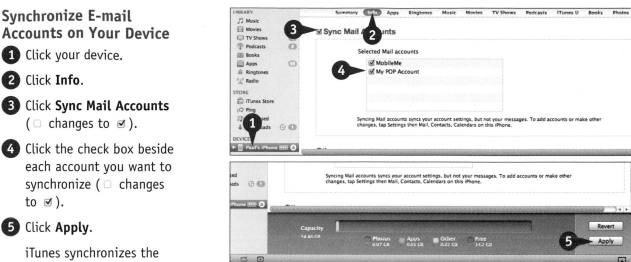

TIP

Is there any other information I can synchronize with my iPhone or iPad?

Yes, you can also synchronize your bookmarks, which are your favorite websites that you have saved using the Safari web browser (see the section "Bookmark Web Pages" in Chapter 4). In iTunes, click your device, click the **Info** tab, scroll down to the Other section, and then click the **Sync Safari bookmarks** check box (☐ changes to ☑).

Other

☑ Sync Safari bookmarks
☐ Sync notes

Synchronize Podcasts

You can synchronize the podcasts in your iTunes Library to your iPod, iPhone, or iPad. Once the synchronization is complete and you have disconnected your device, you can play the synced podcasts on the device.

You can synchronize all your podcasts if your device has enough storage capacity, or you can synchronize just selected episodes.

See the section "Subscribe to a Podcast" in Chapter 7 to learn how to add podcasts to your iTunes Library.

Synchronize Podcasts

1. Click your device in the iTunes Devices list.

2. Click the **Podcasts** tab.

3. Click **Sync Podcasts** (☐ changes to ☑).

4. Click **Automatically include** (☑ changes to ☐).

5 Click a podcast.

6 Click the check box beside each podcast you want to synchronize (☐ changes to ☑).

7 Click **Apply**.

iTunes synchronizes your podcasts to your device.

Is there a way to synchronize just the podcasts that I have not played yet?

Yes. Click **Automatically include** (☐ changes to ☑), click ⇕, and then click one of the "unplayed" options (such as **all unplayed** or **1 most recent unplayed**). A podcast is unplayed if you have not yet played it either in iTunes or your device. If you play an episode on your device, the player sends this information to iTunes when you next sync.

Why does iTunes not sync some of my podcast episodes?

If you selected one of the "unplayed" options, then iTunes does not sync any episode marked as played, which can occur even if you play only a few seconds of a podcast episode within iTunes. To mark a podcast as unwatched, in iTunes choose the Podcasts library, right-click the episode, and then click **Mark as Unplayed**.

Synchronize Games

You can make your video iPod even more fun by synchronizing games from iTunes to the iPod.

If you have a video iPod, you can use it to play games such as Tetris and Scrabble. In the iTunes Store, you can find a wide selection of games that are designed to work with the iPod click wheel.

If you have downloaded games from the iTunes Store to your iTunes Library, you can synchronize those games to your iPod.

Synchronize Games

1 Click your iPod in the iTunes Devices list.

2 Click the **Games** tab.

3 Click **Sync Games** (☐ changes to ☑).

④ Click the check box beside each game you want to synchronize (☐ changes to ☑).

⑤ Click **Apply**.

iTunes synchronizes your games to your iPod.

TIP

How do I get games for my iPod?

You can download games via the iTunes Store. Here are the steps to follow:

① In iTunes, click **iTunes Store**.

② Click the **App Store** menu.

③ Click **iPod Click Wheel Games**.

④ Display the game you want to download.

⑤ Click **Buy Game**.

⑥ Type your iTunes Store password.

⑦ Click **Buy**.

The iTunes Store asks you to confirm the purchase.

⑧ Click **Buy**.

Synchronize Apps

If you have an iPod touch, iPhone, or iPad, you can download small programs — called *apps*, which is short for *applications* — from Apple's App Store to run on your device. You can do this using the App Store on the device, but you can also download apps using your Mac. In that case, you must synchronize the apps with your device.

Synchronize Apps

1 Click your device in the iTunes Devices list.

2 Click the **Apps** tab.

3 Click **Sync Apps** (☐ changes to ☑).

④ Click the check box beside each app you want to synchronize (☐ changes to ☑).

⑤ Click **Apply**.

iTunes synchronizes your apps.

TIP

Can I update my apps using my Mac?

Yes. Updating an app means downloading the latest version of the software, which is almost always free. Here are the steps to follow:

① In iTunes, click **Apps**.

② Click *X* **Updates Available**, where *X* is the number of updates.

③ Locate the app you want to update.

④ Click **Get Update**.

● Alternatively, click **Download All Free Updates** to download every available update.

iTunes downloads the update or updates.

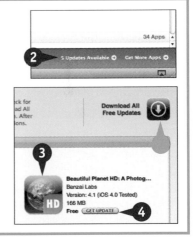

CHAPTER 9

Viewing and Editing Photos

Whether you want to look at your photos, or you want to edit your photos to crop out unneeded portions or fix problems, Mac OS X comes with useful tools for working with your photos. If your Mac comes with the iLife suite, you can also use iPhoto to view and edit photos.

View a Preview of a Photo

M ac OS X offers several tools you can use to see a preview of any photo on your Mac. The Finder application has a number of methods you can use to view your photos, but here you learn about the two easiest methods. First, you can preview any saved image file using the Mac OS X Quick Look feature; second, you can see photo previews by switching to the Cover Flow view.

You can also preview photos using the Preview application.

View a Preview of a Photo

View a Preview with Quick Look

1 Click **Finder** (🖥️) in the Dock.

2 Open the folder that contains the photo you want to preview.

3 Click the photo.

4 Click **Quick Look** (👁️).

You can also right-click the photo and then click **Quick Look**, or press Spacebar.

● Finder displays a preview of the photo.

View a Preview with Cover Flow

1 Click **Finder** (🖥️) in the Dock.

2 Open the folder that contains the photo you want to preview.

3 Click the photo.

4 Click **Cover Flow** (🖼️).

● Finder displays a preview of the photo.

● Use the scroll bar to scroll through the other photos in the folder.

View a Preview in the Preview Application

1 Click **Finder** (⬛) in the Dock.

2 Open the folder that contains the photo you want to preview.

3 Click the photo.

4 Click **File**.

5 Click **Open With**.

6 Click **Preview**.

Note: In many cases, you can also simply double-click the photo to open it in the Preview application.

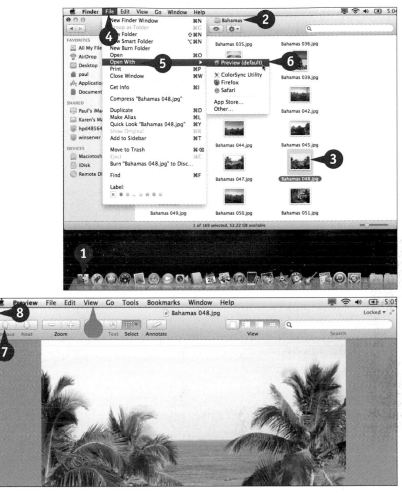

The Preview application opens and displays the photo.

7 Use the toolbar buttons to change how the photo appears in the Preview window. For example, click **Zoom +** to get a closer look at the photos.

● More commands are available on the **View** menu.

8 When you are finished viewing the photo, click **Close** (●).

Is there an easier way to preview multiple photos using the Preview application?

Yes. Instead of constantly starting and quitting Preview for each photo you want to view, you can load multiple photos into the Preview application. In Finder, navigate to the folder that contains the photos, and then select each file that you want to preview and then follow Steps **4** to **6** in this section. Either click and drag the mouse (⬚) over the photos or press and hold ⌘ and click each one. In Preview, click **Next** and **Previous** to navigate the photos.

Is there a way that I can zoom in on just a portion of a photo?

Yes. In Preview, click **Tools** and then click **Select Tool** (or either press ⌘+3 or click **Select** in the toolbar). Click and drag your mouse (⬚) to select the portion of the photo that you want to magnify. Click **View** and then click **Zoom to Selection** (or press ⌘+*).

View a Slide Show of Your Photos

Instead of viewing your photos one at a time, you can easily view multiple photos by running them in a slide show.

You can run the slide show using the Preview application. The slide show displays each photo for a few seconds, and then Preview automatically displays the next photo. Quick Look also offers several on-screen controls that you can use to control the slide show playback. You can also configure Quick Look to display the images full-screen.

View a Slide Show of Your Photos

1. Click **Finder** (icon) in the Dock.

2. Open the folder that contains the photos you want to view in the slide show.

3. Select the photos you want to view.

4. Click **File**.

5. Click **Open With**.

6. Click **Preview**.

The Preview window appears.

7. Click **View**.

8. Click **Slideshow**.

You can also select Slideshow by pressing Shift + ⌘ + F.

Preview opens the slide show window.

 9 Move the mouse ( ).

● Preview displays the slide show controls.

10 Click **Play**.

Preview begins the slide show.

● Click **Next** to move to the next photo.

● Click **Back** to move to the previous photo.

● Click **Pause** to suspend the slide show.

11 When the slide show is over or when you want to return to Finder, click **Close** or press `Esc`.

TIPS

Can I jump to a specific photo during the slide show?
Yes. With the slide show running, press `Return` to stop the show and display thumbnail views of all the slide show images. Use the arrow keys to select the photo that you want to view in the slide show, and then press `Return`. Preview returns you to the slide show and displays the selected photo. Click **Play** to resume the slide show from that photo.

What keyboard shortcuts can I use when viewing a slide show?
Press `→` to display the next photo, and press `←` to display the previous photo. Press `Spacebar` to pause the slide show, and press `Spacebar` to resume. Press `Esc` to end the slide show.

Open and Close iPhoto

If your Mac has iLife installed, the suite includes the iPhoto application, which offers special tools for viewing, managing, and editing your photos. You can also purchase iPhoto separately through the App Store. With iPhoto you can import photos from a digital camera, view and organize the photos on your Mac, and edit and repair photos.

To begin using the program, you must first learn how to find and open the iPhoto window. When you finish using the program, you can close the iPhoto window to free up computer processing power.

Open and Close iPhoto

Open iPhoto

1 In the Dock, click **iPhoto** (⬛).

The iPhoto window appears.

The first time you launch iPhoto, the program asks if you want to use iPhoto when you connect your digital camera.

2 Click **Yes**.

The first time you launch iPhoto, the program asks if you want to view your photos on a map.

3 If you have a GPS-enabled camera (such as an iPhone 4, 3GS, or 3G, or an iPad 2 with 3G) or if you want to enter location data by hand, click **Yes**.

Close iPhoto

1 Click **iPhoto**.

2 Click **Quit iPhoto**.

Are there other methods I can use to open iPhoto?

Yes. If you do not have  in the Dock, there are a couple of methods you can use to open iPhoto. If you have used iPhoto recently, a reasonably fast method is to click , click **Recent Items**, and then click **iPhoto**. Alternatively, click **Spotlight** (Q), type **iphoto**, and then click **iPhoto** in the search results.

Are there faster methods I can use to close iPhoto?

Probably the fastest method you can use to quit iPhoto is to click . Alternatively, right-click the **iPhoto** icon () and then click **Quit**. Finally, if your hands are closer to the keyboard than to the mouse, you can quit iPhoto by switching to the applications and pressing +.

Import Photos from a Digital Camera

You can import photos from a digital camera and save them on your Mac. If you have the iLife suite installed on your Mac, you can use the iPhoto application to handle importing photos. iPhoto is also available separately through the App Store. iPhoto enables you to add a name and a description to each import, which helps you to find your photos after the import is complete.

To perform the import, you will need a cable to connect your digital camera to your Mac. Most digital cameras come with a USB cable.

Import Photos from a Digital Camera

Import Photos from the Digital Camera

1 Connect one end of the cable to the digital camera.

2 Connect the other end of the cable to a free USB port on your Mac.

3 Turn the camera on and put it in either playback or computer mode.

Your Mac launches the iPhoto application.

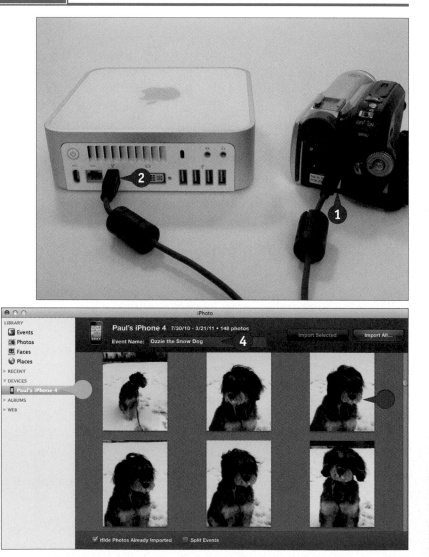

● Your digital camera appears in the Devices section.

● iPhoto displays previews of the camera's photos.

4 Use the Event Name text box to type a name for the group of photos you are going to import.

5 Select the photos that you want to import.

Note: To select photos, either click and drag the mouse ( ) around the photos you want, or press and hold ⌘ and click each photo.

6 Click **Import Selected**.

● If you want to import all the photos from the digital camera, click **Import All** instead.

iPhoto imports the photos from the digital camera.

iPhoto asks if you want to delete the original photos from the digital camera.

7 If you no longer need the photos on the camera, click **Delete Photos**.

● If you prefer to keep the photos on the camera, click **Keep Photos** instead.

View the Imported Photos

1 Click **Events**.

2 Double-click the event name that you specified in Step 4 on the previous page.

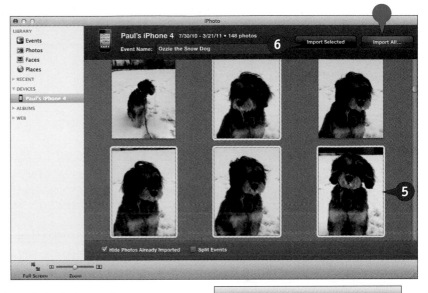

165

View Your Photos

If you want to look at several photos, you can use the iPhoto application, which is available with Apple's iLife suite or separately via the App Store.

iPhoto offers a feature called full-screen mode, which hides everything else and displays your photos using the entire screen. Once you activate full-screen mode, iPhoto offers several on-screen controls that you can use to navigate backward and forward through the photos in a folder. iPhoto's full-screen mode also shows thumbnail images of each photo, so you can quickly jump to any photo you want to view.

View Your Photos

1. In iPhoto, click **Events**.

2. Double-click the event that contains the photos you want to view.

3. Double-click the first photo you want to view.

iPhoto displays the photo.

 Click **Next** () to view the next photo in the event.

● You can also click **Previous** () to see the previous photo in the Event.

Note: You can also navigate photos by pressing and .

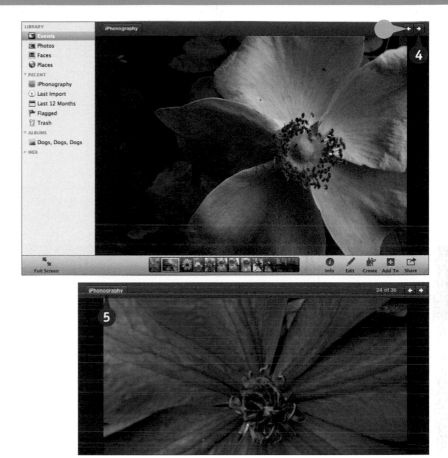

5 When you are done, click the name of the event.

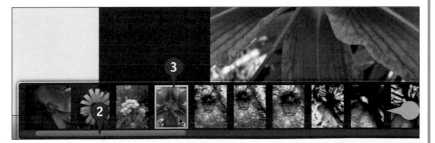

TIP

Is there a way that I can jump quickly to a particular photo in full-screen mode?
Yes. Follow these steps:

1 Move the mouse (↖) to the top of the screen.

● iPhoto displays thumbnail images of the Event's photos.

2 Use the horizontal scroll bar to bring the thumbnail of the photo you want into view.

3 Click the photo's thumbnail.

iPhoto displays the photo in full-screen mode.

Create an Album

You can use the iPhoto application to organize your photos into albums. You can get iPhoto either via the iLife suite, which is installed on all new Macs, or via the App Store.

In iPhoto, an *album* is a collection of photos that are usually related in some way. For example, you might create an album for a series of vacation photos, for photos taken at a party or other special event, or for photos that include a particular person, pet, or place.

Using your iPhoto Library, you can create customized albums that include only the photos that you want to view.

Create an Album

Create the Album

1 Click **File**.

2 Click **New**.

3 Click **Album**.

Note: You can also start a new album by pressing ⌘+N.

4 Type a name for the new album.

5 Press Return.

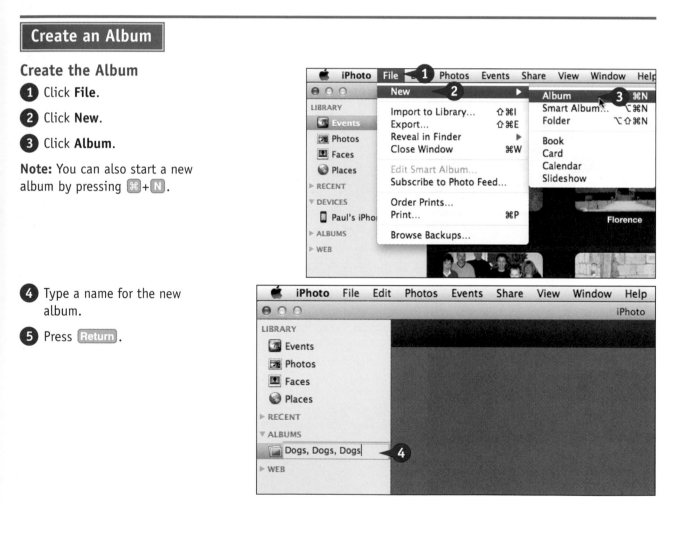

Add Photos to the Album

1 Click **Photos**.

2 Click ► beside an event that contains photos you want to work with (► changes to ▼).

3 Click and drag a photo and drop it on the new album.

4 Repeat Steps **2** and **3** to add other photos to the album.

5 Click the album.

● iPhoto displays the photos you added to the album.

Is there any way to make iPhoto add photos to an album automatically?

Yes, you can create a *smart album* where the photos that appear in the album have one or more properties in common, such as the description, rating, date, or text in the photo title. Click **File**, click **New**, and then click **Smart Album** (you can also press `Option`+`⌘`+ `N`). Use the Smart Album dialog to create one or more rules that define which photos you want to appear in the album.

Crop a Photo

If you have a photo containing elements that you do not want or need to see, you can often cut out those elements. This is called *cropping*, and you can do this with iPhoto, which comes with the iLife suite or via the App Store.

When you crop a photo, you specify a rectangular area of the photo that you want to keep. iPhoto discards everything outside of the rectangle.

Cropping is a useful skill to have because it can help give focus to the true subject of a photo. Cropping is also useful for removing extraneous elements that appear on or near the edges of a photo.

Crop a Photo

1 Click the photo you want to crop.

2 Click **Edit** (✏).

iPhoto displays its editing tools.

3 Click **Crop** (▣).

iPhoto displays a cropping rectangle on the photo.

④ Click and drag a corner or side to define the area you want to keep.

Note: Remember that iPhoto keeps the area inside the rectangle.

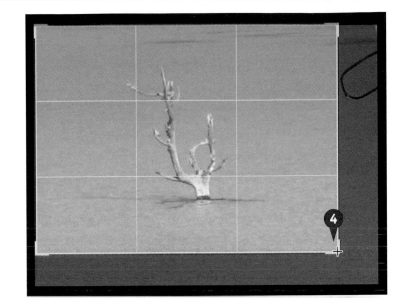

⑤ Click **Done**.

iPhoto saves the cropped photo.

⑥ Click ( ).

iPhoto exits edit mode.

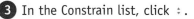

TIP

Is there a quick way to crop a photo to a certain size?

Yes, iPhoto enables you to specify either a specific size, such as 640 x 480, or a specific ratio, such as 4 x 3 or 16 x 9. Follow these steps:

① Follow Steps **1** to **3** to display the Crop tool.

② Click the **Constrain** check box (☐ changes to ☑).

③ In the Constrain list, click ⬦.

④ Click the size or ratio you want to use.

⑤ Click **Done**.

⑥ Click ✎.

iPhoto exits edit mode.

Rotate a Photo

You can rotate a photo using the iPhoto application, which comes with all new Macs as part of iLife, and is also available separately via the App Store.

Depending on how you held your camera when you took a shot, the resulting photo might show the subject sideways or upside down. This may be the effect you want, but more likely this is a problem. To fix this problem, you can use iPhoto to rotate the photo so that the subject appears right-side up. You can rotate a photo either clockwise or counterclockwise.

Rotate a Photo

1 Click the photo you want to rotate.

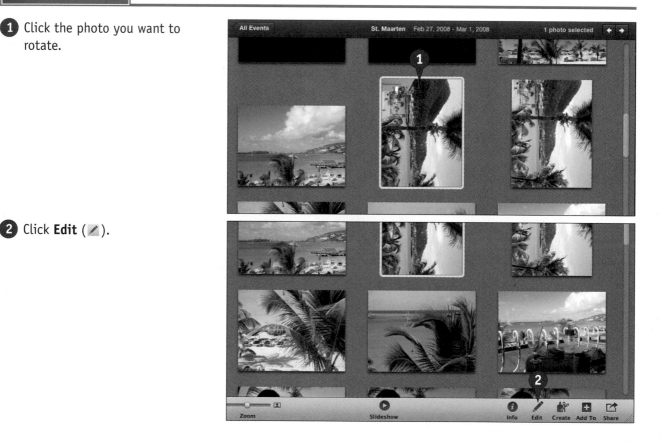

2 Click **Edit** (✏).

iPhoto displays its editing tools.

3 Click **Rotate** ().

● iPhoto rotates the photo 90 degrees counterclockwise.

4 Repeat Step **3** until the subject of the photo is right-side up.

5 Click ✎.

iPhoto exits edit mode.

TIP

Can I rotate a photo clockwise instead?
Yes, you can:

1 With the editing tools displayed, press and hold the `Option` key.

● The Rotate icon changes from 🔄 to 🔄.

2 With `Option` held down, click **Rotate** to rotate the photo clockwise by 90 degrees.

Note: You can also right-click the photo and then click **Rotate Clockwise**.

Straighten a Photo

You can straighten a crooked photo using the iPhoto application, which comes with all new Macs as part of iLife, and is also available separately via the App Store.

If you do not use a tripod when taking pictures, getting your camera perfectly level when you take a shot is very difficult and requires lots of practice and a steady hand. Despite your best efforts, you might end up with a photo that is not quite level. To fix this problem, you can use iPhoto to nudge the photo clockwise or counterclockwise so that the subject appears straight.

Straighten a Photo

1 Click the photo you want to straighten.

2 Click **Edit** ().

iPhoto displays its editing tools.

3 Click **Straighten** (▣).

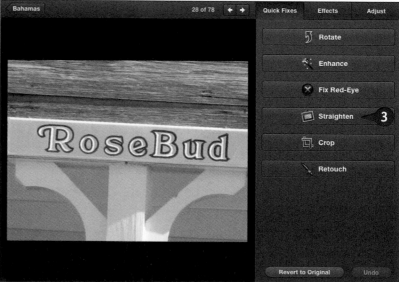

iPhoto displays a grid over the photo.

④ Click and drag the **Angle** slider.

Drag the slider to the left to angle the photo counterclockwise.

Drag the slider to the right to angle the photo clockwise.

⑤ Click **Done**.

⑥ Click .

iPhoto exits edit mode.

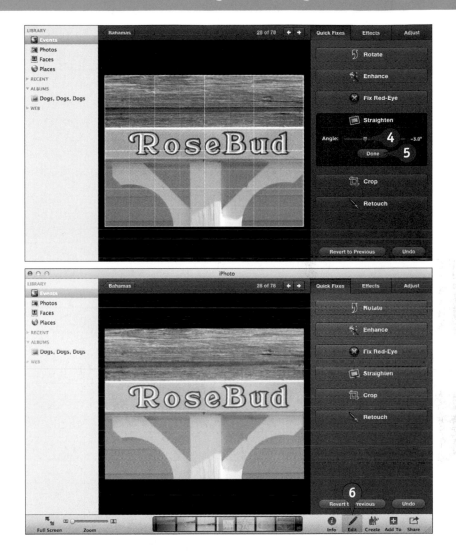

TIP

How do I know when my photo is level?
Use the gridlines that iPhoto places over the photo. Locate a horizontal line in your photo, and then rotate the photo so that this line is parallel to the nearest horizontal line in the grid. You can also match a vertical line in the photo with a vertical line in the grid.

Remove Red Eye from a Photo

You can remove red eye from a photo using the iPhoto application, which comes with all new Macs as part of iLife, and is also available separately via the App Store.

When you use a flash to take a picture of one or more people, in some cases the flash may reflect off the subjects' retinas. The result is the common phenomenon of *red eye*, where each person's pupils appear as red instead of black.

If you have a photo where one or more people have red eyes due to the camera flash, you can use iPhoto to remove the red eye and give your subjects a more natural look.

Remove Red Eye from a Photo

1 Click the photo that contains the red eye.

2 Click **Edit** (✏).

iPhoto displays its editing tools.

● If needed, you can click and drag this slider to the right to zoom in on the picture.

● You can click and drag this rectangle to bring the red eye into view.

3 Click **Fix Red-Eye** (✖).

iPhoto displays its Red-Eye controls.

● You may be able to fix the red eye automatically by clicking the **Auto-fix red-eye** check box. If that does not work, continue with the rest of these steps.

4 Move the red eye pointer over a red eye in the photo.

5 Click the red eye.

● iPhoto removes the red eye.

6 Repeat Steps **4** and **5** to fix any other instances of red eye in the photo.

7 Click **Done**.

8 Click .

iPhoto exits edit mode.

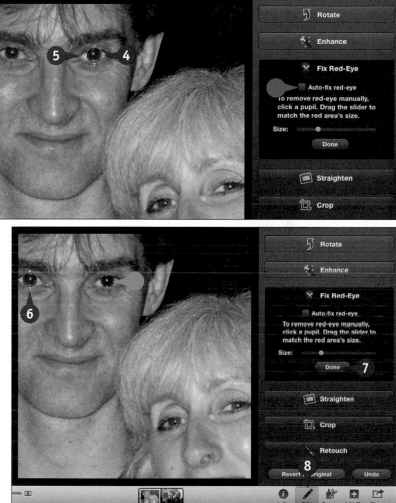

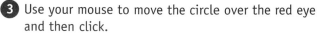

TIP

Why does iPhoto remove only part of the red eye in my photo?
The Red-Eye tool may not be set to a large enough size. The tool should be approximately the same size as the subject's eye:

1 Follow Steps **1** to **3** to display the Red-Eye controls.

2 Click and drag the Size slider until the Red-Eye tool is the size of the red-eye area.

3 Use your mouse to move the circle over the red eye and then click.

iPhoto removes the red eye that occurs within the circle.

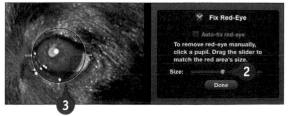

Add Names to Faces in Your Photos

You can make your photos easier to manage and navigate by adding names to the faces that appear in each photo. This is sometimes called *tagging*, and it enables you to navigate your photos by name. For example, you can view all your photos in which a certain person appears.

To add names to the faces in your photos, you must be using iPhoto '09 or later. To check this, click **iPhoto** in the menu bar and then click **About iPhoto**.

Add Names to Faces in Your Photos

1 Click the photo that you want to tag.

2 Click **Info** (ⓘ).

3 Click *X* **unnamed** (where *X* is the number of faces iPhoto identifies in the photo).

iPhoto displays its naming tools.

4 Click **unnamed**.

5 Type the person's name.

6 Press **Return**.

7 Repeat Steps **3** to **5** to name each person in the photo.

● If iPhoto did not mark a face in the photo, click **Add a face**, size and position the box over the face, and then type the name in the **click to name** box.

8 Click **Info**.

iPhoto exits naming mode.

How do I view all the photos that contain a particular person?

One method you can use is to open a photo, click **Info** (●), and then click the **Show All** arrow (●) that appears beside the person's name. You can also follow these steps:

1 Click **Faces** in the iPhoto Sidebar.

● iPhoto displays the names and sample photos of each person you have named.

2 Double-click the person you want to view.

iPhoto displays all the photos that contain the person.

Map Your Photos

You can view your photos by location if you edit each photo to include the location where you took the image.

If your camera does not add location data automatically, you can tell iPhoto the locations where your photos were taken, and then display a map that shows those locations. This enables you to view all your photos taken in a particular place.

To map your photos, you must be using iPhoto '09 or later. To check this, click **iPhoto** in the menu bar and then click **About iPhoto**.

Map Your Photos

1. Click the event that you want to map.

   If you want to map a single photo, open the event and then open the photo.

2. Click **Info** ( ).

3. Click **Assign a Place**.

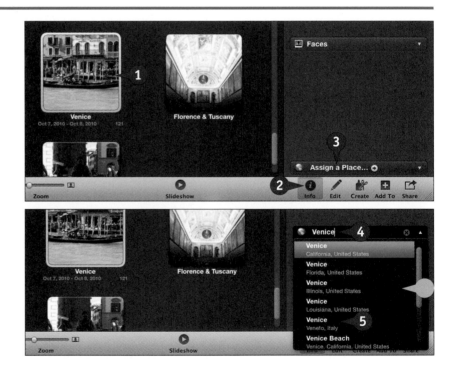

4. Type the location.

   ● iPhoto displays a list of locations that match your typing.

5. When you see the place you want to use, click it.

iPhoto displays the location on a Google map.

⑥ Click and drag the pin to the correct location, if necessary.

⑦ Click **Info**.

iPhoto closes the info window.

TIPS

Is there a way to have the location data added automatically?

Yes. If you have a GPS-enabled device — such as an iPhone 3G or later, or an iPad 2 with 3G — iPhoto automatically picks up location data from the photos. However, for this to work, you must activate this feature. Click **iPhoto** in the menu bar, click **Preferences**, and then click the **Advanced** tab. Click the **Look up Places** ⁞ and then click **Automatically**. Note that you may still have to add or edit location names for your photos.

How do I view all the photos that were taken in a particular place?

Click **Places** in the iPhoto Sidebar to see a map of the world with pins for each of your photo locations. Position the mouse (⬉) over the location's pin, and then click the **Show All** arrow (▶). iPhoto displays all the photos that were taken in that location.

E-mail a Photo

You can use the iPhoto application to create a message to send a photo to another person via e-mail. iPhoto comes with all new Macs as part of iLife, and is also available separately via the App Store.

If you have a photo that you want to share with someone, and you know that person's e-mail address, you can send the photo in an e-mail message. Using iPhoto, you can specify which photo you want to send, and iPhoto will create a new message.

Even if a photo is very large, you can still send it via e-mail because you can use iPhoto to shrink the copy of the photo that appears in the message.

E-mail a Photo

1 Click the photo you want to send.

2 Click **Share**.

3 Click **Email**.

● You can also click **Share** (⬆) and then click **Email**.

● iPhoto creates a new message.

● The photo appears in the message body.

④ Use the To text box to type the address of the message recipient.

⑤ Use the Subject text box to type the message subject.

⑥ Click here and then type your message text.

● You can use these controls to format the text.

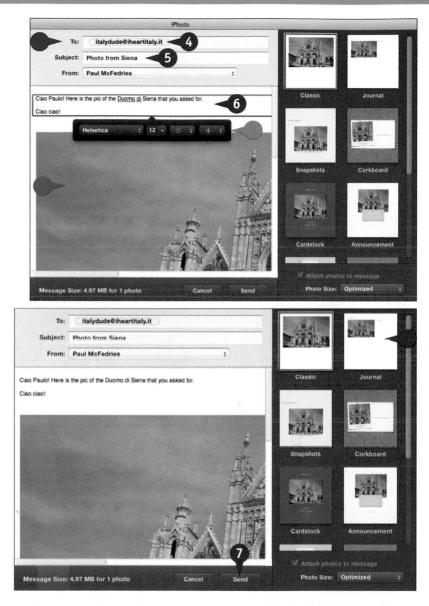

● You can click these thumbnails to apply a special effect to the message.

⑦ Click **Send**.

iPhoto sends the message.

TIP

How do I change the size of the photo?
You need to be careful when sending photos because a single image can be several megabytes in size. If your recipient's e-mail system places restrictions on the size of messages it can receive, your message might not go through.

To change the size of the photo, click the **Photo Size** ⬦ and then click the size you want to use for the sent photo, such as Small or Medium. Note that this does not affect the size of the original photo, just the copy that is sent with the message.

Take Your Picture

You can use your Mac to take a picture of yourself. If your Mac comes with a built-in iSight camera, or if you have an external camera attached to your Mac, you can use the camera to take a picture of yourself using the Photo Booth application.

Once you have taken your picture, you can e-mail that picture, add it to iPhoto, or set is as your user account or iChat buddy picture.

Take Your Picture

Take Your Picture with Photo Booth

① In the Dock, click **Photo Booth** (🖼).

The Photo Booth window appears.

● The live feed from the camera appears here.

② Click **Take a still picture** (▣).

● Click **Take four quick pictures** (▦) if you want Photo Booth to snap four successive photos, each about 1 second apart.

● Click **Take a movie clip** (▤) if you want Photo Booth to capture the live camera feed as a movie.

Click **Take Photo** (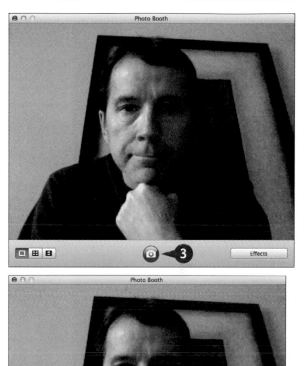).

Note: You can also press ⌘+Ⓣ or click **File** and then click **Take Photo**.

Photo Booth counts down 3 seconds and then takes the photo.

Note: When the Mac is taking your picture, be sure to look into the camera, not into the screen.

Work with Your Photo Booth Picture

● Photo Booth displays the picture.

1 Click the taken picture.

● Click **Email** ( ) to send the photo in an e-mail message.

● Click **iPhoto** ( ) to add the photo to iPhoto.

● Click **Account Picture** ( ) to set the photo as your user account picture.

● Click **Buddy Picture** ( ) to set the photo as your iChat buddy picture.

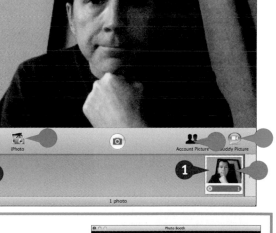

 TIP

Can I make my photos more interesting?
Definitely. Photo Booth comes with around two dozen special effects. Follow these steps:

1 In Photo Booth, click **Effects**.

2 Click an icon to select a different page of effects.

● You can also use the arrow buttons to change pages.

3 Click the effect you want to use.

Create a DVD of Your Photos

You can create a slide show of photos and burn it to a recordable DVD disc for playback on your Mac or on your home or portable DVD player. You can also send the DVD to a friend or relative.

After you start the slide show, the feature automatically advances and displays each photo on the disc as a slide.

To create a DVD of your photos, you must have a DVD drive attached to your Mac, you must have a blank DVD disc, and you must have the iDVD application, which comes with the iLife suite installed on all new Macs.

Create a DVD of Your Photos

 1 In iPhoto, select the event that you want to add to the DVD.

If you want only certain photos on your DVD, open the event and select the photos.

 2 Click **Share**.

3 Click **iDVD**.

iDVD loads, starts a new project, and populates the project with the photos.

4 Click **Themes**.

5 Click the theme you want to use.

6 Double-click the menu title.

7 Use the pop-up menus to set the title font.

8 Type a new title and then click outside the title box.

9 Click **Media**.

10 Click **Photos**.

11 Click and drag a photo and drop it on the theme's Drop Zone 1.

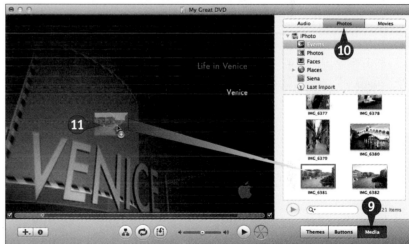

TIP

How do I remove the Apple logo from the main menu?
Follow these steps:

1 Click **iDVD**.

2 Click **Preferences**.

3 Click **General**.

4 Click **Show Apple logo watermark** (☑ changes to ☐).

5 Click ● .

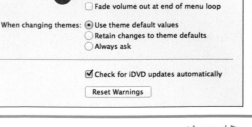

continued ▶

Although the default slide show settings are fine for most projects, iDVD offers a number of options for customizing the slide show display.

For example, by default iDVD times the duration of each image so that the total duration is the same length as the music you have selected (see the second tip on the next page). However, you can change the duration that each image appears. (Note that the longer the duration, the fewer images you can place on the disc.)

Also, by default iDVD does not apply a transition effect between photos, but you can choose from a dozen transition effects to add visual interest to the slide show.

Create a DVD of Your Photos (continued)

● iDVD displays the photo in the drop zone.

12 Double-click the subtitle.

● iDVD displays the slide show editor.

13 To change the order in which the photos appear during the slide show, click and drag a photo thumbnail and drop it in the new location.

14 To remove a photo from the slide show, click the photo and then press Del.

15 In the Slide Duration pop-up menu, click ⁝ and then click the amount of time you want to see each photo.

16 In the Transition pop-up menu, click ⁝ and then click the type of transition you want to see between each photo.

17 Insert a blank DVD.

Note: If you see a dialog asking what you want to do with the blank DVD, click **Ignore**.

18 Click **File**.

19 Click **Burn DVD**.

Note: You can also press ⌘+R or click the **Burn** button (⊙).

TIPS

How can I get my photos to play in a continuous loop?
In the iDVD window, follow Step **12** to display the project's slide show. Click **Settings** (⚙) and then click the **Loop slideshow** check box (☐ changes to ☑). Click **OK** to put the new setting into effect.

Can I add a music soundtrack to my slide show?
Yes. In the iDVD window, display the slide show editor, click **Media**, and then click **Audio**. Locate the song you want to use. Click and drag the song from the Audio list and drop it on the audio icon (⚫). To remove the song, click and drag it from the audio icon and drop it outside of the audio icon.

CHAPTER 10

Playing and Creating Digital Video

Your Mac comes with the tools you need to play movies and digital video as well as to create your own digital video movies. Using the iMovie application, you can import camcorder video; apply scene transitions; add titles, credits, and a soundtrack; and more.

Play a DVD Using DVD Player

If your Mac has a DVD drive, you can insert a DVD movie disc into the drive and then use the DVD Player application to play the movie on your Mac.

You can either watch the movie in full-screen mode where the movie takes up the entire Mac screen, or you can play the DVD in a window while you work on other things. DVD Player has features that enable you to control the movie playback and volume.

Play a DVD Using DVD Player

Play a DVD Full-Screen

1 Insert the DVD disc into your Mac's DVD drive.

DVD Player runs automatically and starts playing the DVD full-screen.

2 If you get to the DVD menu, click **Play** to start the movie.

3 Move the ⬉ to the bottom of the screen.

The playback controls appear.

● Click to pause the movie.

● Click to fast-forward the movie.

● Click to rewind the movie.

● Drag the slider to adjust the volume.

● Click to display the DVD menu.

● Click to exit full-screen mode.

192

Play a DVD in a Window

1 Insert the DVD disc into your Mac's DVD drive.

DVD Player runs automatically and starts playing the DVD full-screen.

2 Press ⌘+F.

You can also press Esc or move the 🕈 to the bottom of the screen and then click **Exit full screen**.

DVD Player displays the movie in a window.

● DVD Player displays the Controller.

3 When you get to the DVD menu, click **Play Movie** to start the movie.

● Click to pause the movie.

● Click and hold to fast-forward the movie.

● Click and hold to rewind the movie.

● Drag the slider to adjust the volume.

● Click to display the DVD menu.

● Click to stop the movie.

● Click to eject the DVD.

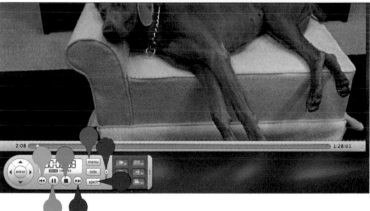

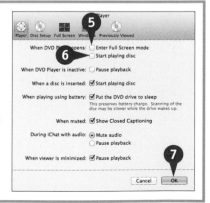

TIP

How can I always start my DVDs in a window?

1 Press ⌘+F to switch to the window view.

2 Click **DVD Player** in the menu bar.

3 Click **Preferences** to open the DVD Player preferences.

4 Click the **Player** tab.

5 Click **Enter Full Screen mode** (☑ changes to ☐).

6 If you want to control when the playback starts, also click **Start playing disc** (☑ changes to ☐).

7 Click **OK** to put the new settings into effect.

Play Digital Video with QuickTime Player

Your Mac comes with an application called QuickTime Player that can play digital video files in various formats. You will mostly use QuickTime Player to play digital video files stored on your Mac, but you can also use the application to play digital video from the web.

QuickTime Player enables you to open video files, navigate the digital video playback, and control the digital video volume.

Although you learn only how to play digital video files in this task, the version of QuickTime that comes with Mac OS X 10.7 (Lion) comes with many extra features, including the capability to record movies and audio and to cut and paste scenes.

Play Digital Video with QuickTime Player

1 Click **Finder** ().

2 Click **Applications**.

3 Double-click **QuickTime Player**.

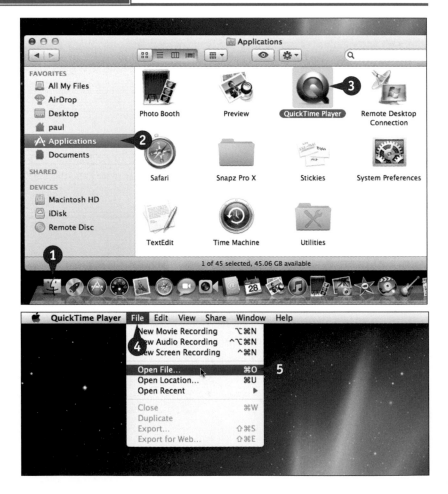

The QuickTime Player application appears.

4 Click **File**.

5 Click **Open File**.

You can also press ⌘+O.

194

The Open dialog appears.

6 Locate and click the video file you want to play.

7 Click **Open**.

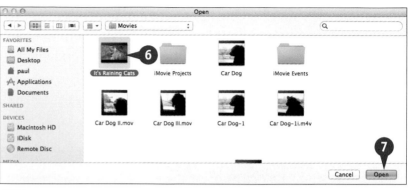

QuickTime opens a new player window.

8 Click **Play** ().

● Click here to fast-forward the video.

● Click here to rewind the video.

● Click and drag this slider to adjust the volume.

If you want to view the video in full-screen mode, press ⌘+F.

TIP

Can I use QuickTime Player to play a video from the web?
Yes, as long as you know the Internet address of the video, QuickTime Player can play most video formats available on the web. In QuickTime Player, click **File** and then click **Open Location** (or press ⌘+U). In the Open URL dialog, type or paste the video address in the **Movie Location** text box, and then click **Open**.

Create a New Movie Project

If you have the iLife suite installed on your Mac, the suite includes iMovie, which enables you to import video from a digital camcorder or video file and use that footage to create your own movies. You do this by first creating a project that holds your video clips, transitions, titles, and other elements of your movie.

When you first start iMovie, the program creates a new project for you automatically. Follow the steps in this section to create subsequent projects.

Create a New Movie Project

1 Click the **iMovie** icon () in the Dock.

The iMovie window appears.

2 Click **File**.

3 Click **New Project**.

You can also press ⌘+N.

The New Project dialog appears.

4 Use the Name text box to type a name for your project.

5 Click the **Aspect Ratio** ⁝ and then click the ratio you prefer: Widescreen (16:9) or Standard (4:3).

6 If you want to apply a theme to your project, click the one you want in the Project Themes list.

7 If you want iMovie to automatically insert transitions between all your clips, click **Automatically add** (▢ changes to ☑) and then click ⁝ to choose the type of transition.

If you chose a theme in Step **6**, the name of the check box changes to **Automatically add transition and titles**, and iMovie selects it by default.

8 Click **Create**.

iMovie creates your new project.

TIPS

What are the iMovie themes?

One of the goals of iMovie is to make digital video editing as effortless as possible. To that end, iMovie offers several themes that you can apply to a project. Each theme comes with its own set of titles and transitions that get added automatically, saving you lots of work. There are seven themes in all, including Photo Album, Bulletin Board, Comic Book, and Scrapbook. If one of them is suitable for your project, applying it cuts down on your production time.

How do I switch from one project to another?

You use the Project Library, which is a list of your movie projects. To display it, click **Window** and then click **Show Project Library**. You can also click the **Project Library** button in the top left corner of the iMovie window. In the Project Library, double-click the project you want to work with.

Import a Video File

With the iMovie application, you can import digital video from a camera for use in your movie project.

If you have video content on a USB digital camcorder or smartphone (such as an iPhone 3GS or later), you can connect the device to your Mac and then import some or all of the video to your iMovie project. If your Mac has a built-in iSight camera, you can also use iMovie to import live images from that camera to use as digital video footage in your movie project.

Import a Video File

Import all Clips

1 Connect the video device to your Mac.

iMovie displays its Import From dialog.

2 Click **Import All**.

iMovie prompts you to create a new event.

3 Click **Create new Event** (○ changes to ⊙).

4 Use the Create new Event text box to type a name for the import event.

● If you want to add the video to an existing event, click **Add to existing Event** (○ changes to ⊙) and then choose the event from the pop-up menu.

5 Click **Import**.

198

Import Selected Clips

1 Connect the video device to your Mac.

iMovie displays its Import From dialog.

2 Click **Manual**.

3 Deselect the check box under each clip you do not want to import (☑ changes to ☐).

4 Click **Import Checked**.

iMovie prompts you to create a new event.

5 Click **Create new Event** (○ changes to ⊙).

6 Use the Create new Event text box to type a name for the import event.

7 Click **Import**.

iMovie begins importing the clips.

8 Click **OK**.

9 Click **Done**.

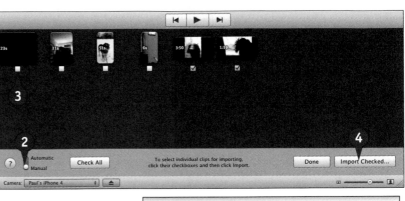

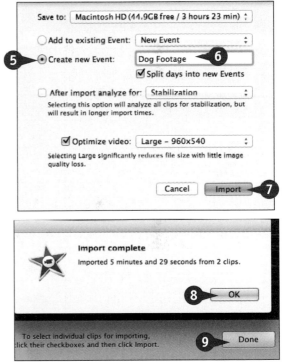

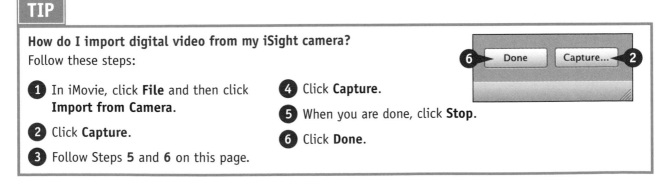

TIP

How do I import digital video from my iSight camera?
Follow these steps:

1 In iMovie, click **File** and then click **Import from Camera**.

2 Click **Capture**.

3 Follow Steps **5** and **6** on this page.

4 Click **Capture**.

5 When you are done, click **Stop**.

6 Click **Done**.

Add Video Clips to Your Project

To create and work with a movie project in iMovie, you must first add some video clips to that project.

A *video clip* is a segment of digital video. You begin building your movie by adding one or more video clips to your project.

When you import digital video as described in the previous section, iMovie automatically breaks up the video into separate clips, with each clip being the footage shot during a single recording session. You can then decide which of those clips you want to add to your project, or you can add only part of a clip.

Add Video Clips to Your Project

Add an Entire Clip

1 Click the Event Library item that contains the video clip you want to add.

2 Press and hold **Option** and click the clip.

● iMovie selects the entire clip.

3 Click and drag the selected clip and drop it in your project at the spot where you want the clip to appear.

● iMovie adds the entire video clip to the project.

● iMovie adds an orange bar to the bottom of the original clip to indicate that it has been added to the project.

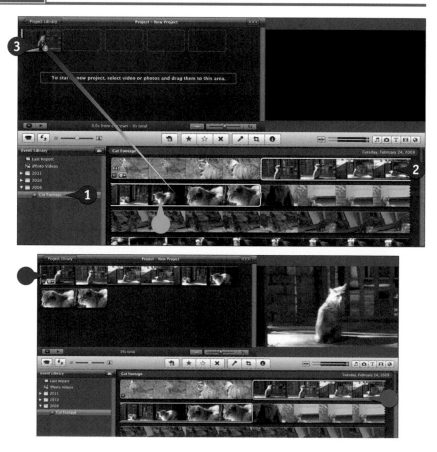

Add a Partial Clip

1 Click the Event Library item that contains the video clip you want to add.

2 Click the clip at the point where you want the selection to begin.

3 Click and drag the right edge of the selection box to the point where you want the selection to end.

4 Click and drag the selected clip and drop it in your project at the spot where you want the clip to appear.

● iMovie adds the selected portion of the video clip to the project.

● iMovie adds an orange bar to the bottom of the original clip to indicate that it has been added to a project.

TIPS

Is it possible to play a clip before I add it?
Yes. The easiest way to do this is to click the clip at the point where you want the playback to start and then press Spacebar. iMovie plays the clip in the Viewer in the top right corner of the window. Press Spacebar again to stop the playback. If you want to see only a portion of the clip, follow Steps 2 and 3 on this page to make your selection, right-click the clip, and then click **Play Selection**.

I added a clip in the wrong place. Can I move it?
Yes. In your project, click the added clip to select it. Use your mouse (↖) to click and drag the clip and then drop the clip in the correct location within the project. If you want to delete the clip from the project, click it, click **Edit**, and then click **Delete Entire Clip** (or press Option+Del).

Trim a Clip

If you have a video clip that is too long or contains footage you do not need, you can shorten the clip or remove the extra footage. Removing parts of a video clip is called *trimming* the clip.

Trimming a clip is particularly useful if you recorded extra, unneeded footage before and after the action you were trying to capture. By trimming this unneeded footage, your movie will include only the scenes you really require.

Trim a Clip

1 In your project, click the clip you want to trim.

● iMovie selects the entire clip.

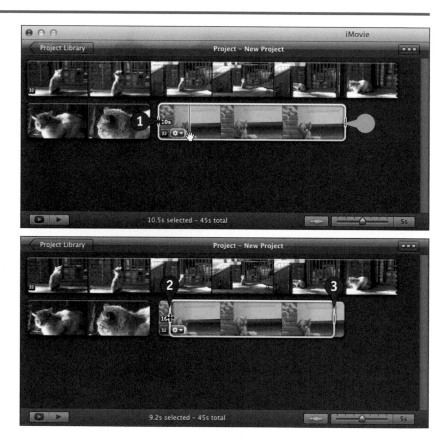

2 Use your mouse (▸) to click and drag the left edge of the selection box to the starting position of the part of the clip you want to keep.

3 Use your mouse (▸) to click and drag the right edge of the selection box to the ending position of the part of the clip you want to keep.

4 Click **Clip**.

5 Click **Trim to Selection**.

Note: You can also press ⌘+B .

● iMovie trims the clip.

TIP

Is it possible to trim a certain number of frames from a clip?

Yes, iMovie enables you to trim one frame at a time from either the beginning or the end of the clip.

1 In your project, click the clip you want to trim.

iMovie selects the entire clip.

2 Click **Clip**.

3 Click **Trim Clip End**.

4 Select the trim direction:

● To trim from the beginning, click **Move Left** (or press Option+◀).

● To trim from the end, click **Move Right** (or press Option+ ▶).

iMovie trims the clip.

5 Repeat Step **4** until you reach the number of frames that you want to trim.

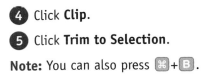

Add a Transition Between Clips

You can use the iMovie application to enhance the visual appeal of your digital movie by inserting transitions between some or all of the project's video clips.

By default, iMovie jumps immediately from the end of one clip to the beginning of the next clip, a transition called a *jump cut*. You can add more visual interest to your movie by adding a transition between the two clips.

iMovie offers 24 different transitions, including various fades, wipes, and dissolves. More transitions are available if you applied a theme to your iMovie project.

Add a Transition Between Clips

① Click the **Transitions Browser** button (⊞), or press ⌘+④.

● iMovie displays the available transitions.

Note: To see a preview of a transition, position your mouse (▸) over the transition thumbnail.

② Use your mouse (▸) to click and drag a transition and drop it between the two clips.

● iMovie adds an icon for the transition between the two clips.

3 Position your mouse (➤) over the beginning of the transition and move the ➤ to the right.

● iMovie displays a preview of the transition.

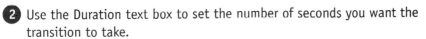

TIP

Can I change the duration of the transition?
Yes. The default length is half a second, but you can increase or decrease the duration by following these steps:

1 Double-click the transition icon in your project.

The Inspector appears.

2 Use the Duration text box to set the number of seconds you want the transition to take.

3 If you want to change only the current transition, click **Applies to all transitions** (☑ changes to ☐).

4 Click **Done**.

Add a Photo

You can use the iMovie application to enhance your movie projects with still photos.

Although most movie projects consist of several video clips, you can also add a photo to your project. By default, iMovie displays the photo for 4 seconds.

You can also specify how the photo fits in the movie frame: You can adjust the size of the photo to fit the frame, you can crop the photo, or you can apply a Ken Burns effect — which automatically pans and zooms the photo — to animate the static photo.

Add a Photo

1. Click the **Photos Browser** button (📷), or press ⌘+2.

● iMovie displays the available photos.

2. Click the event or album that contains the photo you want to add.

3. Click and drag the photo and drop it inside your project.

● iMovie adds the photo to the movie.

4. Click the photo.

5. Click the **Crop** button (🔳).

iMovie displays the cropping options for the photo.

6 Click **Ken Burns**.

● You can also click **Fit** to have iMovie adjust the size of the photo to fit the movie frame.

● You can also click **Crop** and then click and drag the cropping rectangle to specify how much of the photo you want to appear in the movie frame.

7 Click and drag the green rectangle to set the start point of the Ken Burns animation.

8 Click and drag the red rectangle to set the end point of the Ken Burns animation.

Note: Click and drag the corners and edges of the rectangle to change the size; click and drag the interior of the rectangles to change the position.

● The arrow shows the direction of motion.

9 Click **Done**.

TIP

Can I change the length of time that the photo appears in the movie?
Yes. The default length is 4 seconds, but you can increase or decrease the duration by following these steps:

1 Double-click the photo in your project.

2 Click **Clip**.

3 Use the Duration text box to set the number of seconds you want the photo to appear.

4 To change the duration for all the photos in your project, click **Applies to all stills** (☐ changes to ☑).

5 Click **Done**.

Add a Music Track

Using the iMovie application, you can enhance the audio component of your movie by adding one or more songs that play in the background.

With iMovie you can also add sound effects and other audio files that you feel would enhance your project's audio track.

To get the best audio experience, you can adjust various sound properties. For example, you can adjust the volume of the music clip or the volume of the video clip. You can also use iMovie to adjust the time it takes for the song clip to fade in and fade out.

Add a Music Track

1 Click the **Music and Sound Effect Browser** button (🎵), or press ⌘+1.

● iMovie displays the available audio files.

2 Click the folder, category, or playlist that contains the track you want to add.

3 Use your mouse (▶) to click and drag the song and drop it on a video clip.

● iMovie adds the song to the movie.

Note: iMovie treats the song like a clip, which means you can trim the song as needed, as described earlier in the "Trim a Clip" section.

4 Double-click the music clip.

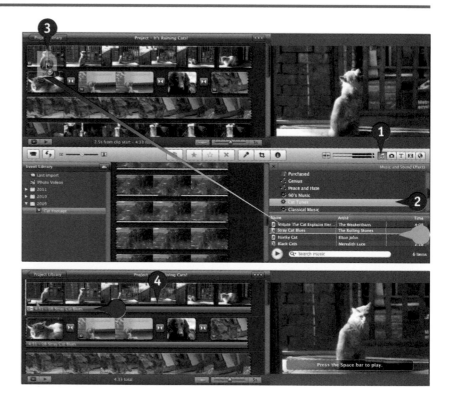

iMovie displays the Inspector.

5 Click the **Audio** tab.

6 Use the **Volume** slider to adjust the volume of the music clip.

7 If you want to reduce the video clip volume, click **Ducking** (☐ changes to ☑) and then click and drag the slider.

8 To adjust the fade-in time, click **Fade In: Manual** (☐ changes to ☑) and then click and drag the slider.

9 To adjust the fade-out time, click **Fade Out: Manual** (☐ changes to ☑) and then click and drag the slider.

10 Click **Done**.

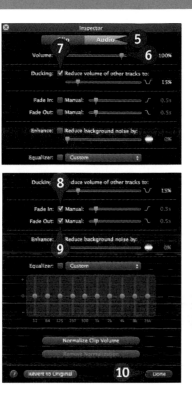

TIP

When I add a video clip before the music clip, the music does not play with the new video clip. How can I work around this?

You need to add your song as a background track instead of a clip. Follow these steps:

1 Click 🎵.

2 Use your mouse (▸) to click and drag a song.

3 Drop the song on the project background, not on a clip or between two clips.

● The background turns green when you have the song positioned correctly.

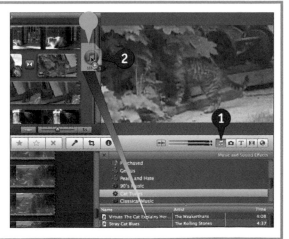

Record a Voiceover

You can use the iMovie application to augment the audio portion of your movie with a voiceover. A *voiceover* is a voice recording that you make using audio equipment attached to your Mac.

A voiceover is useful for explaining a video clip, introducing the movie, or giving the viewer background information about the movie.

To record a voiceover, your Mac must either have a built-in microphone, such as the one that comes with the iSight camera, or an external microphone connected via an audio jack, USB port, or Bluetooth.

Record a Voiceover

1 If your Mac does not have a built-in microphone, attach a microphone.

Note: You may need to configure the microphone as the sound input device. Click **System Preferences** (⚙), click **Sound**, click **Input**, and then click your microphone.

2 Click the **Voiceover** button (✎).

The Voiceover dialog appears.

3 Click the spot in the movie at which you want the voiceover to begin.

iMovie counts down and then begins the recording.

④ Speak your voiceover text into the microphone.

● The progress of the recording appears here.

⑤ When you are finished, click **Recording**.

● iMovie adds the voiceover to the clip.

⑥ Click **Close** (☒).

You can double-click the voiceover to adjust the audio, as described in the previous section.

TIP

Is there a way to tell if my voice is too loud or too soft?
Yes, you can use the controls in the Voiceover dialog. You check your voice level by talking into the microphone and then watching the Left and Right volume meters:

● If you see no green bars or just a few green bars, your voice level is too low.

● If you see yellow or red bars, your voice level is too high.

Use the Input Volume slider to adjust the voice level up or down, as needed.

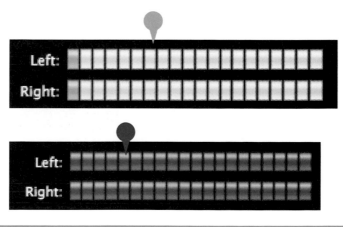

Add Titles and Credits

Y ou can use the iMovie application to enhance your movie project with titles and scrolling credits.

You can get your movie off to a proper start by adding a title and a subtitle at or near the beginning of the movie. iMovie offers a number of title styles that you can choose from, and you can also change the title font.

You can also enhance your movie with *scrolling credits*. This is a special type of title that you place at the end of the movie and that scrolls the names of the people responsible for the project.

Add Titles and Credits

① Click the **Titles browser** button (T).

● iMovie displays the available title types.

② Use your mouse ( ) to click and drag a title and drop it where you want the titles to appear.

Note: To see just the titles, drop the title thumbnail at the beginning of the movie or between two clips. To superimpose the titles on a video clip, drop the title thumbnail on the clip.

● If you want to add credits, click and drag the **Scrolling Credits** thumbnail and drop it at the end of the movie.

● iMovie adds a clip for the title.

3 Replace this text with the movie title.

4 Replace this text with the movie subtitle.

5 Click **Done**.

Note: iMovie treats the title like a clip, which means you can lengthen or shorten the title duration by clicking and dragging the beginning or end, as described earlier in the "Trim a Clip" section.

TIP

How do I change the font of the titles?

The Text menu offers several font-related commands, including Bold, Italic, Bigger, and Smaller. You can also click the **Show Fonts** command to display the Fonts dialog. If you do not see the Fonts dialog shown here, you can switch to iMovie's predefined fonts by clicking **iMovie Font Panel**. You can then click a typeface, font color, and type size; click **Done** (●) to close the dialog.

Play the Movie

The iMovie application offers the Viewer pane, which you can use to play your movie.

While you are building your iMovie project, it is a good idea to occasionally play some or all of the movie to check your progress. For example, you can play the entire movie to make sure the video and audio are working properly and are synchronized correctly. You can also play parts of the movie to ensure that your transitions appear when you want them to.

Play the Movie

Play from the Beginning

1 Click **View**.

2 Click **Play from Beginning**.

Note: You can also press ▢ or click the **Play Project from beginning** button (▶).

Play from a Specific Location

1 Position the mouse ▸ over the spot where you want to start playing the movie.

2 Press Spacebar.

214

Play a Selection

1 Select the video clips you want to play.

Note: See the first Tip below to learn how to select multiple video clips.

2 Click **View**.

3 Click **Play Selection**.

Note: You can also press /.

How do I select multiple video clips?

To select multiple video clips, press and hold ⌘ and then click anywhere inside each clip you want to select. If you select a clip by accident, ⌘+click it again to deselect it. If you want to skip just a few clips, first press ⌘+A to select all the clips, and then press and hold ⌘ and click the clips you do not want in the selection.

Can I enlarge the size of the playback pane?

Yes, you can play your movie in full-screen mode. To do this, click **View** and then click **Play full-screen**. You can also press ⌘+G or click the **Play Project full screen** button (⊡).

Create a DVD of Your Movie

When your movie project is complete, you can burn it to a recordable DVD disc for playback on your Mac or on your home or portable DVD player. You can also send the DVD to a friend or relative.

You can customize your DVD by choosing a theme, modifying the menu title, and adding a photo to the theme's drop zone, if it has one.

To create a DVD of your movie, you must have a DVD burner attached to your Mac, and you must have a blank DVD disc.

Create a DVD of Your Movie

1 Insert a blank DVD in your Mac's DVD drive.

If your Mac asks what action you want to take with the blank DVD, click **Ignore**.

2 Click **Share**.

3 Click **iDVD**.

iMovie creates your movie.

The iDVD window appears with your movie already added to the project.

4 Double-click the menu title.

5 Use the pop-up menus to set the title font.

6 Type a new title and then click outside the title box.

7 Click **Themes**.

8 Click the theme you want to use.

Note: If iDVD displays the Change Project Aspect Ratio dialog, click **Change**.

⑨ Click **File**.

⑩ Click **Burn DVD**.

You can also click the **Burn** button (🔘) or press ⌘+Ⓡ.

iDVD burns the movie to the DVD.

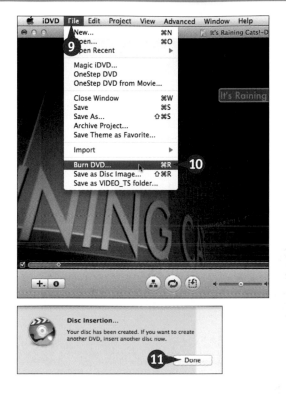

⑪ Click **Done**.

TIPS

How do I publish my movie to YouTube?
First, you need a YouTube account. If you do not have a YouTube account, go to the YouTube website (www.youtube.com), click the **Sign Up** link, and follow the instructions. In iMovie, click **Share** and then click **YouTube**. Click **Add**, type your YouTube user name, and then click **Done**. Type your YouTube password, choose the size to publish (Mobile or Medium), click **Next**, and then click **Publish**.

How do I publish my movie to MobileMe?
If you have a MobileMe account, click **System Preferences** (🔘), click **MobileMe**, and then click **Sign In**. In iMovie, click **Share** and then click **MobileMe**. Click the sizes you want to publish (Tiny, Mobile, Medium, or Large), and then click **Publish**.

CHAPTER 11

Customizing Mac OS X to Suit Your Style

Mac OS X comes with several features that enable you to customize your Mac. Not only can you change the appearance of Mac OS X to suit your taste, but you can also change the way Mac OS X works to make it easier and more efficient for you to use.

Display System Preferences

You can find many of the Mac OS X customization features in System Preferences, a collection of settings and options that control the overall look and operation of Mac OS X.

You can use System Preferences to change the desktop background, specify a screen saver, set your Mac's sleep options, add user accounts, and customize the Dock, to name some of the tasks that you learn about in this chapter.

To use these settings, you must know how to display the System Preferences window.

Display System Preferences

Open System Preferences

1 In the Dock, click **System Preferences** ( ).

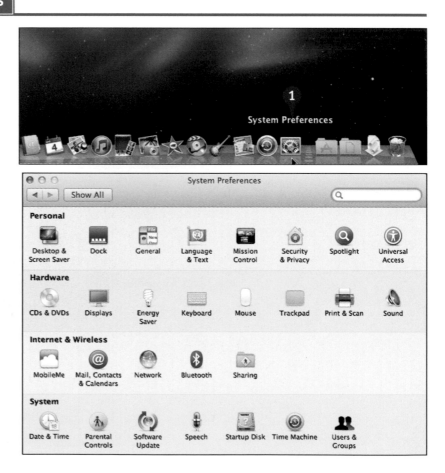

The System Preferences window appears.

Close System Preferences

1 Click **System Preferences**.

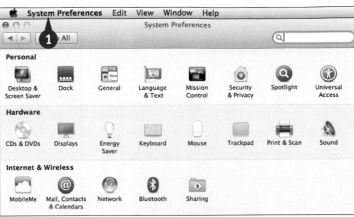

2 Click **Quit System Preferences**.

Are there other methods I can use to open and close System Preferences?

If you have hidden the Dock (as described later in the "Hide the Dock" section) or removed the System Preferences icon from the Dock, you can click ⌘ and then click **System Preferences**. Probably the fastest method you can use to quit System Preferences is to right-click 🖥 and then click **Quit**. Alternatively, if your hands are closer to the keyboard than to the mouse, you can quit System Preferences by switching to the application and pressing ⌘+Q.

Sometimes when I open System Preferences I do not see all the icons. How can I restore the original icons?

When you click an icon in System Preferences, the window changes to show just the options and settings associated with that icon. To return to the main System Preferences window, press ⌘+L or use either of the following techniques:

● Click ◄ until the main window appears.

● Click **Show All**.

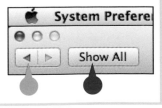

Change the Desktop Background

To give Mac OS X a different look, you can change the default desktop background.

Mac OS X offers a wide variety of desktop background options. For example, Mac OS X comes with several dozen images you can use, from abstract patterns to photos of plants and other natural images. You can also choose a solid color as the desktop background, or you can use one of your own photos.

You can change the desktop background to show either a fixed image or a series of images that change periodically.

Change the Desktop Background

Set a Fixed Background Image

1 Open System Preferences.

Note: See the section "Display System Preferences" earlier in this chapter.

2 Click **Desktop & Screen Saver**.

Note: You can also right-click the desktop and then click Change Desktop Background.

The desktop and screen saver preferences appear.

3 Click **Desktop**.

4 Click the image category you want to use.

5 Click the image you want to use as the desktop background.

Your Mac changes the desktop background.

6 If you chose a photo in Step **5**, click ⫶ and then click an option to determine how your Mac displays the photo.

Note: Another way to set a fixed background image is to select a photo in iPhoto, click **Share**, and then click **Set Desktop**.

Set a Changing Background Image

1 Click **Change picture** (☐ changes to ☑).

2 Click ⫶ in the pop-up menu and then click how often you want the background image to change.

3 If you want your Mac to choose the periodic image randomly, click **Random order** (☐ changes to ☑).

Your Mac changes the desktop background periodically based on your chosen interval.

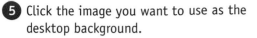

When I choose a photo, what is the difference between the various options for displaying the photo?
Your Mac gives you five options for displaying the photo:

- **Fill Screen**: This option expands the photo by the same amount in all four directions until it fills the entire desktop. This option can cause some edges of the photo to be cropped out.

- **Fit to Screen**: This option expands the photo in all four directions until the photo is either the same height as the desktop or the same width as the desktop.

- **Stretch to Fill Screen**: This option expands the photo in all four directions until it fills the entire desktop. Because the photo is usually expanded more either vertically or horizontally, this option can cause the photo to appear distorted.

- **Center**: This option displays the photo at its actual size and places the photo in the center of the desktop.

- **Tile**: This option repeats your photo multiple times to fill the entire desktop.

Activate the Screen Saver

You can set up Mac OS X to display a *screen saver*, a moving pattern or series of pictures. The screen saver appears after your computer has been idle for a while.

If you leave your monitor on for long stretches while your computer is idle, a faint version of the unmoving image can endure for a while on the screen, a phenomenon known as *persistence*. A screen saver prevents this by displaying a moving image. However, persistence is not a major problem for modern screens, so for the most part you use a screen saver for visual interest.

Activate the Screen Saver

1 Open System Preferences.

Note: See the section "Display System Preferences" earlier in this chapter.

2 Click **Desktop & Screen Saver**.

The desktop and screen saver preferences appear.

3 Click **Screen Saver**.

4 Click the screen saver you want to use.

● A preview of the screen saver appears here.

5 Click and drag the **Start screen saver** slider (▽) to set when the screen saver begins.

Note: The interval you choose is the number of minutes or hours that your Mac must be idle before the screen saver starts.

● If the screen saver is customizable, click **Options** to configure it.

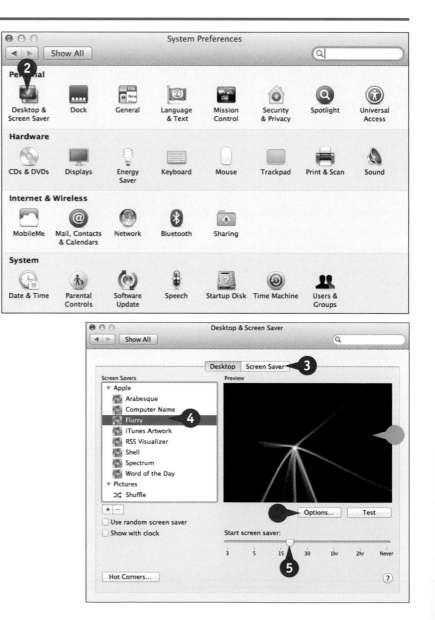

224

● If you also want to see the current time when the screen saver is active, click **Show with clock** (☐ changes to ☑).

● If you want to see a different screen saver each time, click **Use random screen saver** (☐ changes to ☑).

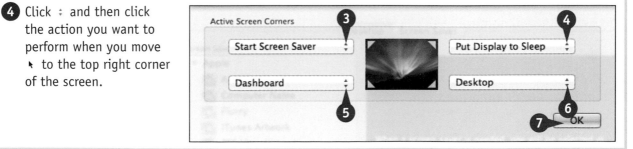

TIP

What are hot corners and how do I configure them?

A *hot corner* is a corner of your Mac's screen that you have set up to perform some action when you move the mouse (➤) to that corner. To configure hot corners, follow these steps:

1 Follow Steps **1** to **4** to select a screen saver.

2 Click **Hot Corners**.

System Preferences displays the Active Screen Corners dialog.

3 In the top left pop-up menu, click ⁞ and then click the action you want to perform when you move ➤ to the top left corner of the screen.

4 Click ⁞ and then click the action you want to perform when you move ➤ to the top right corner of the screen.

5 Click ⁞ and then click the action you want to perform when you move ➤ to the bottom left corner of the screen.

6 Click ⁞ and then click the action you want to perform when you move ➤ to the bottom right corner of the screen.

7 Click **OK**.

Set Your Mac's Sleep Options

You can make Mac OS X more energy efficient by configuring parts of your Mac to go into sleep mode automatically when you are not using them.

Sleep mode means that your display or your Mac is in a temporary low-power mode. This saves energy on all Macs, and also saves battery power on a notebook Mac. For example, you can set up Mac OS X to put the display to sleep automatically after a period of inactivity. Similarly, you can configure Mac OS X to put your entire Mac to sleep after you have not used it for a specified amount of time.

Set Your Mac's Sleep Options

Open the Energy Saver Preferences

① Open System Preferences.

Note: See the section "Display System Preferences" earlier in this chapter.

② Click **Energy Saver**.

The Energy Saver preferences appear.

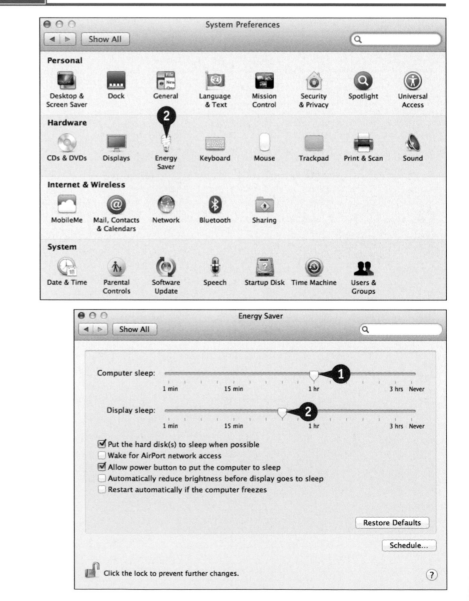

Set Sleep Options for a Desktop Mac

① Click and drag ▽ to set the computer sleep timer.

This specifies the period of inactivity after which your computer goes to sleep.

② Click and drag ▽ to set the display sleep timer.

This specifies the period of inactivity after which your display goes to sleep.

Set Sleep Options for a Notebook Mac

1 Click **Battery**.

2 Click and drag ▽ to set the computer sleep timer for when your Mac is on battery power.

3 Click and drag ▽ to set the display sleep timer for when your Mac is on battery power.

4 Click **Power Adapter**.

5 Click and drag ▽ to set the computer sleep timer for when your Mac is plugged in.

6 Click and drag ▽ to set the display sleep timer for when your Mac is plugged in.

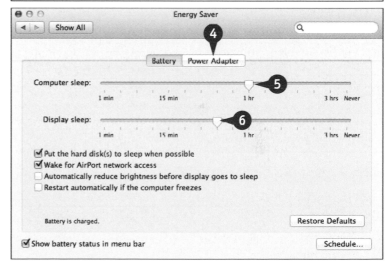

How do I wake up a sleeping display or computer?

If your Mac's display is in sleep mode, you can wake up the display by moving your mouse. If your entire Mac is in sleep mode, you can wake up the computer by clicking the mouse. You can also wake up the display or your entire Mac by pressing a key such as ⌘, Control, Option, or Shift on your keyboard.

I changed the display sleep timer, and now I never see my screen saver. Why?

You have set the display sleep timer to a time that is less than your screen saver timer. For example, suppose you have configured Mac OS X to switch on the screen saver after 15 minutes. If you then set the display sleep timer to a shorter interval, such as 10 minutes, Mac OS X will always put the display to sleep before the screen saver has a chance to kick in. Set the display sleep timer longer than your screen saver timer.

Change the Display Resolution

You can change the resolution of the Mac OS X display. This enables you to adjust the display for best viewing or for maximum compatibility with whatever application you are using.

Increasing the display resolution is an easy way to create more space on the screen for applications and windows because the objects on the screen appear smaller. Conversely, if you are having trouble reading text on the screen, decreasing the display resolution can help because the screen objects appear larger. You can change the Mac OS X display resolution using either the System Preferences window or the menu bar.

Change the Display Resolution

Change Resolution via the Display Preferences

1 Open System Preferences.

Note: See the section "Display System Preferences" earlier in this chapter.

2 Click **Displays**.

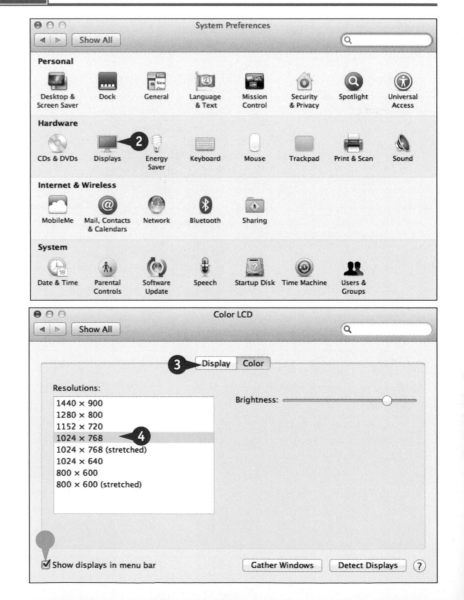

The Displays preferences appear.

3 Click **Display**.

4 Click the resolution you want to use.

Your Mac adjusts the screen to the new resolution.

● To change the resolution using your Mac's menu bar, as described on the next page, click **Show displays in menu bar** (☐ changes to ☑).

Change Resolution via the Menu Bar

1 Click the **Displays** icon (🖥).

Your Mac opens a menu that shows the most commonly or recently used resolutions.

● The resolution with the check mark (✔) is the current resolution.

2 Click the resolution you want to use.

Your Mac adjusts the screen to the new resolution.

TIPS

What do the resolution numbers mean?

The resolution numbers are expressed in *pixels*, short for picture elements, which are the individual dots that make up what you see on your Mac's screen. The pixels are arranged in rows and columns, and the resolution tells you the number of pixels in each row and column. So a resolution of 1024 x 768 means that the display is using 1,024-pixel rows and 768-pixel columns.

Why do some resolutions also include the word "stretched"?

Most older displays are made with the ratio of the width to the height — this is called the *aspect ratio* — set at 4:3. However, most new Mac displays are made with an aspect ratio of 16:10, which is called *widescreen*. Resolutions designed for 4:3 displays — such as 800 x 600 and 1024 x 768 — take up only part of a widescreen display. To make them take up the entire display, choose the *stretched* version of the resolution.

Create an App Folder in Launchpad

You can make Launchpad easier to work with by combining two or more icons into a single storage area called an *app folder*.

Mac OS X Lion displays the Launchpad icons in up to five rows per screen, with up to eight icons in each row, so you can have as many as 40 icons in each Launchpad screen. Also, if you have configured your Mac with a relatively low display resolution, you might see only partial app names in the Launchpad screens.

All of this can make it difficult to locate the app you want. However, by creating app folders, you can organize similar apps and reduce the clutter on the Launchpad screens.

Create an App Folder in Launchpad

① Click **Launchpad** (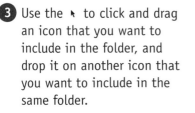).

● Launchpad displays icons for each installed application.

② Click the dot for the Launchpad screen you want to work with.

③ Use the ↖ to click and drag an icon that you want to include in the folder, and drop it on another icon that you want to include in the same folder.

- Launchpad creates the app folder.

- Launchpad applies a name to the folder based on the type of applications in the folder.

- Launchpad adds the icons to the app folder.

④ To specify a different name, click the name and then type the one you prefer.

⑤ Click the Launchpad screen, outside of the app folder.

- Launchpad displays the app folder.

⑥ To add more icons to the new app folder, use the ↖ to click and drag each icon and drop it on the folder.

Note: To launch a program from an app folder, click 🚀, click the app folder to open it, and then click the program's icon.

Can I make changes to an app folder once it has been created?

Yes, you can rename the folder or rearrange the icons within the folder. To get started, click 🚀 to open Launchpad, and then click the app folder to open it. To rename the app folder, click the current name, type the new name, and then press `Return`. To rearrange the icons, use the ↖ to drag and drop the apps within the folder. When you are done, click outside the app folder to close it.

Can I remove an icon from an app folder?

Yes. To begin, click 🚀 to open Launchpad, and then click the app folder to open it. To remove an app from a folder, use the ↖ to click and drag the app out of the folder. Launchpad closes the folder, and you can then drop the icon within the Launchpad screen. Note that if you remove all the icons from an app folder, Launchpad deletes the folder.

Add a User Account

You can share your Mac with another person by creating a user account for that person. This enables the person to log on to Mac OS X and use the system.

The new user account is completely separate from your own account. This means that the other person can change settings, create documents, and perform other OS X tasks without interfering with your own settings or data.

For maximum privacy for all users, you should set up each user account with a password.

Add a User Account

1 Open System Preferences.

Note: See the section "Display System Preferences" earlier in this chapter.

2 Click **Users & Groups**.

- In most Mac OS X systems, to modify accounts you must click the **Lock** icon (🔒) and then enter your administrator password (🔒 changes to 🔓).

3 Click **Add** (+).

The New Account dialog appears.

4 Click ⁝ and then click an account type.

5 Type the user's name.

6 Edit the short user name that Mac OS X creates.

7 Type a password for the user.

8 Retype the user's password.

9 Type a hint that Mac OS X will display if the user forgets the password.

10 Click **Create User**.

● Mac OS X adds the user account to the Accounts preferences window.

New Account: Standard **4**
Full Name: Karen **5**
Account name: karen **6**
Password: ••••••••• **7**
Verify: ••••••••• **8**
Password hint: Mom's maiden name and year of birth **9**
(Recommended)
10
(?) | Cancel | Create User

● ○ ○ Users & Groups
◄ ► Show All | Q

My User
Paul Admin
Other Users
Karen Standard
Guest User Sharing only

Reset Password...

Full name: Karen

Apple ID: Set...

☐ Allow user to reset password using Apple ID
☐ Allow user to administer this computer
☐ Enable parental controls | Open Parental Controls...

Login Options
+ − ✿ ▾

🔓 Click the lock to prevent further changes. (?)

Which account type should I use for the new account?

The Standard account type is a good choice because it can make changes only to its own account settings. Avoid the Administrator option because it is a powerful account type that enables the user to make major changes to the system. If the user is a child, consider the Managed with Parental Controls account type, which enables you to place restrictions on the user's actions and on the content the person can view.

How do I change the user's picture?

In the Accounts preferences, click the user and then click the picture. Mac OS X displays a list of the available images. If you see one you like, click it; otherwise, click **Edit Picture**. If your Mac has a camera attached and the user is nearby, you can click **Take a photo snapshot** to take the user's picture; otherwise, click **Choose**, select an image file, click **Open**, and then click **Set**.

Customize the Dock

You can customize various aspects of the Dock by using System Preferences to modify a few Dock options.

For example, you can make the Dock take up less room on the screen by adjusting the size of the Dock. You can also make the Dock a bit easier to use by turning on the Magnification feature, which enlarges Dock icons when you position the mouse pointer over them.

You can also make the Dock easier to access and use by moving it to another part of the screen.

Customize the Dock

1 Open System Preferences.

Note: See the section "Display System Preferences" earlier in this chapter.

2 Click **Dock**.

Note: You can also open the Dock preferences by clicking , clicking **Dock**, and then clicking **Dock Preferences**.

The Dock preferences appear.

3 Click and drag the **Size** ▽ to make the Dock smaller or larger.

● You can also click and drag the Dock divider; Drag up to increase the Dock size; drag down to decrease the Dock size.

● System Preferences adjusts the size of the Dock.

Note: If your Dock is already as wide as the screen, dragging the Size slider to the right (toward the Large value) has no effect.

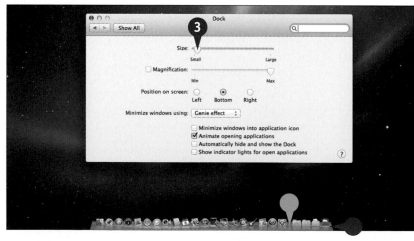

4 Click **Magnification**
(☐ changes to ☑).

5 Click and drag the
Magnification slider (▽) to
set the magnification level.

● When you position the mouse
(▸) over a Dock icon, your
Mac magnifies the icon.

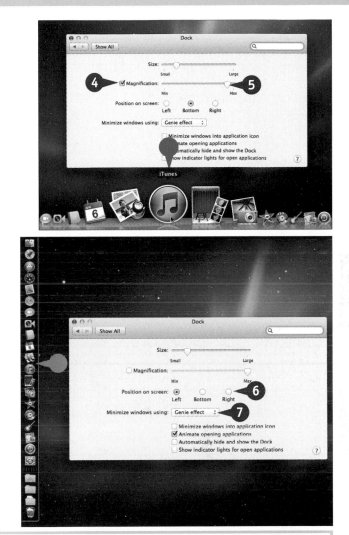

6 Use the **Position on screen**
options to click where you
want the Dock to appear,
such as the **Left** side of the
screen (○ changes to ◉).

● Your Mac moves the Dock to
the new position.

7 In the **Minimize windows
using** pop-up menu, click ⁝
and then click the effect you
want your Mac to use when
you minimize a window:
Genie effect or Scale effect.

TIP

**Is there an easier method I can use to control some of
these preferences?**

Yes, you can control these preferences directly from the Dock.
For example, to set the Dock size, use the ▸ to click and drag
the Dock divider (●) left or right.

For the other preferences, right-click the Dock divider. Click
Turn Magnification On to enable the magnification feature;
click **Turn Magnification Off** to disable this feature. To change
the Dock position, click **Position on Screen** and then click **Left**,
Bottom, or **Right**. To set the minimize effect, click **Minimize
Using** and then click either **Genie Effect** or **Scale Effect**. Finally, you can also click **Dock Preferences** to
open System Preferences's Dock window.

Add an Icon to the Dock

The icons on the Dock are convenient because you can open them with just a single click. You can enhance the convenience of the Dock by adding an icon for an application you use frequently.

The icon remains in the Dock even when the application is closed, so you can always open the application with a single click.

You can add an icon to the Dock even if the program is not currently running.

Add an Icon to the Dock

Add an Icon for a Nonrunning Application

1 Click **Finder** (🖼).

2 Click **Applications**.

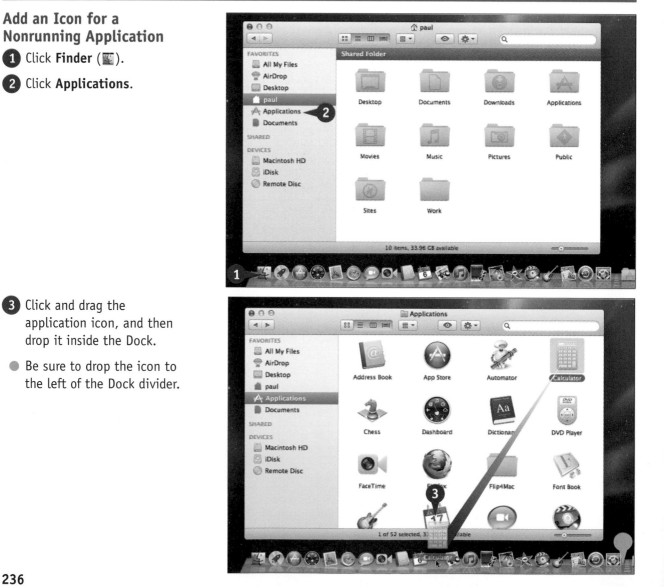

3 Click and drag the application icon, and then drop it inside the Dock.

● Be sure to drop the icon to the left of the Dock divider.

● Mac OS X adds the application's icon to the Dock.

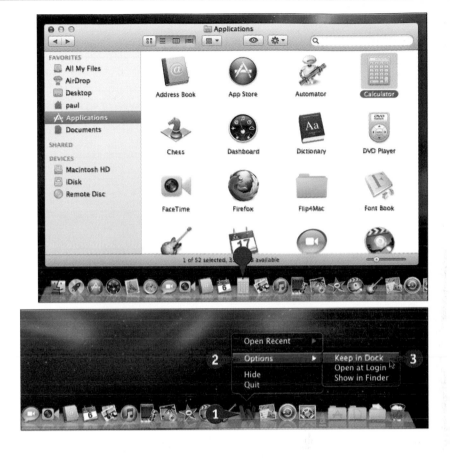

Add an Icon for a Running Application

1 Right-click the application icon in the Dock.

2 Click **Options**.

3 Click **Keep in Dock**.

The application's icon remains in the Dock even after you close the program.

Is there a way to get my Mac to start the application automatically each time I log in to the computer?

Yes. Your Mac maintains a list of *login items*, which are applications that run automatically after you log in. You can configure your application as a login item, and your Mac opens it automatically each time you log in. Right-click the application's Dock icon, click **Options**, and then click **Open at Login**.

How do I remove an icon from the Dock?

Right-click the application's Dock icon, click **Options**, and then click **Remove from Dock**. If the application is currently running, Mac OS X removes the icon from the Dock when you quit the program. Note that you can remove any application icon except Finder (⬛) and Launchpad (◉). Removing an application's Dock icon does not delete the application itself.

Hide the Dock

Ｉf you would like more room on the Mac OS X screen to display your applications, you can hide the Dock to free up some screen space.

When you are working in an application, you might find that you need to maximize the amount of vertical space the application window takes up on-screen. This might come up, for example, when you are reading or editing a long document or viewing a large photo. In such cases, you can size the window to maximum height, but Mac OS X will not let you go past the Dock. You can work around this by hiding the Dock. When the Dock is hidden, it is still easily accessible whenever you need to use it.

Hide the Dock

Turn On Dock Hiding

1 Click .

2 Click **Dock**.

3 Click **Turn Hiding On**.

● You can also right-click the Dock divider and then click **Turn Hiding On**.

● Mac OS X removes the Dock from the desktop.

Display the Dock Temporarily

1 Move the mouse (↖) to the bottom of the screen.

● Mac OS X temporarily displays the Dock.

Note: To hide the Dock again, move the mouse (↖) away from the bottom of the screen.

TIPS

Is there a faster way to hide the Dock?
Yes. You can quickly hide the Dock by pressing Option + ⌘ + D. This keyboard shortcut is a toggle, which means that you can also turn off Dock hiding by pressing Option + ⌘ + D. When the Dock is hidden, you can display it temporarily by pressing Control + F3 (on some keyboards you must press Fn + Control + F3).

How do I bring the Dock back into view?
When you no longer need the extra screen space for your applications, you can turn off Dock hiding to bring the Dock back into view. Click , click **Dock**, and then click **Turn Hiding Off**. Alternatively, display the Dock, right-click the Dock divider, then click **Turn Hiding Off**.

Add a Widget to the Dashboard

The Dashboard is a Mac OS X application that you use to display widgets. You can customize the Dashboard to include any widgets that you find useful or informative.

A widget is a mini-application, particularly one designed to perform a single task, such as displaying the weather, showing stock data, or providing sports scores. When you open the Dashboard, the widgets appear "on top" of your current Mac OS X applications and desktop.

Mac OS X comes with 16 widgets, which include a clock, a calculator, a tile game, and a unit converter. There are also many widgets available online.

Add a Widget to the Dashboard

1 In the Dock click **Dashboard** ().

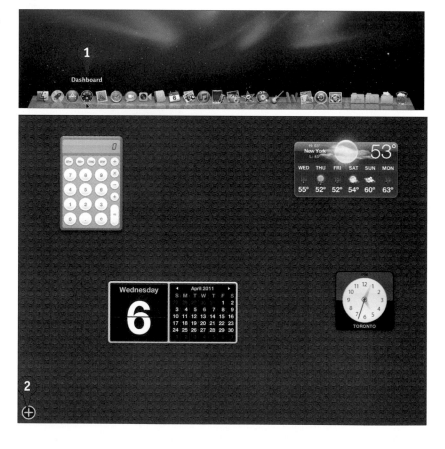

Your Mac displays the Dashboard and its current set of open widgets.

2 Click **Add** ().

Your Mac displays its collection of widgets.

③ Use the arrows (◄ and ►) to scroll to the widget you want to add.

④ Click the widget.

● Your Mac adds the widget to the Dashboard.

⑤ Click the **Close** button (⊗).

⑥ Use the mouse (↖) to click and drag the widget to the position you prefer.

● If the widget is configurable, it displays an *i* when you position the mouse (↖) over the widget.

⑦ Click the *i*.

⑧ Configure the widget as needed.

⑨ Click **Done**.

⑩ Move the ↖ to the bottom of the screen.

⑪ Click ⊗.

Your Mac closes the Dashboard.

Are there faster methods I can use to open the Dashboard?

If your hands are on the keyboard, you can display the Dashboard quickly on most Macs by pressing F2. On some keyboards, you must press Fn+F2 instead. Note, too, that you can also press F2 (or Fn+F2) to close the Dashboard. On most Apply keyboards, you can also press F4 to open and close the Dashboard.

How do I remove a widget from the Dashboard?

The Dashboard gives you a couple of ways to remove widgets. If you just want to remove a single widget, press and hold Option, position the mouse (↖) over the widget, and then click the **Close** button (⊗) that the Dashboard displays in the upper left corner of the widget. If you want to remove more than one widget, click ⊕ to display the available widgets, and then click ⊗ in each widget that you want to remove.

Install a Program Using the App Store

You can enhance and extend Mac OS X by installing new programs from the App Store.

Mac OS X comes with an impressive collection of applications — or *apps* — particularly if your Mac came with the iLife suite preinstalled. However, Mac OS X does not offer a complete collection of apps. For example, Mac OS X lacks apps in categories such as games, personal finance, and social networking.

To fill in these gaps — or to look for apps that go beyond what the default Mac OS X programs can do — you can use the App Store to locate, purchase, and install new programs.

Install a Program Using the App Store

1 In the Dock, click **App Store** ( ).

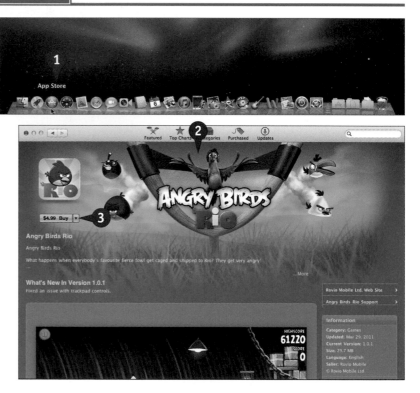

The App Store window appears.

2 Locate the app you want to install.

3 Click the price button.

Note: If the app is free, click the Free button instead.

The App Store prompts you to log in with your Apple ID.

4 Type your Apple ID.

5 Type your password.

6 Click **Sign In**.

The App Store asks you to confirm the purchase.

7 Click **Buy**.

● The App Store begins downloading the app.

● When the progress meter disappears, your app is installed. Click Launchpad (●) and then click the app to run it.

TIP

How do I use an App Store gift card to purchase apps?
If you have an App Store or iTunes gift card, you can redeem the card to give yourself store credit in the amount shown on the card. To redeem the card, first scratch off the sticker on the back to reveal the code. Click ● to open the App Store, click **Redeem** (●), type the code, and then click **Redeem**.

In the App Store window, the Account item (●) shows your current store credit balance.

CHAPTER 12

Performing Mac OS X Maintenance

To keep your Mac running smoothly, maintain top performance, and reduce the risk of computer problems, you need to perform routine maintenance chores. This chapter shows you how to empty the trash, delete unnecessary files, uninstall applications, and more.

Empty the Trash

You can free up disk space on your Mac by periodically emptying the trash. When you delete a file or folder, Mac OS X does not immediately remove the file from your Mac's hard disk. Instead, Mac OS X moves the file or folder to the Trash. This is useful if you accidentally delete an item because it means you can open the Trash and restore the item. However, all those deleted files and folders take up disk space, so you need to empty the trash periodically to regain that space.

You should empty the trash at least once a week.

Empty the Trash

1 Click **Finder** (🖳).

2 Click **Finder** from the menu.

3 Click **Empty Trash**.

● You can also right-click the **Trash** icon (🗑) and then click **Empty Trash**.

Note: Another way to select the Empty Trash command is to press Shift + ⌘ + Del .

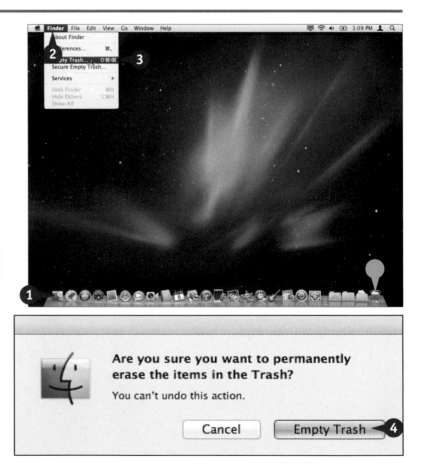

Mac OS X asks you to confirm.

4 Click **Empty Trash**.

Mac OS X empties the trash (🗑 changes to 🗑).

Organize Your Desktop

You can make your Mac OS X desktop easier to scan and navigate by organizing the icons. The Mac OS X desktop automatically displays icons for objects such as your external hard drives, inserted CDs and DVDs, disk images, and attached iPods. The desktop is also a handy place to store files, file aliases, copies of documents, and more. However, the more you use your desktop as a storage area, the more the desktop can become disarrayed, making it hard to find the icon you want. You can fix this by organizing the icons.

Organize Your Desktop

1 Click the desktop.

2 Click **View**.

3 Click **Arrange By**.

4 Click **Name**.

You can also right-click the desktop, click **Arrange By**, and then click **Name**, or press Option + ⌘ + 1.

● If you just want to nudge each icon into the nearest row and column, click **Clean Up** instead.

● Your Mac organizes the icons alphabetically and arranges them in rows and columns from right to left.

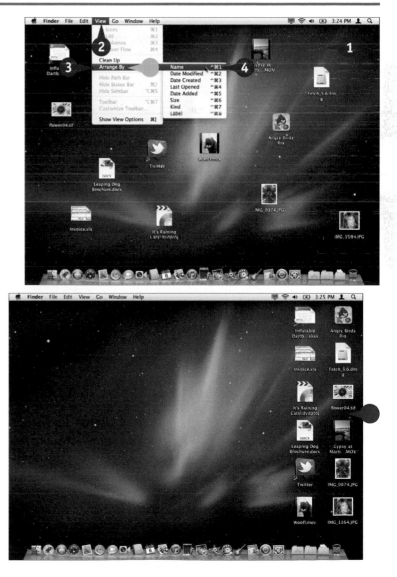

Check Hard Disk Free Space

To ensure that your Mac's hard disk does not become full, you should periodically check how much free space it has left. If you run out of room on your Mac's hard disk, you will not be able to install more applications or create more documents, and your Mac's performance will suffer. To ensure your free space does not become too low — say, less than about 20 or 25GB — you can check how much free space your hard disk has left.

You should check your Mac's hard disk free space about once a month. If you frequently install programs, create large files, or download media, you should check your free space every couple of weeks.

Check Hard Disk Free Space

Check Free Space Using Finder

1 Click **Finder** ().

2 Click **Macintosh HD**.

Note: You can also click any folder on your Mac's hard disk.

3 Read the "available" value, which tells you the amount of free space left on the hard disk.

Display Free Space on the Desktop

1 Display your Mac's HD (hard drive) icon on the desktop, as described in the first tip on the next page.

2 Click the desktop.

3 Click **View**.

4 Click **Show View Options**.

Note: You can also run the Show View Options command by pressing ⌘+J.

The Desktop dialog appears.

5 Click **Show item info**
(☐ changes to ☑).

● Your Mac displays the amount
of free hard disk space under
the Macintosh HD icon.

6 Drag the Icon size ▽ until you
can read all the icon text.

7 If you still cannot read all the
text, click the **Text size** ⁝ and
then click a smaller size.

8 Click **Close** (●).

TIPS

My Mac's hard disk icon does not appear on the desktop. How do I display it?

If you do not see the Macintosh HD icon on your desktop, click the desktop, click **Finder** in the menu bar, and then click **Preferences**. Click the **General** tab, click **Hard disks** (☐ changes to ☑), and then click **Close** (●).

Show these items on the desktop:
☑ Hard disks
☑ External disks
☑ CDs, DVDs, and iPods
☐ Connected servers

What should I do if my Mac's hard disk space is getting low?

First, you should empty the trash, as described earlier in this chapter. Next, you should uninstall any applications that you no longer use, as described in the next section. If you have any documents that you are sure you no longer need — particularly large media files — you should either move them to an external hard disk or USB flash drive, or send them to the trash and then empty the Trash folder.

Uninstall Unused Applications

If you have an application that you no longer use, you can free up some disk space and reduce clutter in the Applications folder by uninstalling that application.

When you install an application, the program stores its files on your Mac's hard disk, and although most programs are quite small, many require hundreds of megabytes of disk space. Uninstalling applications you do not need frees up the disk space they use and removes their icons or folders from the Applications folder.

In most cases you must be logged on to Mac OS X with an administrator account to uninstall applications.

Uninstall Unused Applications

1 Click **Finder** (⬚).

2 Click **Applications**.

③ Click and drag the application or its folder and drop it on the **Trash** icon (🗑).

If your Mac prompts you for an administrator password, type the password, and then click **OK**.

● Your Mac uninstalls the application.

TIPS

Is there another way to uninstall an application?

Yes, in some cases. A few Mac applications come with a separate program for uninstalling the application:

① Follow Steps **1** to **3**.

② If the application has its own folder, examine the contents for an icon with "Uninstaller" in the name.

③ Double-click that icon and then follow the instructions on-screen.

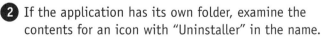

Can I restore an application that I uninstalled accidentally?

If you used the application's uninstall program, the only way to restore the application is to reinstall it. If you sent the application to the Trash, and that was the most recent operation you performed, click **Finder** (🙂), click **Edit**, and then click **Undo Move of "*Application*"** (where *Application* is the name of the application you want to restore). Otherwise, click **Trash** (🗑), and then use the Trash folder to click and drag the application and drop it on Applications.

Set a Software Update Schedule

You can ensure that your Mac and the applications that come with Mac OS X are up to date with the latest features and fixes by setting a schedule for updating the software.

Apple makes Mac OS X updates available from time to time. These updates fix problems, add new features, and resolve security issues. You can reduce computer problems and maximize online safety by setting up Mac OS X to download and install these updates automatically.

By default, Mac OS X checks for updates weekly. You can configure Software Update to check for updates daily or only once a month.

Set a Software Update Schedule

1 Click .

2 Click **System Preferences**.

Note: You can also click **System Preferences** ( ) in the Dock.

The System Preferences window appears.

3 Click **Software Update**.

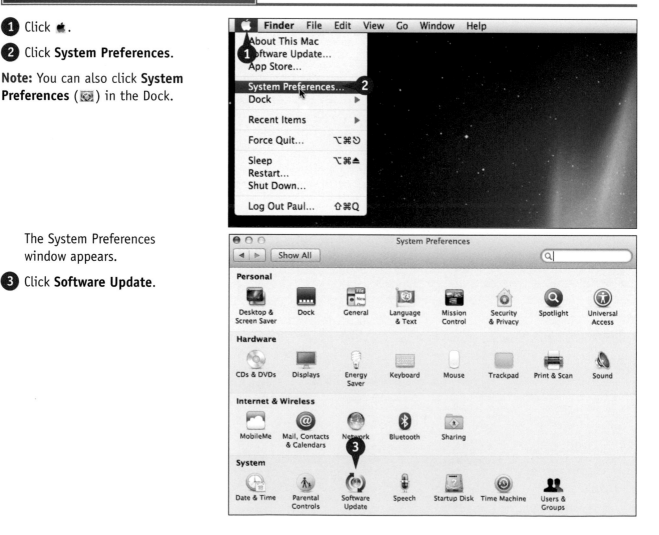

The Software Update preferences appear.

4 Click **Scheduled Check**.

5 Click **Check for updates**
(☐ changes to ☑).

6 In the Check for updates pop-up menu, click ⁞ and then click the schedule you want: **Daily**, **Weekly**, or **Monthly**.

7 Click **Download updates automatically** (☐ changes to ☑).

Your Mac checks for updates on your selected schedule, and downloads updates automatically.

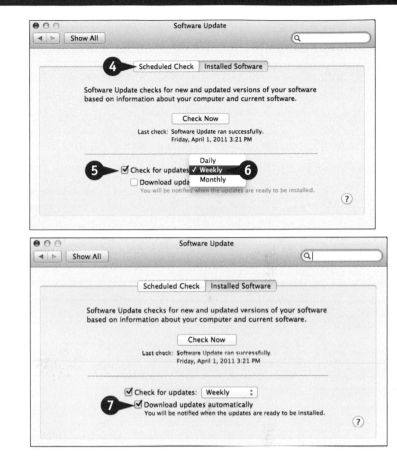

TIPS

Do I have to let my Software Update do the checking automatically?

Technically, no, you do not have to rely on Software Update's automatic checking. Instead, you can check for software updates by hand, as described in the next section. However, this is not a good idea because you should always keep your Mac software up to date, and this might not happen if you try to remember to check for updates yourself.

How does Software Update work?

When the time comes for an update check, Software Update first examines what Apple applications and system software you have installed on your Mac. Then, for each program, Software Update queries an Internet database on Apple's site to see if the program has an update available. If it does, Software Update adds the program to the update list. If the update is considered important, Software Update immediately downloads the update. The Software Update icon then bounces in the Dock to let you know that updates are available.

Update Software by Hand

To make sure that your Mac and the applications that come with Mac OS X are currently up to date with the latest features and fixes, you can update the software by hand.

By default, Mac OS X checks for new software updates automatically on a regular schedule. If you turned off this feature or configured it to be less frequent, you can still keep Mac OS X up to date by checking for — and if necessary, installing — updates yourself.

See the previous section to learn how to configure the Software Update schedule.

Update Software by Hand

1 Connect to the Internet, if you have not already done so.

2 Click the Apple menu.

3 Click **Software Update**.

Your Mac connects with Apple's servers and checks for new updates.

Your Mac lets you know if any software updates are available.

4 If updates are available, click **Show Details**.

Your Mac displays the list of available updates.

● A description of the selected update appears here.

● If you install any updates that display the Restart icon (○), you must restart your Mac to complete the installation.

5 Click the check box for any update you do not want to install (☑ changes to ☐).

6 Click **Install _X_ Items** (where _X_ is the number of updates you have selected).

For some updates, your Mac displays a software license agreement. If you see a license agreement, click **Agree**.

For some updates, your Mac asks for the administrator password.

7 Use the Password text box to type the administrator password.

8 Click **OK**.

For some updates, your Mac prompts you to restart the computer.

9 If you have any unsaved work, save and close those documents.

10 Click **Restart**.

TIPS

Should I always install every available update?

As a general rule, yes. However, some exceptions exist. For example, if an update is available for an application that you never use, you can safely skip that update. Also, if your Internet connection is slow, you may prefer to install the updates one at a time.

Is the Mac OS X Update important?

Yes, any update named Mac OS X Update is very important. These are major updates to your Mac's operating system, and they generally improve system stability and security. Because such an update affects your entire Mac and is usually quite large — often several hundred megabytes — it is best to install this update on its own.

Remove Unneeded Login Items

You can make your Mac start up faster and improve the overall performance of your Mac by removing any login items that you no longer require.

If your Mac OS X user account has login items that you no longer need, those items may slow down your Mac's startup and consume extra system memory. From time to time you should check your user account's login items and remove those you no longer need.

Remove only a login item that you are sure you do not need or that is causing a problem.

Remove Unneeded Login Items

1 Click **🍎**.

2 Click **System Preferences**.

Note: You can also click **System Preferences** (🖼) in the Dock.

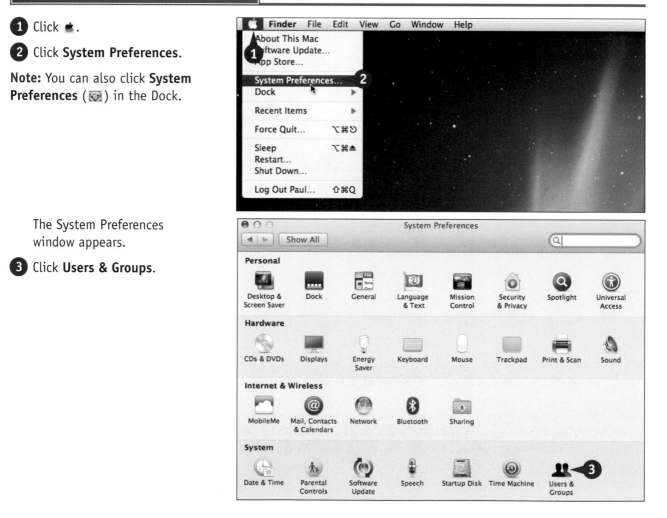

The System Preferences window appears.

3 Click **Users & Groups**.

4 Click your user account.

5 Click **Login Items**.

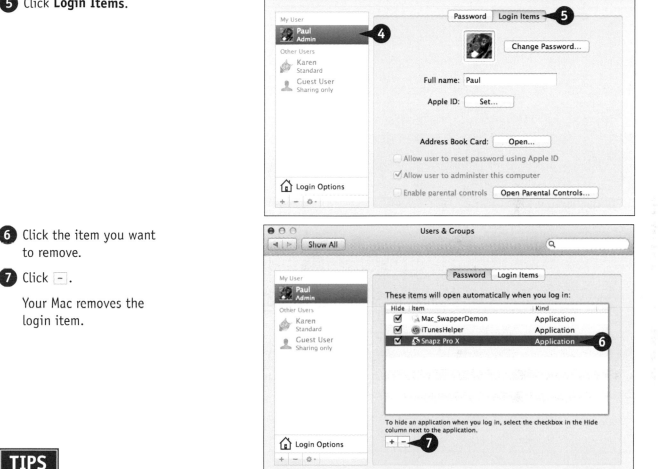

6 Click the item you want to remove.

7 Click ⊟.

Your Mac removes the login item.

TIPS

What is a login item?

When you start your Mac, many behind-the-scenes tasks get performed to set up the computer for your use. One of these tasks is that your Mac checks the list of items that are supposed to open automatically when you log in to your user account. These items are usually applications, but they can also be files, folders, and shared network locations. These are called *login items*.

Can you give me an example of a problem related to a login item?

Yes. If you uninstall an application by moving it to the Trash as described earlier, the application may leave behind one or more login items, and these will cause an error each time you log in. Similarly, if a login item refers to a network resource that no longer exists, you will see an error similar to the one shown here.

Configure Time Machine Backups

One of the most crucial Mac OS X maintenance chores is to configure your system to make regular backups of your files. Macs are reliable machines, but they do crash and all hard disks eventually die, so at some point your data will be at risk. To avoid losing that data forever, you need to configure the Mac OS X Time Machine feature to perform regular backups.

To use Time Machine, your Mac requires a second hard disk. This can be a second internal disk on a Mac Pro, but on most Macs the easiest course is to connect an external hard disk, which is what this task assumes.

Configure Time Machine Backups

1 Connect an external USB or FireWire hard disk to your Mac.

● When your Mac recognizes the external hard disk, it adds an icon for the disk to the desktop.

2 Click **⌘**.

3 Click **System Preferences**.

Note: You can also click **System Preferences** (🔲) in the Dock.

Note: If Mac OS X asks if you want to use the hard disk as your backup disk, click **Use as Backup Disk** and then skip the rest of these steps.

4 Click **Time Machine**.

The Time Machine preferences appear.

5 Click **Select Disk**.

Time Machine displays a list of available disks.

6 Click the external hard disk.

7 Click **Use Backup Disk**.

Time Machine enables backups and prepares to run the first backup automatically in 2 minutes.

8 Click **Close** (●).

TIP

How do Time Machine backups work?

Time Machine makes backing up your Mac easy because backups are handled automatically on the following schedule:

- The initial backup occurs 2 minutes after you configure Time Machine for the first time. This backup includes your entire Mac.

- Time Machine runs another backup every hour. These hourly backups include just those files and folders that you have changed or created since the most recent hourly backup.

- Time Machine runs a daily backup that includes only those files and folders that you have changed or created since the most recent daily backup.

- Time Machine runs a weekly backup that includes only those files and folders that you have changed or created since the most recent weekly backup.

Restore Files Using Time Machine

If you have configured Mac OS X to make regular Time Machine backups, you can use those backups to restore a lost file.

If you accidentally delete a file, you can quickly restore it by opening the Trash folder. However, that does not help you if you have emptied the Trash folder, if you overwrite a file with another file with the same name, or if you improperly edit a file.

Because Time Machine makes hourly, daily, and weekly backups, it stores older copies and older versions of your data. You can use these backups to restore any file that you accidentally delete, overwrite, or improperly edit.

Restore Files Using Time Machine

1 Click **Finder** (🖼).

2 Open the folder you want to restore, or the folder that contains the file you want to restore.

● If you want to restore your entire hard disk, choose **Macintosh HD** in the sidebar.

Note: Restore your entire hard disk only if your original hard disk crashed and you have had it repaired or replaced.

3 Click **Time Machine** (🕰).

The Time Machine interface appears.

● Each window represents a backed-up version of the folder.

● This area tells you when the displayed version of the folder was backed up.

● You can use this timeline to navigate the backed-up versions.

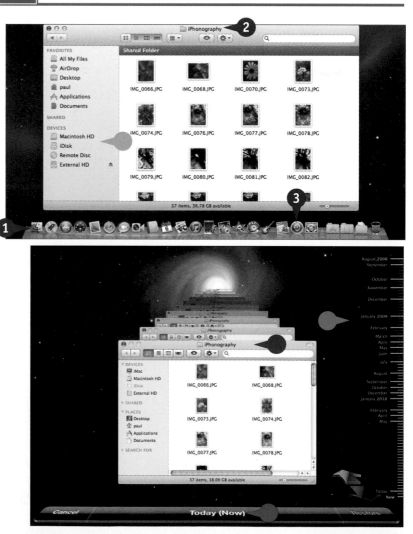

④ Navigate to the date that contains the backed-up version of the folder or file.

Note: See the tip below to learn how to navigate the Time Machine backups.

⑤ If you are restoring a file, click the file.

⑥ Click **Restore**.

If another version of the folder or file already exists, Time Machine asks if you want to keep it or replace it.

⑦ Click **Replace**.

Time Machine restores the folder or file.

TIP

How do I navigate the backups in the Time Machine interface?
Here are the most useful techniques:

- Click the top arrow to jump to the earliest version; click the bottom arrow to return to the most recent version.
- Press and hold the ⌘ key and click the arrows to navigate through the backups one version at a time.
- Use the timeline to click a specific version.
- Click the version windows.

Recondition Your Mac Notebook Battery

To get the most performance out of your Mac notebook's battery, you need to recondition the battery by cycling it. *Cycling* a battery means letting it completely discharge and then fully recharging it again.

Most Mac notebook batteries slowly lose their charging capacity over time. If you can use your Mac notebook on batteries for 4 hours today, later on you'll only be able to run the computer for 3 hours on a full charge. You cannot stop this process, but you can delay it significantly by periodically cycling the battery.

You should cycle your Mac notebook battery once a month or so.

Recondition Your Mac Notebook Battery

Display the Battery Status Percentage

1 Click the **Battery status** icon (▭).

2 Click **Show**.

3 Click **Percentage**.

Your Mac shows the percentage of available battery power remaining.

Cycle the Battery

1 Disconnect your Mac notebook's power cord.

● The Battery Status icon changes from ▭ to ▭ .

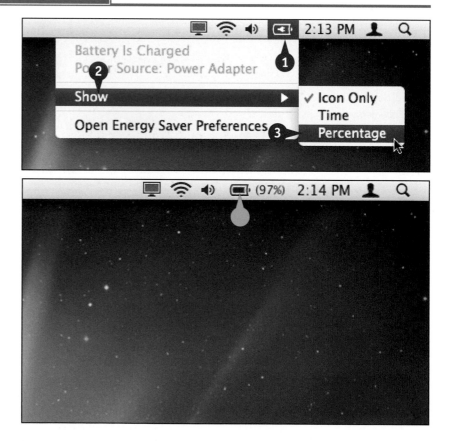

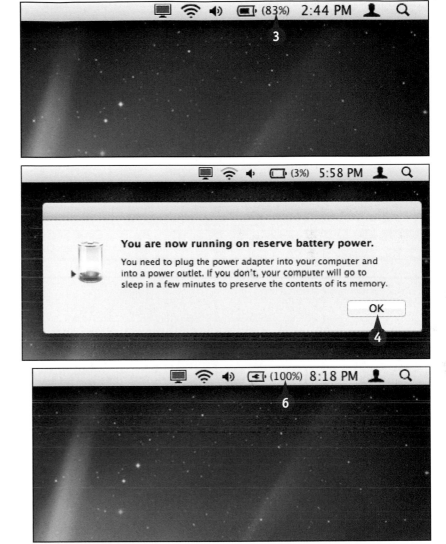

2 Operate your Mac notebook normally by running applications, working with documents, and so on.

3 As you work, keep your eye on the Battery Status percentage.

When the Battery Status reaches 3%, your Mac warns you that it is now running on reserve power.

4 Click **OK**.

5 Reattach the power cord.

Your Mac restarts and the Battery Status icon changes from 🔋 to 🔌.

6 Leave your Mac plugged in at least until the Battery Status shows 100%.

TIPS

I do not see the battery status in my menu bar. How do I display it?
Click **System Preferences** (⚙️) in the Dock to open System Preferences, and then click the **Energy Saver** icon. In the Energy Saver window, click **Battery** and then click the **Show battery status in the menu bar** check box (☐ changes to ☑).

Do Mac notebooks suffer from the memory effect?
Older portable computers used rechargeable nickel metal hydride (NiMH) or nickel cadmium (NiCad) batteries. The NiMH and NiCad types were phased out because they can suffer from a problem called the *memory effect*, where the battery loses capacity if you repeatedly recharge it without first fully discharging it. All the latest Mac notebooks have rechargeable lithium-ion (Li-ion) or lithium-polymer (Li-Po) batteries. These batteries are lighter and last longer than NiMH and NiCad batteries and, most importantly, do not suffer from the memory effect.

CHAPTER 13

Troubleshooting Mac OS X Problems

Mac OS X Lion is a solid operating system, and it should give you many years of dependable performance. However, *all* computers eventually run into problems, and your Mac will likely be no exception. This chapter offers a few tried-and-true troubleshooting techniques.

Restart Your Mac

If a hardware device is having a problem with some system files, it often helps to restart your Mac. By rebooting the computer, you reload the entire system, which is often enough to solve many computer problems.

For a problem device that does not have its own power switch, restarting your Mac might not resolve the problem because the device remains powered up the whole time. You can *power cycle* — shut down and then restart — such devices as a group by power cycling your Mac.

Restart Your Mac

Restart Your Mac

1 Click the **Apple** icon ().

2 Click **Restart**.

Your Mac asks you to confirm.

3 Click **Restart**.

Note: To bypass the confirmation dialog, press and hold Option when you click the **Restart** command.

Power Cycle Your Mac

1 Click .

2 Click **Shut Down**.

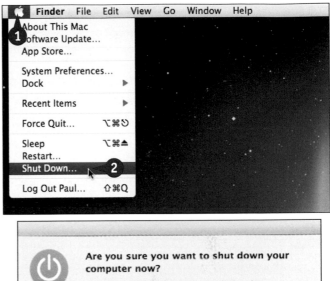

Your Mac asks you to confirm.

Note: To bypass the confirmation dialog, hold down Option when you click **Shut Down**.

3 Click **Shut Down**.

4 Wait for 30 seconds to give all devices time to spin down.

5 Turn your Mac back on.

TIP

What other basic troubleshooting techniques can I use?

- Make sure that each device is turned on, that cable connections are secure, and that insertable devices (such as USB devices) are properly inserted.
- If a device is battery powered, replace the batteries.
- If a device has an on/off switch, power cycle the device by turning it off, waiting a few seconds for it to stop spinning, and then turning it back on again.
- Close all running programs.
- Log out of your Mac — click ; click **Log Out** *User*, where *User* is your Mac user name; and then click **Log Out** — and then log back in again.

Unlock System Preferences

When you open System Preferences and click an icon, you may find that some or all of the controls in the resulting preferences window are disabled. To enable those controls, you need to unlock the preferences.

Remember that having locked system preferences is not a glitch. Instead, it is a security feature designed to prevent unauthorized users from making changes to sensitive system settings. After you unlock most system preferences, Mac OS X automatically locks them again when you exit the System Preferences application.

Unlock System Preferences

1 Click **System Preferences** (![icon]) in the Dock.

The System Preferences window appears.

2 Click the icon of the system preferences you want to work with (such as Users & Groups, as shown here).

The preferences appear.

3 Click the **System Preferences Locked** icon (![lock]).

System Preferences prompts you for an administrator's user name and password.

4 Use the Name text box to type the name of an administrator account on your Mac.

5 Use the Password text box to type the administrator account's password.

6 Click **Unlock**.

● 🔒 changes to 🔓.

● Your Mac enables the preferences.

System Preferences is trying to unlock Users & Groups preferences. Type your password to allow this.

Name: Paul **4**

Password: •••••••• **5**

Cancel   Unlock **6**

Users & Groups

Show All

Password   Login Items

My User
Paul
Admin

Other Users
Karen
Standard

Guest User
Sharing only

Change Password...

Full name: Paul

Apple ID: paulmcfedries@me.com   Change...

Address Book Card: Open...

☐ Allow user to reset password using Apple ID

☑ Allow user to administer this computer

Login Options

☐ Enable parental controls   Open Parental Controls...

+ − ⚙ ·

🔓 Click the lock to prevent further changes.

TIPS

Some preferences are already unlocked. Should I lock them?

The purpose behind locking system preferences is to prevent unauthorized changes to those preferences. If you are the only person who uses your Mac, then you do not need to worry about this, so you can leave those other system preferences unlocked for convenience. However, if other people have access to your Mac, you should probably lock important system preferences by clicking 🔓 (which changes to 🔒).

Is there a way to lock my entire Mac?

Yes, you can configure your Mac to require a password when it wakes up from sleep mode or from the screen saver. Click **System Preferences** (🖥) in the Dock, click **Security & Privacy**, click 🔒, and then type a password. Click **General**, click **Require password** (☐ changes to ☑), click ⁞, and then click **immediately**.

Force a Stuck Application to Close

When you are working with an application, you may find that it becomes unresponsive and you cannot interact with the application or even quit the application normally. In that case, you can use a Mac OS X feature called Force Quit to force a stuck or unresponsive application to close, which enables you to restart the application or restart your Mac.

Unfortunately, when you force an application to quit, you lose any unsaved changes in your open documents. Therefore, make sure the application really is stuck before forcing it to quit. See the second tip on the following page for more information.

Force a Stuck Application to Close

1 Click .

2 Click **Force Quit**.

The Force Quit Applications
window appears.

③ Click the application you
want to shut down.

④ Click **Force Quit**.

Your Mac asks you to confirm
that you want to force the
application to quit.

⑤ Click **Force Quit**.

Your Mac shuts down the
application.

⑥ Click **Close** (⊙) to close the
Force Quit Applications
window.

Force Quit Applications

If an application doesn't respond for a while,
select its name and click Force Quit.

- ⓘ iTunes (not responding) ◀3
- ⓦ Safari
- ▦ System Preferences
- ⓕ Finder

You can open this window by pressing
Command-Option-Escape.   Force Quit ◀4

Force Quit Applications

⑥ **Do you want to force iTunes to quit?**

You will lose any unsaved changes.

Cancel   Force Quit ◀5

Finder

You can open this window by pressing
Command-Option-Escape.   Force Quit

TIPS

**Are there easier ways to run the Force Quit
command?**
Yes. From the keyboard, you can run the Force Quit
command by pressing `Option`+`⌘`+`Esc`. If the
application has a Dock icon, press and hold `Control`+
`Option` and then click the application's Dock icon.
In the menu that appears, click **Force Quit**.

**If an application is not responding, does that
always mean the application is stuck?**
Not necessarily. For example, some application
operations — such as recalculating a large
spreadsheet or rendering a 3-D image — can take a
few minutes, and during that time the application
can appear stuck. Similarly, your Mac may be low on
memory, which can also cause an application to
seem stuck. In this case, try shutting down some of
your other applications to free up some memory.

Repair a Corrupt Preferences File

You can use Mac OS X to reset an application's preferences file, which may help you solve problems you may be having with the application.

One of the most common causes of application instability is a preferences file that has somehow become corrupted. Although there is no easy way to fix a corrupt preferences file directly, you can do so indirectly by deleting the preferences file. The next time you start the application, the application detects that its preferences file is missing, so it automatically rebuilds a new — and uncorrupted — file. The downside to this method is that you may have to reconfigure the application's preferences.

Repair a Corrupt Preferences File

1 If the problem application is still running, shut it down.

Note: If you have trouble closing the application, see the section "Force a Stuck Application to Close."

2 Click **Finder** (🖥).

3 Click your user account folder.

4 Click **Go**.

5 Click **Go to Folder**.

The Go to Folder dialog appears.

6 Type **~/Library/Preferences**.

7 Click **Go**.

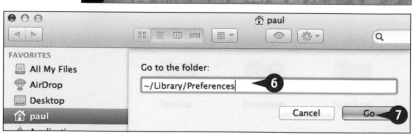

The Preferences folder appears.

8 Click and drag the problem application's preferences file and drop it on the Trash.

Note: See the second Tip below to learn how to locate the correct preferences file.

Your Mac deletes the preferences file.

9 Run the application and set some preferences.

● The application creates a new preferences file.

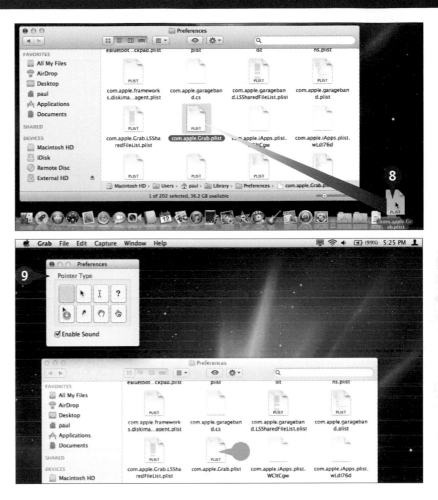

TIPS

What is a preferences file?

A *preferences file* is a document that stores a user's options, settings, and other data related to a particular application. To specify preferences, click the application's name in the menu bar and then click **Preferences**. The application displays a dialog that you use to customize the preferences. When you are done, the application saves the new settings in the preferences file.

How can I tell which preferences file belongs to the problem application?

Most preferences files use the .plist filename extension. In most cases, the filename uses the following general format: com.*company*.*application*.plist. Here, *company* is the name of the software company that makes the application, and *application* is the name of the program. Here are some examples: com.apple.iTunes.plist; com.microsoft.Word.plist; com.palm.HotSync.plist.

Access the Mac OS X Recovery Tools

You can recover from some Mac problems by accessing the recovery tools that are available on systems running Mac OS X Lion.

All Macs that have Mac OS X Lion installed have a hidden area of the hard drive called Recovery HD, which contains a program called Mac OS X Utilities. This program offers various tools that you can use to troubleshoot and recover from problems. For example, if you suspect that your Mac's main hard drive is causing a problem, you can access Recovery HD and use a tool called Disk Utility to repair the drive. Similarly, you can also use Recovery HD to restore your Mac from a Time Machine backup, and to reinstall Mac OS X Lion.

Access the Mac OS X Recovery Tools

Start Mac OS X Utilities

1 Restart your Mac.

2 Press and hold **Option** while your Mac is restarting.

A list of disk drives appears.

3 Double-click **Recovery HD**.

The Mac OS X Utilities application appears.

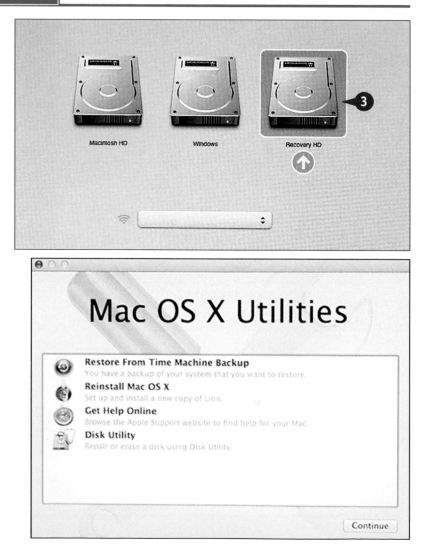

Restart Your Mac

1 Click ⌘.

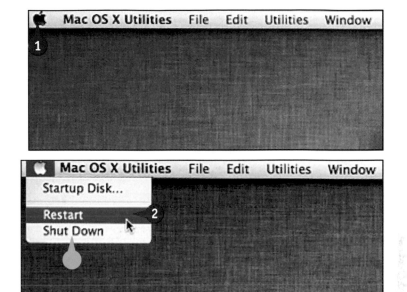

2 Click **Restart**.

● If you prefer to turn off your Mac instead, click **Shut Down**.

TIP

If I cannot start my Mac, is there any way to access troubleshooting information on the web?

Yes. You can start your Mac using Recovery HD and then use the Mac OS X Utilities to access the Web.

First, you must connect to your Wi-Fi network so that you can access its Internet connection. Click the **Wi-Fi Status** icon (🛜), click your Wi-Fi network, and then type your Wi-Fi password, if prompted.

In the Mac OS X Utilities window, click **Get Help Online** and then click **Continue**. Mac OS X Utilities loads Safari and displays some troubleshooting steps. However, you can also use Safari to surf to any site that has the information you seek.

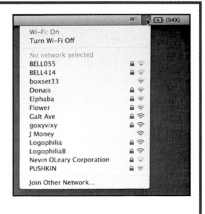

Repair Disk Permissions

Your Mac's files can become corrupted for a variety of reasons. For example, a hard disk glitch could render a file impossible to read; similarly, if Mac OS X or an application crashes, one or more files could develop problems.

If the permissions on one or more of your Mac's system files become corrupted, your Mac may freeze, run slowly, or become unstable. You can often solve these Mac OS X problems by repairing the permissions associated with each file and folder on your Mac's hard disk.

Repair Disk Permissions

1 Click **Finder** (🖥️).

2 Click **Applications**.

3 Open the Utilities folder.

Note: You can also open the Utilities folder by pressing 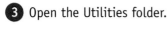.

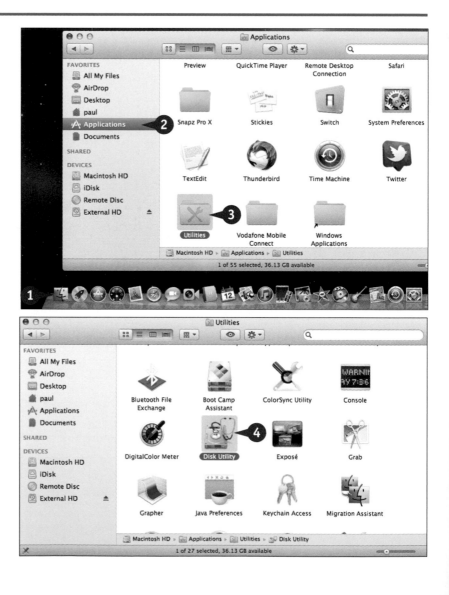

The Utilities folder opens.

4 Double-click **Disk Utility**.

The Disk Utility window appears.

5 Click your Mac's hard disk.

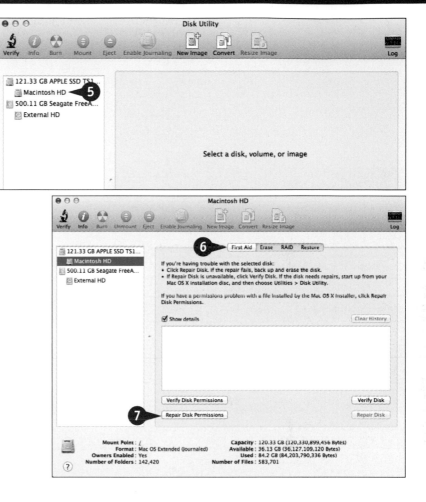

6 Click **First Aid**.

7 Click **Repair Disk Permissions**.

Your Mac repairs the disk permissions.

8 When the repair is complete, press ⌘+Q to quit Disk Utility.

TIPS

What are disk permissions?
All the files on your Mac have *permissions* associated with them. Permissions are a collection of settings that determine what users or groups of users can do with each file. For example, if read-only permissions apply to a file, it means that all users can read only the contents of the file and cannot make any changes to the file or delete it. If the permissions for your Mac's system files change or get corrupted, it can cause all kinds of problems, including application lock-ups and unstable system behavior.

How do I repair permissions if I cannot start my Mac?
Corrupt disk permissions might prevent your Mac from booting. In this case, follow Steps **1** to **3** in the "Access the Mac OS X Recovery Tools" section, click **Disk Utility**, click **Continue,** and then follow Steps **5** to **7** in this section.

Repair a Disk

You can use your Mac OS X install DVD to check for errors on your Mac's hard disk and repair those errors. If your Mac will not start, or if an application freezes, an error on the main hard disk is possibly causing the problem. To see if this is the case, you can try repairing the hard disk using Disk Utility, which you can find in the Utilities folder within your Applications folder.

To repair your Mac's main hard drive, you need to have the original installation DVD that came with your Mac or that you used to install Mac OS X.

Repair a Disk

1 Restart your Mac.

2 Press and hold **Option** while your Mac is restarting.

A list of disk drives appears.

3 Double-click **Recovery HD**.

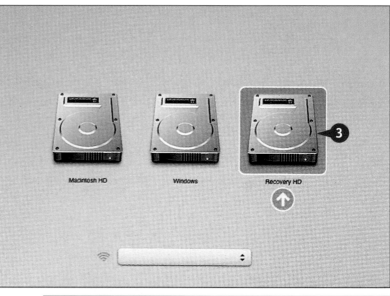

The Mac OS X Utilities application appears.

4 Click **Disk Utility**.

5 Click **Continue**.

The Disk Utility window appears.

6 Click your Mac's hard disk.

7 Click **First Aid**.

8 Click **Repair Disk**.

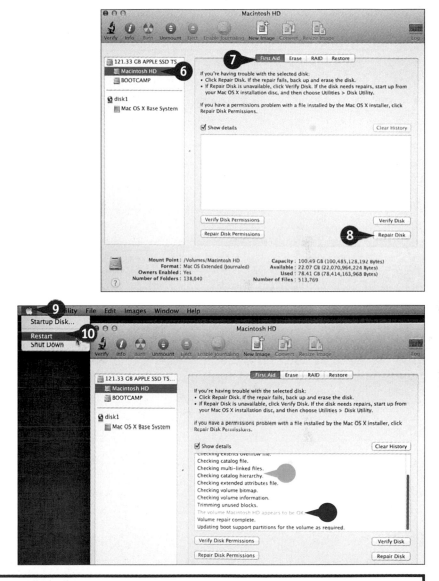

Disk Utility verifies the hard disk and attempts to repair any errors it finds.

● Information on the disk checks appears here.

● The result of the checks appears here.

9 Click .

10 Click **Restart**.

Your Mac restarts.

TIPS

How do I repair errors on a secondary hard disk?

If you are working with your Mac's startup hard disk, you must boot to the Mac OS X Install DVD to repair that disk. For all other hard disks, however, you can perform the repair without rebooting. Click **Finder** (🖥️), click **Applications**, click **Utilities**, and then double-click **Disk Utility**. Click the disk you want to repair, click **First Aid**, and then click **Repair Disk**.

What do I do if Disk Utility finds a problem?

In the best-case scenario, Disk Utility reports either "No repairs were necessary" or "The volume Macintosh HD appears to be OK." Otherwise, Disk Utility attempts to fix any errors it finds. If Disk Utility cannot fix the errors, you must turn to a third-party disk repair application. Two useful tools are DiskWarrior (www.alsoft.com) and TechTool Pro (www.micromat.com).

Reinstall Mac OS X

You can recover from a major problem by reinstalling the Mac OS X Lion operating system. If worse comes to worst and your Mac will not start or if your system is completely unstable, then you need to reinstall the operating system. This places a fresh set of operating system files on your Mac, which should solve the problem.

To reinstall Mac OS X, you need to restart your Mac using the Recovery HD section of the Mac hard drive. Since you will need to download a fresh copy of Mac OS X Lion, you will also need access to a wireless or wired network that is connected to the Internet.

Reinstall Mac OS X

Start Mac OS X Utilities

1 Restart your Mac.

2 Press and hold **Option** while your Mac is restarting.

A list of disk drives appears.

3 Double-click **Recovery HD**.

The Mac OS X Utilities application appears.

Connect to Wi-Fi

1 Click the **Wi-Fi Status** icon ().

2 Click the Wi-Fi network you want to join.

If the network is protected by a password, Mac OS X Utilities prompts you to enter that password.

3 Type the network password.

4 Click **Join**.

The Wi-Fi network "Logophilia" requires a WPA2 password.

Password: ••••••••••• ◄—**3**

☐ Show password

Cancel   Join ◄—**4**

TIPS

Under what circumstances should I reinstall Mac OS X?

The most common scenario is when your Mac does not start, and repairing the hard disk as described in the previous section has no effect. Another common scenario is when your Mac suffers from frequent lockups, application crashes, and other unstable behavior, and repairing preferences files and disk permissions, as described earlier in this chapter, have no effect.

Do I have to use a wireless network connection to access the Internet?

No, this is not necessary. The Mac OS X Install application can work with both wireless and wired connections. If you have a wired network nearby, and that network is connected to the Internet, you can also connect your Mac to that network using a network cable. In this case, you do not need to follow the steps for connecting to a Wi-Fi network.

continued ▶

Once you have established a connection to a network that offers Internet access, you are ready to reinstall Mac OS X Lion. For security reasons, the Mac OS X Install application must transmit your Mac's serial number to Apple. This is safe and no personal information is included in the transmission. The Install application downloads Mac OS X Lion to your computer. This is a very large download, so it might take an hour or two, depending on the speed of your connection. When the download is complete, the installation proceeds automatically.

Once you have finished reinstalling Mac OS X, you will then be able to restore your system using the most recent Time Machine backup.

Reinstall Mac OS X (continued)

Start the Reinstallation

 1 Click **Reinstall Mac OS X**.

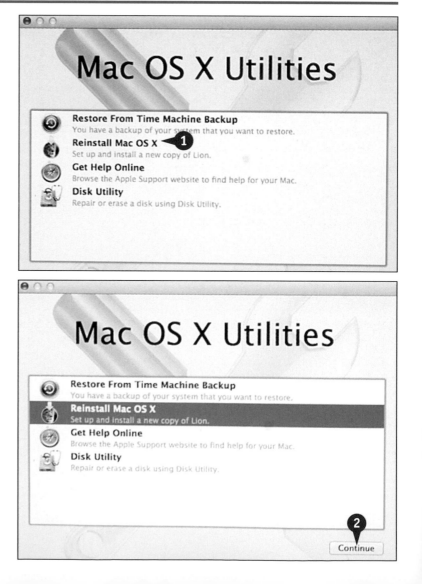

2 Click **Continue**.

The Mac OS X Install application appears.

 Click **Continue**.

Mac OS X Lion

To set up the installation of Mac OS X 10.7, click Continue.

Continue

Mac OS Install warns you that it will send your Mac's serial number to Apple.

4 Click **Continue**.

Mac OS X Install connects to Apple, downloads Mac OS X, and then reinstalls Mac OS X on your Mac.

Install Mac OS X

In order to download and restore Mac OS X, your computer's serial number must be sent to Apple.

Cancel   Continue

TIPS

Why does my Apple Bluetooth mouse not work with the Installer program?
The Mac OS X Installer application does not come with the necessary device drivers to work with the signals that the Apple Bluetooth mouse or any other wireless mouse generates. You cannot reinstall Mac OS X unless your Mac has a trackpad, or a mouse that is physically connected to the computer.

Once Mac OS X is reinstalled, what else do I need to do?
The first thing you should do is restore your Mac from your most recent Time Machine backup. If you have no backup, you should update your Mac's software. To do this, click and then click **Software Update**. Next, you should reinstall any third-party applications that you used on your old Mac OS X installation. Once you have your applications installed, you should check your preferences in each program to make sure they are configured correctly.

CHAPTER 14

Working with Your MobileMe Account

For an annual fee, you can get a MobileMe account, which is a web-based service that gives you e-mail, an address book, a calendar, a web Gallery for sharing photos, and online file storage. You can also use MobileMe to automatically synchronize data between MobileMe and your Mac.

Sign in to MobileMe

Before you can use any of the features associated with your MobileMe account, you must sign in to the service.

MobileMe is a web-based service, so you access it using a web browser. Most modern browsers should work fine with MobileMe, but Apple recommends that you use at least Safari 4 or Firefox 3.5. For the best experience, Apple recommends Safari 5 or later or Firefox 3.6 or later.

You can also access MobileMe using a Windows PC, and in this case Apple's minimum recommendations are Safari 4, Firefox 3.5, or Internet Explorer 7. For best results on a Windows PC, use Safari 5 or later, Firefox 3.6 or later, or Internet Explorer 8 or later.

Sign in to MobileMe

① In your web browser, type **www.me.com**.

② Press **Return**.

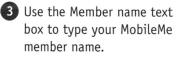

The MobileMe Login page appears.

③ Use the Member name text box to type your MobileMe member name.

④ Use the Password text box to type the password for your MobileMe account.

● If you want MobileMe to sign you in automatically for two weeks, click **Keep me signed in for 2 weeks** (☐ changes to ☑).

5 Click **Sign In**.

Your main MobileMe account page appears.

● When you are done working with your MobileMe account, if you prefer not to remain signed in to your account, click your member name and then click **Sign Out**.

How do I get a MobileMe account?

In your web browser, go to www.apple.com/MobileMe, click **Sign up for MobileMe free trial**, and then fill in the form. You will be able to try out MobileMe free for 60 days, and then to continue you must pay a subscription fee. An Individual subscription currently costs $99 per year, although some online vendors such as Amazon.com may sell for less; a Family Pack subscription currently costs $149 per year and consists of one main account plus four subaccounts.

Can I sign in from my Mac?

Yes. Click **System Preferences** ( ) in the Dock (or click and then click **System Preferences**) and then click **MobileMe**. Type your member name and password, and then click **Sign In** (●).

Are you a MobileMe member?

Sign into your account to set up MobileMe on this computer.

Member Name: myaccount@me.com

Password: ••••••••••

Sign In

Send and Receive MobileMe Mail

You can use the MobileMe Mail feature to work with your MobileMe e-mail account online. Using either your Mac or any computer with web access, you can access MobileMe using a web browser and then perform your e-mail tasks. These include checking for incoming messages, replying to messages you receive, forwarding a received message, and composing and sending a new message.

You can also configure MobileMe Mail to send blind courtesy copies and to automatically send vacation messages.

Send and Receive MobileMe Mail

Display MobileMe Mail

1 Sign in to your MobileMe account.

Note: See the section "Sign in to MobileMe," earlier in this chapter.

2 If you are using another section of MobileMe, click **Switch Apps** (⬚) and then click **Mail** (🗂).

Get Incoming Messages

1 Click **Reload** (↻).

● MobileMe Mail checks for incoming messages and, if there are any, displays them in the Inbox folder.

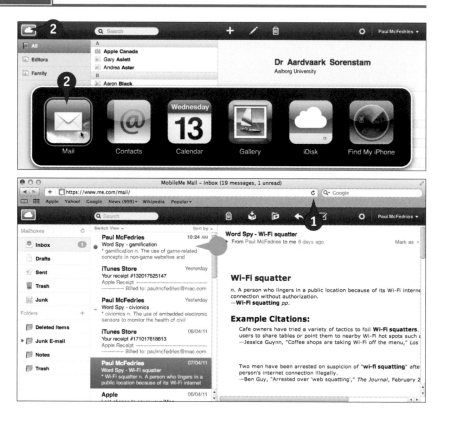

Reply to a Message

1 Click the message.

2 Click **Reply, Reply All, Forward** (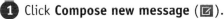).

3 Click **Reply**.

● To reply to the sender and all the recipients of the original message, click **Reply All** instead.

● To pass the message to another person, click **Forward** instead.

4 In the message window that appears (not shown), type your message and then click **Send message** ( ).

Send a New Message

1 Click **Compose new message** ( ).

The New Message window appears.

2 Use the To text box to type the recipient's e-mail address.

● If you want another person to see a copy of the message, type that person's address in the Cc text box.

3 Use the Subject text box to type the subject of the message.

4 Type your message.

5 Click **Send message** ( ).

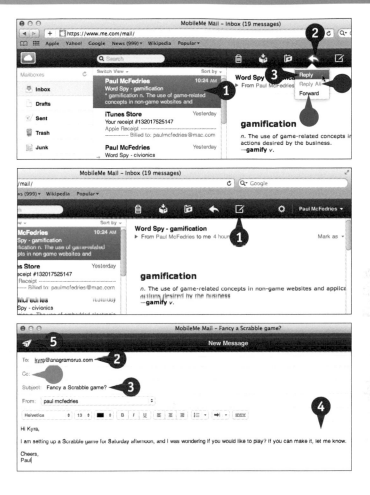

TIP

Can I use MobileMe to send a message to a person without other recipients knowing?

Yes, you can send that person a blind courtesy copy (Bcc), which means that he or she receives a copy of the message, but the other message recipients do not see that person's name or address in the recipient fields. To activate this feature, open MobileMe Mail, click **Actions** ( ), click **Preferences**, and then click the **Composing** tab. Click **Show Bcc field** (☐ changes to ☑) and then click **Done**.

Work with MobileMe Contacts

You can use MobileMe to store information about your friends, family, colleagues, and clients. Using the Contacts application, you can store data such as the person's name, company name, phone numbers, e-mail address, and street address.

The Contacts application also enables you to write notes about a contact, store extra data such as the person's job title and birthday, and assign a picture to a contact.

If you already have contacts in your Mac Address Book, you can synchronize them with MobileMe. See the section "Synchronize Your Mac with MobileMe," later in this chapter.

Work with MobileMe Contacts

Display MobileMe Contacts

1 Sign in to your MobileMe account.

Note: See the section "Sign in to MobileMe," earlier in this chapter.

2 Click **Switch Apps** (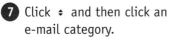).

3 Click **Contacts** (📧).

Create a Contact

1 Click **Create a new contact** (➕).

2 Type the person's first name.

3 Type the person's last name.

4 Type the person's company's name.

5 Click ⬧ and then click a phone number category.

6 Type the phone number.

7 Click ⬧ and then click an e-mail category.

8 Type the person's e-mail address.

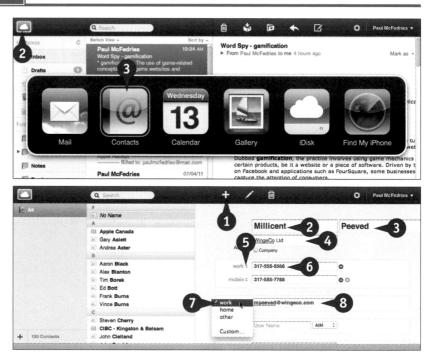

9 Click ✦ and then click a street address category.

10 Use the text boxes in this section to type the person's street address.

11 Type a note about the person.

12 Click **Save**.

MobileMe saves the contact.

Display a Contact

1 Use the scroll bar to locate the contact.

2 Click the contact.

● MobileMe displays the contact's details.

● You can also type part of the contact's name in the Search box.

● To e-mail the contact, click the address.

● To make changes to the contact, click **Edit** (✎).

● To remove the contact, click **Delete** (🗑).

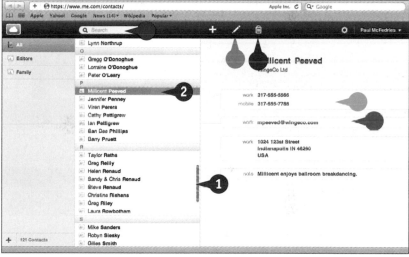

TIPS

How do I add a photo for a contact?
To add a photo to an existing contact, click the contact and then click **Edit**. Click **Add** to open the Add Photo dialog, click **Choose Photo**, click the photo you want to use, click **Choose**, and then click **OK**. Note that you can use only GIF, JPEG, or PNG files that are no larger than 1MB.

Is there any way to store data such as the person's birthday or job title?
Yes, the Contacts application offers a number of other fields, including Birthday, Job Title, Nickname, Prefix, and Suffix. To add a field to an existing contact, click the contact and then click **Edit**. Click **Add Field**, click the field you want, and then edit the field data. Note, too, that you can also add more instances of some fields by clicking the green plus icon (●) to the right of a field.

Manage Your Schedule with MobileMe

You can use MobileMe to manage your schedule. Using the Calendar application, you can add events (appointments and all-day activities) and to-do items (tasks). For events, you can specify the date and time they occur, the event name and location, and notes related to the event.

You can also use the Calendar application to display your schedule by day, by week, or by month.

If you already have events in your Mac iCal application, you can synchronize them with MobileMe. See the section "Synchronize Your Mac with MobileMe," later in this chapter.

Manage Your Schedule with MobileMe

Display MobileMe Calendar

1. Sign in to your MobileMe account.

Note: See the section "Sign in to MobileMe," earlier in this chapter.

2. Click **Switch Apps** (◻).

3. Click **Calendar** (⅟).

Note: If MobileMe asks whether you want to keep a copy of your calendars, click **Keep Local Copy**.

Navigate Calendar

1. Click **Month**.

2. Click the month you want.

● You can also click **Next Month** (▶) and **Previous Month** (◀) to select the month you want.

3. Click the date.

● To see just that date, click **Day**.

● To see the date in the context of its week, click **Week**.

● To return to today's date, click **Today**.

Create an Event

1 Navigate to the date when the event occurs.

2 Click the calendar you want to use.

3 Click **Week**.

4 Position the ⬉ at the time when the event starts.

5 Click and drag the ⬉ down to the time when the event ends.

● Calendar adds the event.

6 Type the event name.

7 Type the event location.

● If the event lasts all day, click **all-day** (☐ changes to ☑).

8 Adjust the start time, if necessary.

9 Adjust the end time, if necessary.

10 Fill in the other event details as needed.

11 Click **OK**.

Note: To edit the event, double-click it.

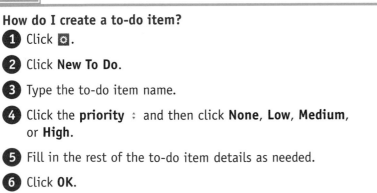

TIP

How do I create a to-do item?

1 Click ⚙.

2 Click **New To Do**.

3 Type the to-do item name.

4 Click the **priority** ⫶ and then click **None**, **Low**, **Medium**, or **High**.

5 Fill in the rest of the to-do item details as needed.

6 Click **OK**.

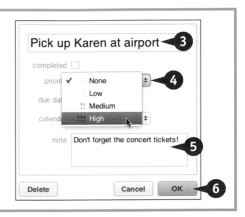

Share Photos with MobileMe

You can use MobileMe to upload photos and share them with others. Using the Gallery application, you can create different photo albums and make those albums available for others to see.

You can also configure a photo album to allow others to download photos from MobileMe to their computers. It is also possible to configure a photo album to allow other people to upload photos to the album, via MobileMe, via e-mail, or via the Photos app on an iPhone, iPad, or iPod touch.

Share Photos with MobileMe

Create a Photo Album

1 Sign in to your MobileMe account.

Note: See the section "Sign in to MobileMe," earlier in this chapter.

2 Click **Switch Apps** ( ).

3 Click **Gallery** ( ).

4 Click **Create a New Album** (+).

5 Type the album name.

6 To allow downloading, click **Downloading of photos or entire album** (☐ changes to ☑).

7 To allow web uploading, click **Uploading of photos via web browser** (☐ changes to ☑).

8 To allow e-mail uploading, click **Adding of photos via email or iPhone** (☐ changes to ☑).

9 Click **Create**.

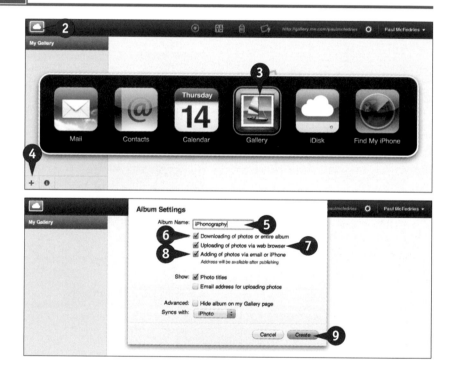

Upload Photos

1 Click the album.

2 Click **Upload** ().

The Uploads window appears.

3 Click **Close window when complete** (☐ changes to ☑).

4 Click **Choose**.

5 Select the photos you want to upload.

Note: To select multiple photos, press and hold ⌘ and click each photo. To select all the folders in the current folder, press ⌘+A.

6 Click **Open**.

MobileMe uploads the photos to the album.

TIPS

Can I upload photos to an album using my iPhone?
Yes, and the following technique also works with the iPad and the iPod touch. On your iPhone's Home screen, tap **Photos**, tap the photo album that contains the photo you want to upload, tap the photo, tap the **Action** icon in the lower left corner, and then tap **Send to MobileMe**. Tap the album you want to use for the photo. In the new e-mail message, type a photo title in the Subject field and then tap **Send**.

How do people view my MobileMe Gallery?
People can view your MobileMe Gallery using any recent web browser. The address of your gallery is shown in the upper right corner of the Gallery application. The format is http://gallery.me.com/*username*, where *username* is your MobileMe username.

Upload Files to Your iDisk

You can store files with your MobileMe account by using the iDisk online storage feature. With iDisk, you upload files from your Mac and store them in iDisk folders such as Pictures, Documents, and Public.

You can use iDisk to make backup copies of important documents. Because you can access your iDisk from any computer over the web, you can also use iDisk to make certain files available to you from any location that has Internet access.

Upload Files to Your iDisk

Display MobileMe iDisk

1 Sign in to your MobileMe account.

Note: See the section "Sign in to MobileMe," earlier in this chapter.

2 Click **Switch Apps** (⬜).

3 Click **iDisk** (⬜).

Upload a File Using MobileMe

1 Click the folder where you want to store the file.

2 Click **Upload** (⬜).

The Uploads window appears.

3 Click **Close window when complete** (☐ changes to ☑).

4 Click **Choose**.

5 Select the file you want to upload.

6 Click **Open**.

MobileMe uploads the file to your iDisk.

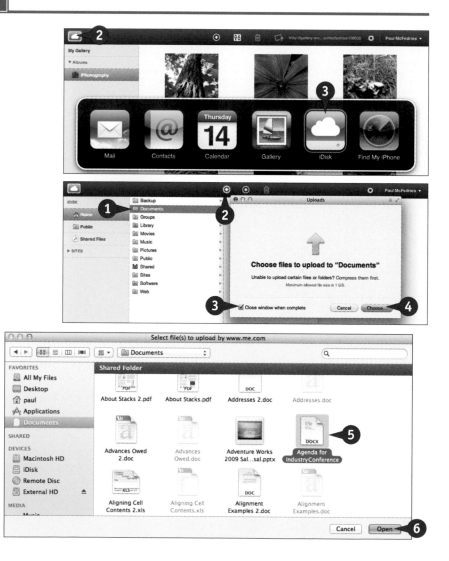

Upload a File Using Your Mac

1 Sign in to your MobileMe account using your Mac.

Note: See the tip in the section "Sign in to MobileMe," earlier in this chapter.

2 Click **Finder** ().

3 Click **iDisk**.

4 Open the folder to which you want to upload the file.

5 Press ⌘+N.

A new Finder window appears.

6 Open the folder that contains the file you want to upload.

7 Click and drag the file and drop it inside the iDisk folder.

Your Mac uploads the file to your iDisk.

You can now access your uploaded files online.

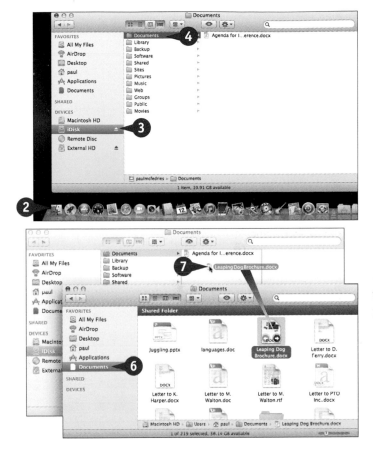

TIP

Can I use iDisk to share files with other people over the web?
Yes. Click the file you want to share and then click **Share File**. In the Sharing dialog that appears, type the contact names or e-mail addresses of the people you want to share the file with, type a short message, and then click **Share** (●).

You can also share files by storing them in the iDisk Public folder. Other people can then see the files by using a web browser to enter the address http://public.me.com/*username*/, where *username* is your MobileMe member name.

Synchronize Your Mac with MobileMe

Y ou can ensure that your Mac and your MobileMe account have the same data by synchronizing the two.

The main items you will want to synchronize are iCal appointments, Address Book contacts, and Mail e-mail accounts. However, there are many other types of data you want synchronize to MobileMe, including Safari bookmarks, Mail notes, Dashboard widgets, and system preferences and passwords.

If you have a second Mac, you can also synchronize it with the same MobileMe account, which ensures that your two Macs use the same data.

Synchronize Your Mac with MobileMe

1 Click the **Apple** icon ( ).

2 Click **System Preferences**.

Note: You can also open System Preferences by clicking its icon ( ) on the Dock.

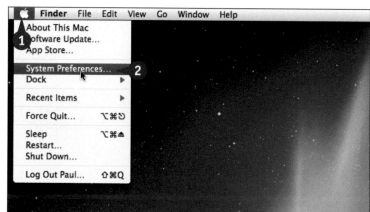

The System Preferences window appears.

3 Click **MobileMe**.

Note: If you see Are You a MobileMe Member?, type your MobileMe member name and password and then click **Sign In**.

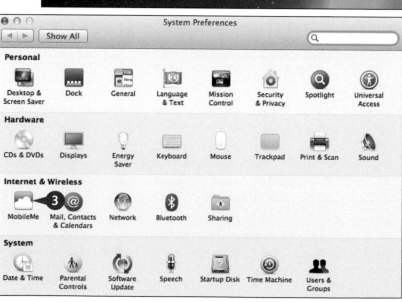

The MobileMe preferences appear.

④ Click **Sync**.

⑤ Click **Synchronize with MobileMe** (☐ changes to ☑).

● Your Mac registers itself with your MobileMe account.

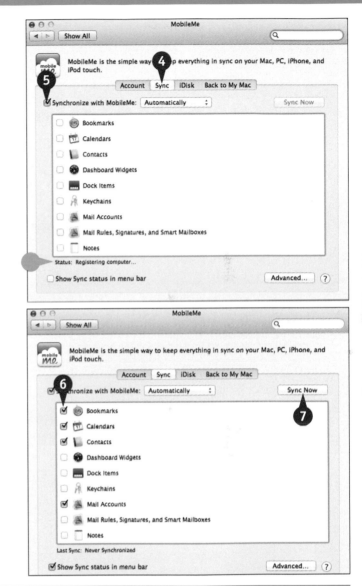

⑥ Click the check box beside each type of data you want to synchronize (☐ changes to ☑).

⑦ Click **Sync Now**.

Your Mac synchronizes the data with your MobileMe account.

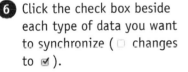

TIPS

Is there a way to have my Mac synchronize with my MobileMe account on a schedule?
Yes, you can configure your MobileMe preferences to perform an automatic synchronization at regular intervals. Follow Steps **1** to **6** to enable the synchronization. In the Synchronize with MobileMe pop-up menu, click ↕ and then click the interval you want: **Every Hour**, **Every Day**, or **Every Week**.

What happens if I modify an appointment, contact, bookmark, or other data in MobileMe?
The synchronization process works both ways. That is, all the Mac data you selected to synchronize is sent to your MobileMe account. However, the data on your MobileMe account is also sent to your Mac. This means that if you modify, add, or delete data on your MobileMe account, those changes are also reflected in your Mac data.

CHAPTER 15

Networking with Mac OS X

If you have multiple computers in your home or office, you can set up these computers as a network to share information and equipment. This chapter gives an overview of networking concepts and shows you how to connect to a network, work with the other computers on your network, and share your Mac's resources with other network users.

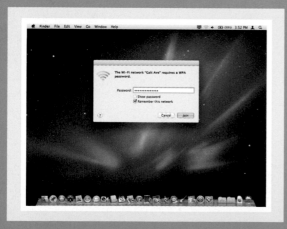

Understanding Networking

A network is a collection of computers and other devices that are connected. You can create a network using cable hookups, wireless hookups, or a combination of the two. In both cases, you need special networking equipment to make the connections.

A network gives you a number of advantages. For example, once you have two or more computers connected on a network, those computers can share documents, photos, and other files. You can also use a network to share equipment, such as printers and optical drives.

Share Files

Networked computers are connected to each other, and so they can exchange files with each other along the connection. This enables people to share information and to collaborate on projects. Mac OS X includes built-in security, so that you can control what files you share with other people.

On	Service
☐	Screen Sharing
☑	File Sharing
☐	Printer Sharing
☐	Scanner Sharing
☐	Web Sharing
☐	Remote Login
☐	Remote Management
☐	Remote Apple Events
☐	Xgrid Sharing
☐	Internet Sharing
☐	Bluetooth Sharing

File Sharing: On

Other users can access shared folders on this computer, and administrators all volumes, at afp://192.168.1.142/ or "Paul's MacBook Air".

Options...

Shared Folders:
- Documents
- Karen's Public Folder
- Paul's Public Folder

Users:
| Paul | Read & Write |
| Everyone | Read Only |

Share Equipment

Computers connected over a network can share some types of equipment. For example, one computer can share its printer, which enables other network users to send their documents to that printer. Networked computers can also share hard drives, CD or DVD drives, and document scanners.

On	Service
☐	Screen Sharing
☐	File Sharing
☑	Printer Sharing
☑	Scanner Sharing
☐	Web Sharing
☐	Remote Login
☐	Remote Management
☐	Remote Apple Events
☐	Xgrid Sharing
☐	Internet Sharing
☐	Bluetooth Sharing

Printer Sharing: On

Printer Sharing allows others on your network to use printers connected to this computer.

Open Print & Scan Preferences...

Printers:
- ☑ Photosmart Pre...

Users:
| Everyone | Can Print |

Wired Networking

Network Cable

A *network cable* is a special cable designed for exchanging information. One end of the cable plugs into the Mac's network port. The other end plugs into a network connection point, which is usually the network's router (discussed next), but it could also be a switch, hub, or even another Mac. Information, shared files, and other network data travel through the network cables.

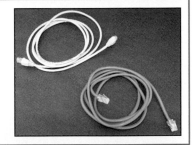

Router

A *router* is a central connection point for all of the computers on the wired portion of the network. For each computer, you run a network cable from the Mac's network port to a port in the router.

When network data travels from computer A to computer B, it first goes out through computer A's network port, along its network cable, and into the router. Then the router passes the data along computer B's network cable and into its network port.

Wireless Networking

Wireless Connections

A *wireless network* is a collection of two or more computers that communicate with each other using radio signals instead of cable. The most common wireless technology is Wi-Fi (rhymes with hi-fi) or 802.11. There are three main types — 802.11b, 802.11g, and 802.11n — each of which has its own range and speed limits. The other common wireless technology is Bluetooth, which enables devices to communicate directly with each other.

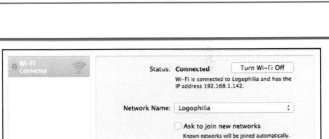

Wireless Access Point

A *wireless access point* (WAP) is a device that receives and transmits signals from wireless computers to form a wireless network. Many WAPs also accept wired connections, which enables both wired and wireless computers to form a network. If your network has a broadband modem, you can connect the modem to a type of WAP called a *wireless gateway,* which extends Internet access to all of the computers on the network.

Connect a Bluetooth Device

You can make wireless connections to devices such as mice, keyboards, headsets, and cell phones by using the Bluetooth networking technology.

The networking tasks that you learn about in the rest of this chapter require special equipment to connect your computers and devices. However, with Bluetooth devices, the networking is built in, so no extra equipment is needed. For Bluetooth connections to work, your Mac must support Bluetooth (all newer Macs do) and your device must be Bluetooth enabled. Also, your Mac and the Bluetooth device must remain within about 30 feet of each other.

Connect a Bluetooth Device

Connect a Generic Bluetooth Device

1 Click **System Preferences** (⬚) in the Dock.

2 Click **Bluetooth**.

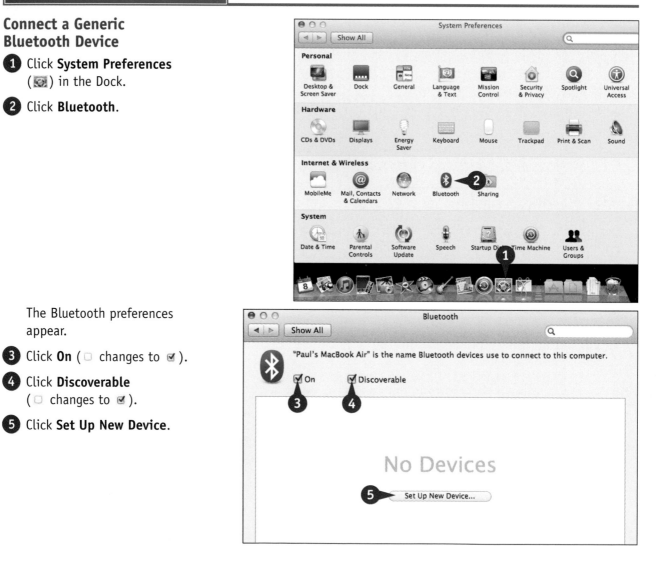

The Bluetooth preferences appear.

3 Click **On** (☐ changes to ☑).

4 Click **Discoverable** (☐ changes to ☑).

5 Click **Set Up New Device**.

The Bluetooth Setup Assistant appears.

6 Perform whatever steps are necessary to make your Bluetooth device discoverable.

Note: For example, if you are connecting a Bluetooth mouse, the device often has a separate switch or button that makes the mouse discoverable, so you need to turn on that switch or press that button.

● A list of the available Bluetooth devices appears here.

7 Click the Bluetooth device you want to connect.

8 Click **Continue**.

9 Perform the steps required to pair your Mac and your device.

Your Mac connects with the device.

10 Click **Quit**.

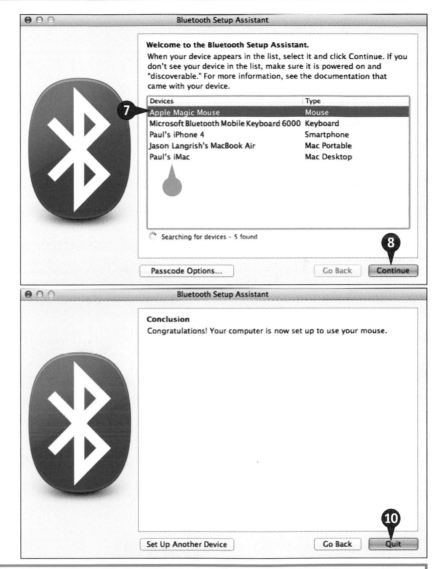

Bluetooth Setup Assistant

Welcome to the Bluetooth Setup Assistant.
When your device appears in the list, select it and click Continue. If you don't see your device in the list, make sure it is powered on and "discoverable." For more information, see the documentation that came with your device.

Devices	Type
Apple Magic Mouse	Mouse
Microsoft Bluetooth Mobile Keyboard 6000	Keyboard
Paul's iPhone 4	Smartphone
Jason Langrish's MacBook Air	Mac Portable
Paul's iMac	Mac Desktop

Searching for devices - 5 found

Passcode Options...   Go Back   Continue

Bluetooth Setup Assistant

Conclusion
Congratulations! Your computer is now set up to use your mouse.

Set Up Another Device   Go Back   Quit

TIPS

What does it mean to make a device "discoverable"?
This means that you configure the device to broadcast that it is available for a Bluetooth connection. Controlling the broadcast is important because you usually want to use a Bluetooth device such as a mouse or keyboard with only a single computer. By controlling when the device is discoverable, you ensure that it works only with the computer you want it to.

What does "pairing" mean?
As a security precaution, many Bluetooth devices do not connect automatically to other devices. This makes sense because otherwise it means a stranger with a Bluetooth device could connect to your cell phone or even your Mac. To prevent this, most Bluetooth devices require you to enter a password before the connection is made. This is known as *pairing* the two devices.

continued ▶

Connect a Bluetooth Device

A Bluetooth mouse and a Bluetooth headset do not require any extra pairing steps, so you can skip the rest of this section if you are pairing one of these devices. In these pages you learn the pairing instructions for a Bluetooth keyboard and a Bluetooth cell phone.

In most cases, pairing is accomplished by your Mac generating a 6- or 8-digit *passkey* that you must then type into the Bluetooth device (assuming that it has some kind of keypad). In other cases, the device comes with a default passkey that you must enter into your Mac to set up the pairing.

Connect a Bluetooth Device (continued)

Connect a Bluetooth Keyboard

1 Turn the keyboard on, if required.

2 Turn on the switch that makes the keyboard discoverable, if required.

3 Follow Steps **1** and **2** from earlier in this section and click **Add** (+).

The Bluetooth Setup Assistant appears.

4 Click your Bluetooth keyboard.

5 Click **Continue**.

The Bluetooth Setup Assistant displays a passkey.

6 Use the Bluetooth keyboard to type the displayed passkey.

7 Press <kbd>Return</kbd>.

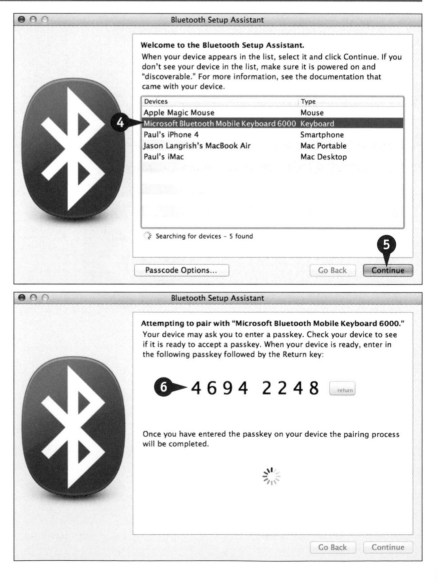

Connect a Bluetooth Cell Phone

1 Turn on the cell phone.

2 Make the cell phone discoverable.

3 Follow Steps **1** and **2** from earlier in this section and click **Add** (+).

The Bluetooth Setup Assistant appears.

4 Click your Bluetooth phone.

5 Click **Continue**.

The Bluetooth Setup Assistant displays a passkey.

6 Use the Bluetooth phone's keypad to type the displayed passkey.

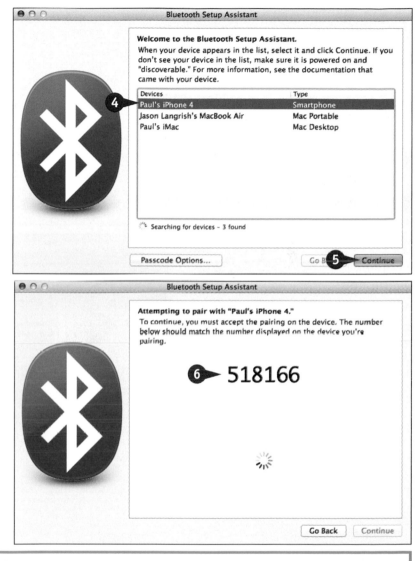

How do I remove a Bluetooth device?

1 Click the **Bluetooth status** icon ( ) in the menu bar.

2 Click **Open Bluetooth Preferences**.

Note: You can also click , click **System Preferences**, and then click **Bluetooth**.

The Bluetooth preferences appear.

3 Click the device you want to remove.

4 Click **Remove** (−).

Your Mac asks you to confirm.

5 Click **Remove**, and your Mac removes the device.

Connect to a Wireless Network

If your Mac has built-in wireless networking capabilities, you can use them to connect to a wireless network that is within range. This could be a network in your home, your office, or a public location such as a coffee shop. In most cases, this will also give you access to the wireless network's Internet connection.

Most wireless networks have security turned on, which means you must know the correct password to connect to the network. However, after you have connected to the network once, your Mac remembers the password, and will connect again automatically the next time the network comes within range.

Connect to a Wireless Network

1 Click the **Wi-Fi status** icon
( ) in the menu bar.

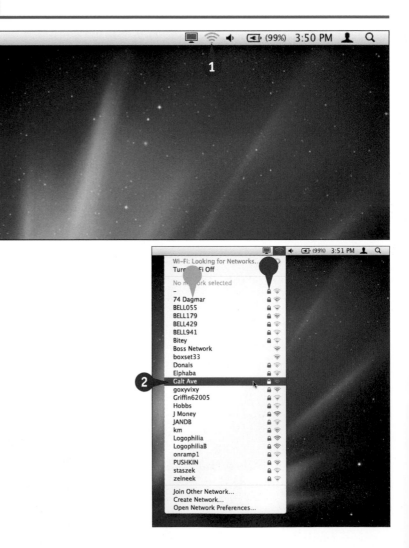

Your Mac locates the wireless networks within range of your Mac.

● The available networks appear in the menu.

● Networks with a Lock icon
( ) require a password to join.

2 Click the wireless network you want to join.

If the wireless network is secure, your Mac prompts you for the password.

③ Use the Password text box to type the network password.

● If the password is very long and you are sure no one can see your screen, you can click **Show password** (☐ changes to ☑) to see the actual characters instead of dots. This helps to ensure you type the password correctly.

④ Click **Join**.

Your Mac connects to the wireless network.

● The Wi-Fi status icon changes from 🛜 to 🛜 to indicate the connection.

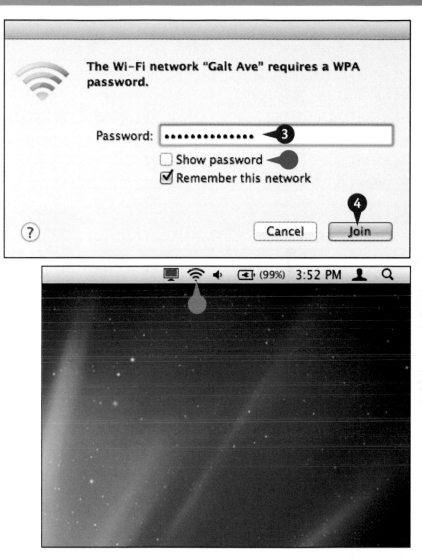

I know a particular network is within range, but I do not see it in the list. Why not?
As a security precaution, some wireless networks do not broadcast their availability. However, you can still connect to such a network, assuming you know its name and the password, if one is required. Click 🛜 and then click **Join Other Network**. Use the Network Name text box to type the name of the network, click the **Security** ⟂, and then click the network's security type. Follow Steps **3** and **4** to join the network.

I do not see the Wi-Fi status icon on my menu bar. How do I display the icon?
You can do this using System Preferences. Click its icon (🖼) in the Dock (or click 🍎 and then click **System Preferences**) to open the System Preferences window. Click **Network**, click Wi-Fi, and then click the **Show Wi-Fi status in menu bar** check box (☐ changes to ☑).

Connect to a Network Resource

To see what other network users have shared on the network, you can use the Network folder to view the other computers and then connect to them to see their shared resources.

To get full access to a Mac's shared resources, you must connect with a user name and password for an administrator account on that Mac. To get access to the resources that have been shared by a particular user, you must connect with that user's name and password.

Note, too, that your Mac can also connect to the resources shared by Windows computers.

Connect to a Network Resource

1 Click **Finder** (⬚).

2 Click **Go**.

3 Click **Network**.

Note: Another way to run the Network command is to press Shift+⌘+K.

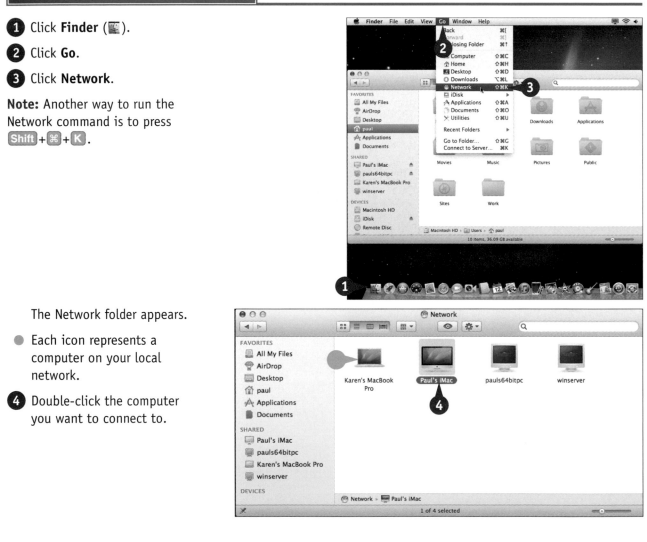

The Network folder appears.

● Each icon represents a computer on your local network.

4 Double-click the computer you want to connect to.

Your Mac connects to the network computer using the Guest account.

Note: The Guest account has only limited access to the network computer.

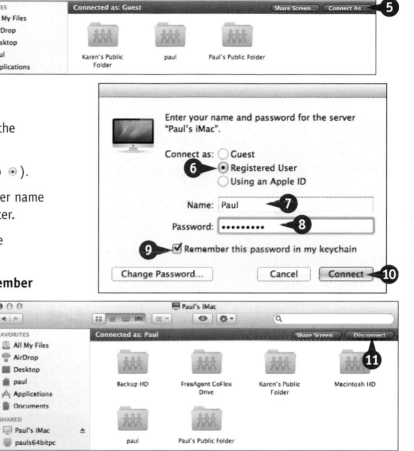

5 Click **Connect As**.

Your Mac prompts you to connect to the network computer.

6 Click **Registered User** (○ changes to ⊙).

7 Use the Name text box to type the user name of an account on the network computer.

8 Use the Password text box to type the password of the account.

9 To store the account data, click **Remember this password in my keychain** (□ changes to ☑).

10 Click **Connect**.

Your Mac connects to the computer and shows the shared resources that you can access.

11 When you are done, click **Disconnect**.

TIPS

Is there a faster way to connect to a network computer?
Yes. If your Mac detects network computers sharing resources, it usually displays the names of those computers in Finder's sidebar area, under the Shared section. Click the computer you want to connect with (●) and then follow Steps **5** to **10** to connect as a registered user.

How can I connect to a computer that does not appear in the Network folder?
If you are sure that the computer is sharing resources on the network, right-click **Finder** (🖥), and then click **Connect to Server**. In the Connect to Server dialog, use the Server Address text box to type the address: For a Mac, type the Mac's network name followed by **.local**; for a Windows PC, type **smb://** followed by the PC's name; for any computer, type its IP address. Click **Connect**.

Change Your Password

You can make your Mac and your shared folders more secure by changing your password. For example, if you turn on file sharing as described in the next section, you can configure each shared folder so that only someone who knows your user account password can get full access to the data in that shared folder.

Similarly, you should change your password if other network users know your current password and you no longer want those users to have access to your shared folders. Finally, you should also change your password if you feel that your current password is not secure enough. See the Tip on the next page to learn how to create a secure password.

Change Your Password

1 Click **System Preferences** (⚙).

2 Click **Users & Groups**.

The Users & Groups preferences appear.

● Your user account is selected automatically.

● If you want to work with a different user account, you must click the **Lock** icon (🔒) and then enter your administrator password (🔒 changes to 🔓).

3 Click **Change Password**.

The Change Password dialog appears.

4 Type your current password.

5 Type your new password.

6 Retype the new password.

Old password:	●●●●●●●●● ◀ **4**
New password:	●●●●●●●●●●● ◀ **5** 🔑
Verify:	●●●●●●●●●●● ◀ **6**
Password hint: (Recommended)	
	Cancel Change Password

7 Type a hint that Mac OS X will display if you forget the password.

8 Click **Change Password**.

Mac OS X changes your password.

Old password:	●●●●●●●●●
New password:	●●●●●●●●●●● 🔑
Verify:	●●●●●●●●●●●
Password hint: (Recommended)	Mom's maiden name, year of birth, and month of birth ◀ **7**
	Cancel Change Password ◀ **8**

TIP

How do I create a secure password?

A secure password requires only two characteristics: It must be relatively long — at least eight characters; and it must include characters from at least three of the following four sets: lowercase letters, uppercase letters, numbers, and non-alphanumeric symbols such as $ and @. If you want Mac OS X to create a secure password for you, follow these steps:

1 Follow Steps **1** to **4** in this section.

2 Click the **Password Assistant** icon (🔑).

The Password Assistant dialog appears.

3 Click the **Type** ⁞ and then click a password type.

4 Click and drag the **Length** slider to set the password length you want to use.

5 Click the **Suggestion** ⁞ and then click the password you want to use.

6 Click **Close** (●).

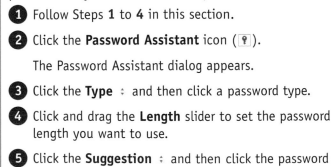

Turn On File and Printer Sharing

You can share your files with other network users. This enables those users to access your files over the network. Before you can share these resources, you must turn on your Mac's file-sharing feature.

To learn how to share a particular folder, see the section "Share a Folder," later in this chapter. You can also share your printer with other network users. This enables those users to send print jobs to your printer over the network. Before this can happen, you must turn on your Mac's printer-sharing feature. To learn how to share a particular printer, see the section "Share a Printer," later in this chapter.

Turn On File and Printer Sharing

① Click **System Preferences** (![icon]) in the Dock.

The System Preferences window appears.

② Click **Sharing**.

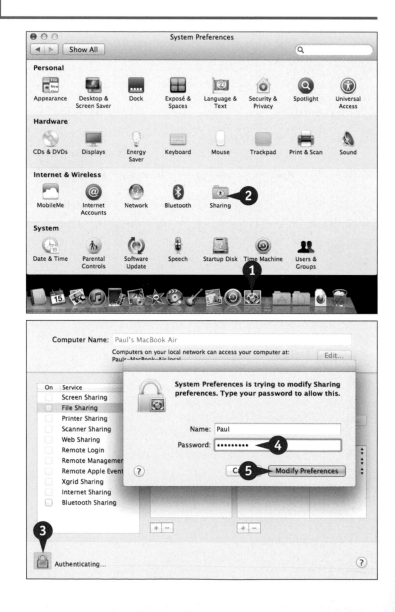

The Sharing preferences appear.

③ Click the **Lock** icon (🔒).

④ Type your administrator password.

⑤ Click **Modify Preferences**.

Mac OS X unlocks the Sharing preferences (🔒 changes to 🔓).

6 Click the **File Sharing** check box (☐ changes to ☑).

You can now share your folders, as described in the next section.

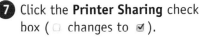

7 Click the **Printer Sharing** check box (☐ changes to ☑).

You can now share your printers, as described later in this chapter.

Another user has asked me for my Mac's IP address. How do I look that up?

Your Mac gives you a couple of ways to do this. Follow Steps **1** and **2** in this section, click **File Sharing** (click the name, not the check box); the series of digits after afp:// is your IP address (such as 192.168.1.142). Alternatively, open System Preferences, click **Network**, click **Ethernet** (or click **Wi-Fi** if you have a wireless network connection), and then read the IP Address value.

What is the Public folder and how do I access it?

Your user account's Public folder is a special folder that you use to share files with other people on the network or on your Mac. If someone connects to your Mac using your user name and password, he or she has full access to the Public folder. Everyone else can only read the contents of the folder or add files to the Drop Box folder. To access the folder, click **Finder** ( ), click your user name, and then open the Public folder.

Share a Folder

You can share one of your folders on the network, enabling other network users to view and optionally edit the files you place in that folder.

Mac OS X automatically shares your user account's Public folder, but you can share other folders. Sharing a folder enables you to work on a file with other people without having to send them a copy of the file.

Mac OS X gives you complete control over how people access your shared folder. For example, you can allow users to make changes to the folder, or you can prevent changes.

Share a Folder

1 Open and unlock the Sharing preferences.

Note: See the section "Turn On File and Printer Sharing" to learn how to display and unlock the Sharing preferences.

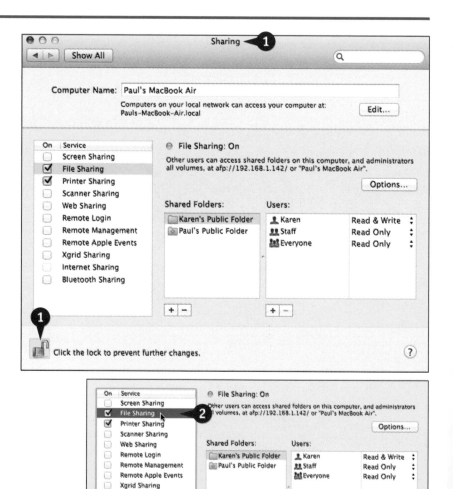

2 Click **File Sharing**.

Note: Be sure to click the **File Sharing** text, not the check box. This ensures that you do not accidentally uncheck the check box.

3 Under Shared Folders, click + .

An Open dialog appears.

4 Click the folder you want to share.

5 Click **Add**.

Your Mac begins sharing the folder.

Note: You can also click and drag a folder from a Finder window and drop it on the list of shared folders.

● The folder appears in the Shared Folders list.

6 Click the folder.

7 For the Everyone user, click the current permission and then click the permission you want to assign.

● The current permission is indicated with a check mark (✓).

Mac OS X assigns the permission to the user.

● You can also click + under the Users list to add more users.

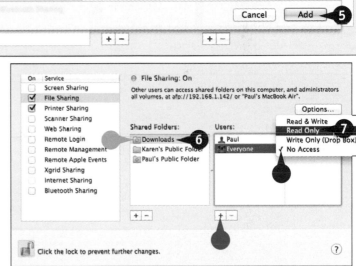

TIPS

What are the differences between the various types of permissions I can assign to users?

Permissions define what users can and cannot do with the shared folder:

• **Read & Write**: Users can open files, add new files, rename or delete existing files, and edit file contents.

• **Read Only**: Users can open files, but cannot add, delete, rename, or edit files.

• **Write Only (Drop Box)**: Users can add files to the folder as a Drop Box, but cannot open the folder.

• **No Access**: Users cannot open (or even see) the folder.

Can I share folders with Windows users?

Yes. In the Sharing window, click **Options** and then click the **Share files and folders using SMB** check box (☐ changes to ☑). Click your user account (☐ changes to ☑), use the Password text box to type your account password, click **OK**, and then click **Done**. Windows users must enter their user name and password to see their shared folders.

Share a Printer

If you have a printer connected to your Mac, you can share the printer with the network. This enables other network users to send their documents to your printer.

Sharing a printer saves you money because you only have to purchase one printer for all the computers on your network. Sharing a printer also saves you time because you only have to install, configure, and maintain a single printer for everyone on your network.

See the next section, "Add a Shared Printer," to learn how to configure Mac OS X to use a shared network printer.

Share a Printer

1 Click ⌘.

2 Click **System Preferences**.

Note: You can also click **System Preferences** ( ) in the Dock.

The System Preferences window appears.

3 Click **Sharing**.

4 Click **Printer Sharing**.

Note: Be sure to click the **Printer Sharing** text, not the check box. This ensures that you do not accidentally uncheck the check box.

5 Click the check box beside the printer you want to share (☐ changes to ☑).

Is there another method I can use to share a printer?
Yes, you can follow these steps:

1 Click .

2 Click **System Preferences**.

3 Click **Print & Fax**.

4 Click the printer you want to share.

5 Click the **Share this printer on the network** check box (☐ changes to ☑).

Add a Shared Printer

If another computer on your network has an attached printer that has been shared with the network, as described in the previous section, you can add that shared printer to your Mac. This enables you to send a document from your Mac to that shared printer, which means you can print your documents without having a printer attached directly to your Mac.

Before you can print to a shared network printer, you must add the shared printer to Mac OS X.

Add a Shared Printer

① Click **System Preferences** () in the Dock.

The System Preferences window appears.

② Click **Print & Scan**.

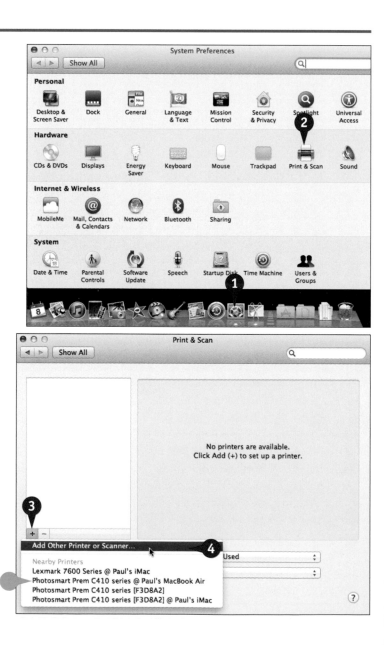

③ Click **+**.

● If you see the printer you want to add, click it and skip the rest of these steps.

④ Click **Add Other Printer or Scanner**.

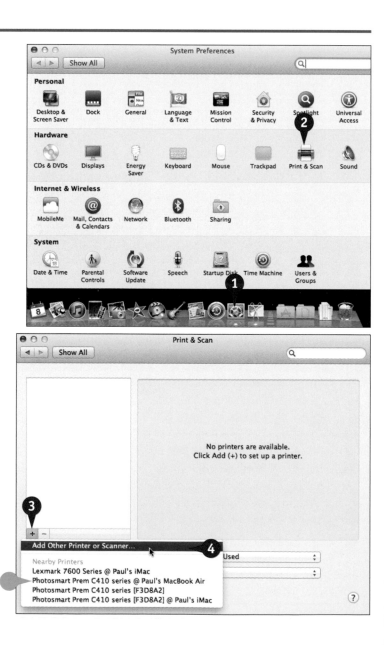

5 Click **Default**.

6 Click the shared printer.

● Look for the word *Shared* in the printer description.

7 Click **Add**.

Note: If Mac OS X alerts you that it must install software for the printer, click **Install**.

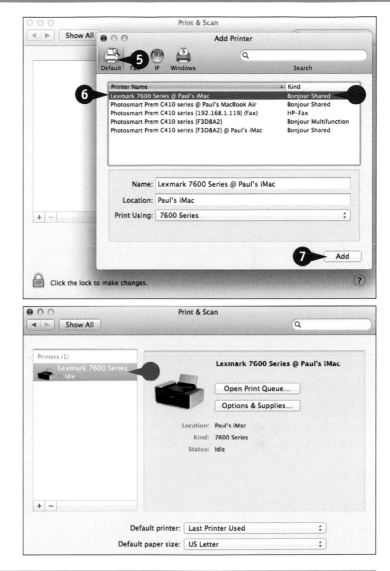

● Mac OS X adds the printer.

TIPS

Can I add a shared Windows printer?
Yes, if you have Windows computers on your network you can connect to any printers that they share. Follow Steps **1** to **4** and then click the **Windows** tab. Click the Windows workgroup, click the computer with the shared printer, log on to the Windows computer, and then click the shared printer you want to use. In the Print Using list, click **+**, click **Other**, and then click the printer in the list that appears. Click **Add**.

How do I print to the shared network printer that I added?
In any application that supports printing, click **File** and then click **Print**. You can also press ⌘+P. In the Print dialog, use the Printer pop-up menu to click **+** and then click the shared printer you added in this section. Choose any other printing options you require, and then click **Print**.

Share a Screen with Another Mac

Y ou can configure Mac OS X to share your Mac's screen with other computers on your network. Sharing your screen means that whatever is displayed on your Mac's desktop is also displayed inside a window on the other user's Mac. This is useful if you need to demonstrate something on the screen because it means the other user can watch the demonstration without having to be physically present in front of your Mac.

Once you have shared your screen, it also means the other user can work your Mac just as though he or she was sitting in front of it. This is useful if that person needs to troubleshoot a problem.

Share a Screen with Another Mac

Turn On Screen Sharing

1 Open and unlock the Sharing preferences.

Note: See the section "Turn On File and Printer Sharing" to learn how to display and unlock the Sharing preferences.

The Sharing preferences appear.

2 Click **Screen Sharing** (□ changes to ☑).

Mac OS X configures the desktop for sharing.

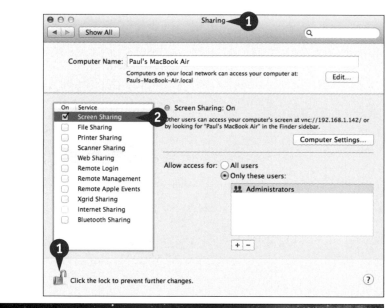

View a Shared Screen

1 On another Mac, click **Finder** ( ).

2 In the sidebar, click the Mac with the shared screen.

3 Click **Share Screen**.

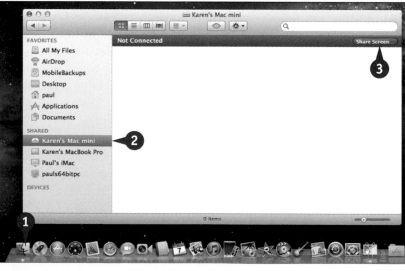

Mac OS X prompts you to log in to the remote computer.

④ Type the password for an administrative account on the Mac that is sharing the screen.

⑤ Click **Connect**.

● Mac OS X displays the shared screen in a window.

Can I take a picture of the shared Mac screen?

Yes. This is a good idea if the shared screen is displaying a message or other data that you want to preserve in an image. In the Screen Sharing window, click **Connection**, click **Save Screen Capture As**, and then save the image file to the Mac.

Is it possible to copy data either from or to the Mac with the shared screen?

Yes, you can copy data either way. This is useful if you have text or an image on one Mac and you need to use it on the other. If you want to send data to the Mac with the shared screen, copy the data that you want to send, click **Edit**, and then click **Send Clipboard**. If you want to receive data from the Mac with the shared screen, use that Mac to copy the data that you want to receive. In the Screen Sharing window, click **Edit**, and then click **Get Clipboard**.

Index

Read Less–Learn More®

There's a Visual book for every learning level...

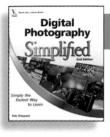

Simplified®

The place to start if you're new to computers. Full color.

- Computers
- Creating Web Pages
- Digital Photography
- Excel
- Internet
- Laptops
- Mac OS
- Office
- PCs
- Windows
- Word

Teach Yourself VISUALLY™

Get beginning to intermediate-level training in a variety of topics. Full color.

- Access
- Algebra
- Astronomy
- Bass Guitar
- Beadwork
- Bridge
- Car Care and Maintenance
- Chess
- Circular Knitting
- Collage & Altered Art
- Computers
- Crafting with Kids
- Crocheting
- Digital Photography
- Digital Video
- Dog Training
- Drawing
- Dreamweaver
- Excel
- Flash
- Golf
- Guitar
- Hand Dyeing
- Handspinning
- HTML
- iLife
- iPad
- iPhone
- iPhoto
- Jewelry Making & Beading
- Knitting
- Lightroom
- Macs
- Mac OS
- Office
- Outlook
- Photoshop
- Photoshop Elements
- Piano
- Poker
- PowerPoint
- Quilting
- Scrapbooking
- Sewing
- Web Design
- Windows
- Wireless Networking
- Word
- WordPress

Top 100 Simplified® Tips & Tricks

Tips and techniques to take your skills beyond the basics. Full color.

- Digital Photography
- eBay
- Excel
- Google
- Office
- Photoshop
- Photoshop Elements
- PowerPoint
- Windows

...all designed for visual learners—just like you!

Master VISUALLY®

Your complete visual reference. Two-color interior.

- 3ds Max
- Creating Web Pages
- Dreamweaver and Flash
- Excel
- iPod and iTunes
- Mac OS
- Office
- Optimizing PC Performance
- Windows
- Windows Server

Visual Blueprint™

Where to go for professional-level programming instruction. Two-color interior.

- ActionScript
- Ajax
- ASP.NET 2.0
- Excel Data Analysis
- Excel Pivot Tables
- Excel Programming
- HTML
- JavaScript
- Mambo
- Mobile App Development
- Perl and Apache
- PHP & MySQL
- SEO
- Ubuntu Linux
- Vista Sidebar
- Visual Basic
- XML

Visual™ Quick Tips

Shortcuts, tricks, and techniques for getting more done in less time. Full color.

- Beading
- Crochet
- Digital Photography
- Excel
- Golf
- Internet
- iPhone
- iPod & iTunes
- Knitting
- Mac OS
- Office
- Paper Crafts
- PowerPoint
- Quilting
- Sewing
- Windows
- Wire Jewelry

Visual®
An Imprint of ⊕**WILEY**
Now you know.

For a complete listing of Visual books, go to wiley.com/go/visual

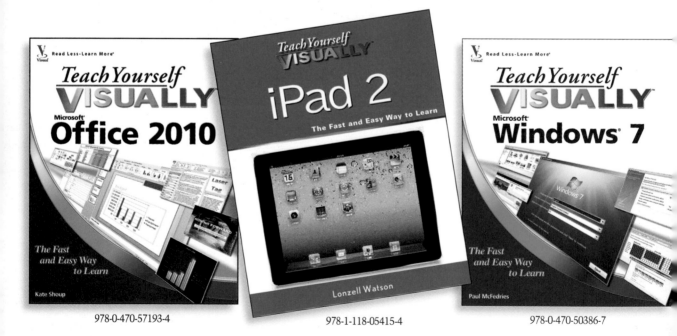